RECOV
HISPA
OF TEXAS

Hispanic History of Texas Project

Roberto R. Calderón
University of North Texas

Antonia Castañeda
Independent Scholar

Monica Perales
University of Houston

Gerald Poyo
St. Mary's University

Raúl Ramos
University of Houston

Antonio Saborit
INAH Dirección de Estudios Históricos

Emilio Zamora
The University of Texas at Austin

RECOVERING THE HISPANIC HISTORY OF TEXAS

Monica Perales and Raúl A. Ramos, Editors

Recovering the U.S. Hispanic Literary Heritage

Arte Público Press
Houston, Texas

Recovering the Hispanic History of Texas is made possible through grants from the City of Houston through the Houston Arts Alliance, the Exemplar Program, a program of Americans for the Arts in collaboration with the LarsonAllen Public Services Group, funded by the Ford Foundation and by the Summerlee Foundation.

Recovering the past, creating the future

Arte Público Press
University of Houston
452 Cullen Performance Hall
Houston, Texas 77204-2004

Cover design by Pilar Espino

Recovering the Hispanic history of Texas / edited by Monica Perales and
    Raúl A. Ramos.
    p.   cm.
Includes bibliographical references.
ISBN: 978-1-55885-591-5 (pbk: alk. paper)
ISBN: 978-1-55885-691-2 (cloth: alk. paper)
    1. Mexican Americans—Texas—History. 2. Mexican Americans—
Texas—Historiography. 3. Mexican American women—Texas—History.
4. Mexican American women—Texas—Historiography. 5. Hispanic
Americans—Texas—History. 6.   Hispanic   Americans—Texas—
Historiography. 7.   Texas—History. 8.   Texas—Historiography.
9. Texas—Ethnic relations. 10. Texas—Social conditions. I. Perales,
Monica. II. Ramos, Raúl A.
F395.M5R43 2010
976.4'0046872—dc22
                                                                2010000601
                                                                CIP

♾ The paper used in this publication meets the requirements of the American National Standard for Information Sciences—Permanence of Paper for Printed Library Materials, ANSI Z39.48-1984.

10 11 12 13 14 15 16   10 9 8 7 6 5 4 3 2 1

CONTENTS

Unearthing Voices

INTRODUCTION

Building a Project to Expand Texas History

Monica Perales and Raúl A. Ramos
The University of Houston

I N A STATE KNOWN FOR ITS SWELTERING SUMMERS, THERE WAS SOMETHING ELSE generating a great deal of heat in Texas in the summer of 2009. The members of a panel of experts providing recommendations to the Texas Board of Education on its K-12 social studies curriculum standards engaged in a debate over what students in the state's public schools should be learning about history. Some reviewers lamented that the experts paid insufficient attention to the nation's "founding fathers" while they overemphasized what the reviewers deemed were less historically significant individuals, such as Thurgood Marshall and César Chávez. Others pointed to the need for an even greater focus on the multicultural origins of the nation and called for a more thorough understanding of the roles that ethnic minorities and women have played in the social, political, and economic life of the nation. Several members of the panel emphasized the need for students to engage primary documents and criticized the current state curriculum for spending too much time on interpretations of documents and what they believed to be an inordinate amount of emphasis on less "factual" historical productions including poetry, folktales, and art.[1] This was not the first time in recent years that Texans became fascinated with historical narratives and documents. Just two years before, the Texas Historical Commission caused a stir over the proposed purchase of an often cited, but never before seen, letter by Davy Crockett, a central character in one of the state's most revered defining myths, for a reported $500,000. After forensic tests proved inconclusive in verifying the authenticity of the letter—said to be the last letter Crockett wrote before perishing at the Alamo—the Texas Historical Commission passed on the purchase.[2]

While these controversies could be written off simply as another battle in the "culture wars," there was something more fundamental at stake. These two episodes raise some important questions about the politically charged nature of the historical enterprise in Texas and the extent to which history is deeply enmeshed in debates about national and state identity in the present day. They also tell us something about the nature of "historical work," and, in a related fashion, the nature of the archival process. What is the purpose of history, and who gets to write it? More importantly, how does history get written, and whose historical text represents the "authentic" voice of the past that is thus worthy of preserving?

As one of the first collections of scholarship produced under the auspices of the Hispanic History of Texas Project, the essays in this volume seek to make an important intervention into these very questions. An extension of the Recovering the U.S. Hispanic Literary Heritage Project, Hispanic History of Texas's goal is not only to identify, preserve, and publish documents that uncover the myriad historical voices and experiences of ethnic Mexicans in Texas, but also to promote research that highlights the complex roles ethnic Mexican men and women have played in the shaping of the cultural, economic, and political fabric of the region. The essays in this book—by both established and up-and-coming scholars—are examples of the kinds of innovative work the Hispanic History Project seeks to inspire. By employing a wide range of historical sources and in the spirit of true interdisciplinarity, the authors seek to forge new ground and take the study of Mexicans, Texas, and the Borderlands into new and exciting terrain.

At its heart, this type of project is about more than simply recovering the voices of lost historical actors and simply adding to an existing story. The essays in this volume seek to reimagine the dominant narrative of Texas history and also to transform the very way in which the archival enterprise is viewed and knowledge is produced. Chicana/o scholars have theorized the importance of rethinking the meanings attached to historical artifacts and source materials. As historian Emma Pérez explains, the archive is not a value-neutral repository of incontrovertible truth. Rather, it is a social and cultural product that presents a particular point of view and reifies a distinct narrative, often to the exclusion of other points of view that challenge, disprove, or otherwise upset that common story.[3] While archives certainly contain important historical materials that shed light into the events of the past, they also obscure as much as they reveal. More often than not, archives contain the materials produced by the privileged and governing classes of society. They place emphasis on government documents, letters, books, and memoirs of political leaders or titans of industry—mostly men, and even more often Euro-Americans. Finding Mexican-origin perspectives in the archives is not impossible, but the task is made all the more difficult by the lasting legacy of conquest and the failure to recognize both the potential and the limitations of existing resources. Chicana/o scholars, inspired by the "new" social history, have long understood the value of alternative sources—oral histories, published and unpublished Spanish language writings and periodicals, folklore, photography, and other personal materials.

This is by no means a call for an end to the archive as we presently know it. However, it is critical to reimagine the archive as something more than the brick-and-mortar building, to expand its boundaries into communities and individuals who have, for generations, been the keepers of history. To do so creates a space for producing new narratives that challenge the older versions that range from incomplete to purposefully exclusionary. Making this broader connection between the professional archive and the countless personal archives in Mexican communities across the state, thereby opening up the field for the creation of new and multiple narratives, is one of the primary endeavors of the Hispanic History of Texas Project.

Challenging paradigms is no easy task, particularly in a state whose creation epic has played boldly on the silver screen and has fundamentally shaped its cultural and racial politics and sense of identity. Yet the seeds have been planted. Beyond recovering and preserving documents and providing resources and research opportunities, the Hispanic History of Texas Project endeavors to open a wider intellectual space through organizing and participating in conferences and meetings wherein new scholarship can be shared and can have a positive and lasting impact. In 2008, the Hispanic History of Texas Project partnered with the Texas State Historical Association to cosponsor the annual meeting convened in Corpus Christi. Of the more than sixty panels, roundtables, and events, twenty-two were Recovery Project panels, radically transforming the composition of the conference itself. The essays selected for this volume represent some of the excellent scholarship presented at that meeting. The Recovery Project has similarly partnered with other organizations, including the Western Historical Association, as well as hosting its own meetings in an effort to make the study of Hispanic people central to the study of Texas, the Borderlands, and the West.

This volume and project come out of several analytical and narrative trajectories. The essays primarily engage themes within the field of Chicana/o Studies, especially as it has developed around Texas subjects. Each of the authors approaches the field from the related perspectives of history of the American West and Borderlands history generally. The insights introduced here, however, remind readers of the inherent overlap between fields and disciplines, and likewise, the difficulty of producing scholarship in isolation. As such, this volume attempts to create a space for dialogue across and within fields and disciplines. Moreover, it suggests to us the richly textured narratives that emerge from such an approach. By opening up the conversation, we gain greater insight and perspective.

These articles emerge from a longer tradition of challenging dominant historical narratives by exploring novel forms of critical analysis. A half-century ago, Jovita González and Américo Paredes articulated an oppositional narrative to the popular and academic tropes explaining the historical and social location of ethnic Mexicans in Texas. At the University of Texas at Austin, they wrote both scholarly pieces and fictionalized accounts that defined another way of being in Texas. In 1930, while a graduate student, González presented a master's thesis, "Social Life in Cameron, Starr, and Zapata Counties," which recast the Texas narrative in terms of Tejana/o history and society.[4] For González, the history of the region was bound in the ethnic and racial tension of conquest. She wrote, "Place these two [Mexicans and Anglos] side by side after a war in which one considers itself the victim and views the other as aggressor, and the natural result will not be peace."[5] González also took another approach toward suggesting alternate perspectives on early Texas history through fiction in *Caballero: A Historical Novel* (cowritten with Eve Raleigh) and the collection *Dew on the Thorn.*[6] Written during the Great Depression, these works represented nuanced readings of the complex social landscape Tejanos faced after American annexation. This stood in contrast to the larger than life heroes and triumphalist narrative of Texas at the time. Fiction provided González an avenue to circumvent established paths of academic authority. Yet González's fiction was only published recently, thanks to the recovery efforts of scholars engaged in broader projects.

Américo Paredes took a similar tack by publishing an academic analysis in *With His Pistol in His Hand: A Border Ballad and Its Hero* while also writing a work of fiction, *George Washington Gómez: A Mexicotexan Novel.* In *With His Pistol,* Paredes employs a popular corrido about Gregorio Cortez, performed for decades in South Texas as a critique of the production of historical memory and the Texas mythos. Paredes elevates the song to the level of historical text by using it to recast the story of Cortez and in turn making it the subject of ethnomusical analysis. Using the ballad as a historical text expanded expectations of what constituted "legitimate" historical evidence and in turn situated accepted evidence in a critical frame. The resulting critique of received knowledge that came from broadening the evidentiary base led to a demystification of the dominant Texas narrative. Or as Paredes summed up, "And had the Alamo, Goliad, and Mier not existed, they would have been invented, as indeed they seem to have been in part."[7] And while Paredes could and did directly destabilize the dominant Texas narrative, he pursued fiction as an avenue to explore the impact and weight of the narrative on identity formation. Paredes traces the coming of age of an ethnic Mexican boy in South Texas as he confronts the contradictions and inequities of everyday life. Like *Caballero*, it took decades and a changed literary landscape before Paredes saw the publication of *George Washington Gómez*.

Both González and Paredes used historical fiction to propose alternate constructions of ethnic identity. Set in the context of their academic production, these works suggest that they sensed limits to the explanatory power of scholarly production. The question remains, though, whether these limits were structural or analytical. Were the limits related to marginalization within the academy or a lack of sources related to what was archived and how it had been organized? There is also the matter of recovery. Silenced for decades because of the racial and political climate in which they lived, González and Paredes found ways of challenging the dominant narrative, but it was only after many years that their critiques and alternative perspectives could be seen and appreciated. Fiction was a way around the power structure, and, in this way, fictional works do allow the author to break from the empirical constraints and authoritative perspective expected in academic work. On the other hand, alternate figurations had to make their way into popular and official history through gatekeepers in universities. The extent to which these alternate voices enter into wider debates about power and knowledge is shaped by those stories deemed legitimate and authoritative. We must, in a sense, imagine how this new history appears as we seek to expand archives and the historical record.

A second generation coming after the Chicana/o movement has continued to confront the dominant narratives within the academy. Those working on Texas have developed a deep literature on Mexican Texas aimed at shifting the discourse.[8] Following the general movement incorporating social science analysis in the field of history, these works made use of census data and social theories to paint a broader picture of Mexicans in Texas and racial and ethnic relations generally. By using quantitative evidence and revisiting events from multiple contexts, these historians created a space for ethnic Mexicans in Texas history and situated the region's myths into a broader framework.[9] The current generation of historians follows their lead by employing social analysis while consciously engaging textual and narrative critiques to bring broader meaning to this subject. The authors in this volume connect with these developments in a variety of ways.

Historians of the American West have also moved Texas history in a direction that attempts to account for complex social and cultural interactions, particularly in border regions. Through a methodology perhaps best epitomized by Richard White's *The Middle Ground: Indians, Empires, and Republics in the Great Lakes Region, 1650–1815*, historians have started to recast conquest and colonization through a lens that takes subaltern agency seriously and makes room for mutual impacts between groups.[10] White's now-standard text provides a generation of scholars a model of new possibilities for exploring the idea of a geographic, metaphorical, or symbolic space wherein mutual misunderstandings create new meanings. Historians of the West have produced an increasing number of works of comparative race and ethnicity as well as novel formulations of indigenous communities. Post-*Middle Ground* history allows for the merging of social science with the fictionalized narratives of González and Paredes by presenting a narrative that accounts for nuance and ambiguity in social relations. More to the point of our project, all these historians have continued to emphasize the importance of expanding the evidentiary base to make sense of these worlds.

A rich literature on textual critiques of Texas myths and dominant narratives has shown one direction that historians can follow to extract meaning and significance from alternative sources of Texas history. José David Saldívar, Emma Pérez, and Richard Flores excavate power relations and subject positions through discourses of the past and present in both history and literature.[11] In their hands, Chicano history and border analysis provides insight beyond the lives of those in the region and exposes the lines of authority. The Recovering the Hispanic History of Texas Project seeks to both expand the evidentiary base and broaden the definition of what constitutes evidence. These essays touch on the rich analysis that is possible with a fresh and dynamic reexamination of the past. The Project attempts to increase investment and participation in redefining Texas history. Scrutinized from the "outside" as parochial or provincial—and fiercely guarded from within as exceptional and sacred—Texas's dynamic and diverse history deserves more. In the hands of previous scholars, and of the authors included here, we seek to recover Texas history in a more fundamental way.

As we think imaginatively about the nature of historical record collecting, the Project and this volume make a case for expanding the lines of inquiry beyond the static categories to which we have long been attached. Recent scholarship has pointed to the imperative need to break free from the kinds of binaries that have limited immigration, border, Chicana/o, and ultimately, Texas history: immigrant versus settler, citizen versus "alien," Mexican versus American. For generations, scholars examined the history of Mexican-origin people through the prism of immigration, assimilation, and the nation state. While this work contributed in fundamental ways to our understanding of the Mexican experience and laid the foundation for the work we engage in today, the global realities of the twenty-first century compel us to forge new intellectual terrain. What happens when we ask different questions and try to answer them from a different perspective? By using new methodologies and using categories like gender and sexuality, migration, transnationalism, and globalization as critical analytical devices, we recover a whole new set of stories and experiences and gain a better understanding of the world in which we live.[12] Taking this call to heart, the essays in this volume seek to forge new paths into historical territories, both familiar and not, in order to provide different insight into history. The question is not, "What is Texas?" but rather, "Where is Texas?"

The essays that follow have been divided into three sections. In "Creating Social Landscapes," the authors each reveal the complex ways in which the diverse peoples of the Texas borderlands negotiated difference and forged common ground in a changing political, social, and economic landscape. Francis X. Galán explores the oft-forgotten Texas–Louisiana borderland in the late eighteenth and early nineteenth centuries, where Native Americans, Tejanos, and Euro-Americans forged a peaceful relationship on the fringes of the Mexican frontier. Exploring the intersection of Mexican and Native local healing practices and professionalized medicine of the United States Army, Mark Allan Goldberg reveals how health and healing became critical sites wherein issues of racial and national difference were debated and how disease and health came to be important markers for defining the national body. Emilio Zamora illuminates the profoundly transnational character of ethnic Mexican's social world, as evidenced by the plans to commemorate the 100th anniversary of Mexican independence by funding the construction of schools in Mexico. Highlighting both conflict and consensus, the essays in this section challenge us to conceive of Texas not as a place defined by geographic and national boundaries alone, but as multiple landscapes shaped by myriad processes of intercultural exchange, interaction, and conflict.

The next section, "Racialized Identities," encourages a critical examination of lived experiences in those Texas landscapes. The essays in this section challenge the notion of race as a simple or fixed category. More importantly, they expand our understanding of civil rights mobilization, showing the various ways in which people of color demanded racial justice, particularly in the state's public schools. Virginia Raymond introduces us to the fascinating Alberta Zepeda Snid, a mother and activist, who played a pivotal role in the 1968 rebellion at Edgewood High School and the community's subsequent challenge of the Texas school finance system in *Rodríguez v. San Antonio ISD*. Although Snid's name has disappeared from the record, Raymond uncovers a more multiracial, gendered, and politically diverse response to educational reform in Texas. Dennis Bixler-Márquez recounts the educational reforms enacted in Crystal City as a result of the political successes of the Raza Unida Party. His analysis of the making of the documentary film, *The Schools of Crystal City*, and the context from which it emerged is enhanced by his own experience as an active participant in the Leadership Training Institute (LTI) at Stanford University. Both essays shift our attention to the locations where identities are constructed and politicized.

The final section, "Unearthing Voices," takes up the vital question of recovery, not only in terms of bringing lost voices to the fore, but also in terms of bringing new interpretations as well. James Crisp revisits well-known documents attributed to Tejanos to explore nuance and ambiguity evident when translating Spanish into English. Crisp argues that Anglophone historians have conveniently misconstrued these texts to support the dominant narrative of Texas history when closer scrutiny reveals they present an alternate understanding of the past. In a similar vein, Norma Mouton uses oral history and sermons to uncover the previously untold story of Reverend Gregorio M. Valenzuela, a prominent Mexican Protestant minister, shedding new insight into the religious and cultural diversity of Mexicans in Texas. Donna Kabalen de Bichara takes on the writings of two Mexican writers—Leonor Villegas de Magnón and Jovita Idar—to explore how these women crafted a rich bilingual and bicultural space through their writings. Although both women are well-known in literary circles, these privileged women also provide insight into the hidden feminine spaces in the borderlands.

The essays contained in this volume make important strides toward envisioning a new kind of history of, and for, Texas. They show the transformative power of reconfiguring the dominant themes and narratives and what is possible when scholars employ new methods, take interdisciplinarity to heart, and think creatively and critically about the archive and historical artifacts. The result is a volume that is far from conclusive, but one that we hope points the way to a different path and that encourages work that further challenges scholars to think beyond the old paradigms.

Notes

[1] "The Culture Wars' New Front: U.S. History Classes in Texas," *Wall Street Journal* 14 July 2009 <http://online.wsj.com/article/SB124753078523935615.html>, accessed 14 July 2009. The controversy made its way into the national spotlight, raising concerns about how curriculum changes in Texas would affect textbooks sold to other schools across the country. On May 21, 2010, the

State Board of Education voted 9-to-5 along partisan lines to adopt the more conservative standards. "Texas Approves Textbook Changes," *New York Times* 22 May 2010 <http://www.ny times.com/2010/05/22/education/22texas.html?src=un&feedurl=http%3A%2F%2Fjson8.nytimes. com%2Fpages%2Feducation%2Findex.jsonp>, accessed 12 June 2010.

[2] In his article in *Texas Monthly*, Gregory Curtis argues that the letter in question was probably a copy, made many years later, of a letter from Crockett to his daughter. In it, Crockett wrote of Texas that "I must say as to what I have seen of Texas it is the garden spot of the world the best land and best prospect for health I ever saw is here and I do believe it is a fortune to any man to come here." Gregory Curtis, "What a Crockett!" *Texas Monthly January* 2008 <http://www.texasmonthly.com/2008-01-01/curtis.php?click_code=b5199a5b9230d0cb538fa 24c5469346d#>, accessed 28 July 2009.

[3] Emma Pérez, *The Decolonial Imaginary: Writing Chicanas into History* (Bloomington: Indiana UP, 1999).

[4] The thesis has been republished as Jovita González Mireles and María Eugenia Cotera, *Life Along the Border: A Landmark Tejana Thesis.* (College Station: Texas A & M UP, 2006).

[5] González, *Life Along the Border*, 51.

[6] Jovita González Mireles, Eve Raleigh, José Eduardo Limón, and María Eugenia Cotera. *Caballero: A Historical Novel* (College Station: Texas A & M UP, 1996); Jovita González Mireles, and José Eduardo Limón. *Dew on the Thorn* (Houston, Tex: Arte Publico P, 1997).

[7] Américo Paredes, *With His Pistol in His Hand: A Border Ballad and Its Hero* (Austin: U of Texas P, 1970), 19.

[8] For examples, see Arnoldo De León, *They Called Them Greasers: Anglo Attitudes Toward Mexicans in Texas, 1821–1900* (Austin: U of Texas P, 1983) and *The Tejano Community, 1836–1900* (Dallas, TX: Southern Methodist UP, 1997); Mario T. García, *Desert Immigrants: The Mexicans of El Paso 1880–1920* (New Haven, CT: Yale UP, 1981) and *Mexican Americans: Leadership, Ideology and Identity, 1930–1960* (New Haven, CT: Yale UP, 1993); Gilberto Hinojosa, *A Borderlands Town in Transition: Laredo, 1755–1870* (College Station: Texas A&M UP, 1983); David Montejano, *Anglos and Mexicans in the Making of Texas, 1836–1986* (Austin: U of Texas P, 1987); and Neil Foley, *The White Scourge: Mexicans, Blacks and Poor Whites in Texas Cotton Culture* (Berkeley: U of California P, 1999).

[9] Martha Menchaca, *Recovering History, Constructing Race: The Indian, Black, and White Roots of Mexican Americans* (Austin: U of Texas P, 2002).

[10] Richard White, *The Middle Ground: Indians, Empires, and Republics in the Great Lakes Region, 1650–1815* (Cambridge UP, 1991). For a reflection of the intellectual impact of his book, see Richard White, "Creative Misunderstandings and New Understandings," *The William and Mary Quarterly*, January 2006 <http://www.historycooperative.org/journals/wm/63.1/white.html>, accessed 17 September 2009.

[11] José David Saldívar, *Border Matters: Remapping American Cultural Studies* (Berkeley: U of California P, 1997), Pérez, *Decolonial Imaginary*; Richard Flores, *Remembering the Alamo: Memory, Modernity, and the Master Symbol* (Austin: U of Texas P, 2002).

[12] For examples of this new scholarship, see Denise Segura and Patricia Zavella, eds. *Women and Migration in the U.S.-Mexico Borderlands: A Reader* (Durham, NC: Duke UP, 2007); Samuel Truett and Elliott Young, eds. *Continental Crossroads: Remapping U.S.-Mexico Borderlands History* (Durham, NC: Duke UP, 2004).

CREATING SOCIAL LANDSCAPES

entertainment design ornament

Lost in Translation: Tejano Roots on the
Louisiana-Texas Borderlands, 1716-1821

Francis X. Galán
Our Lady of the Lake University

IN THE SUMMER OF 1821 AT NATCHITOCHES, LOUISIANA, A SMALL PARTY OF
Tejanos under the leadership of Erasmo Seguín met with a young, ambitious
Stephen F. Austin and escorted him along the Camino Real into Nacogdoches
and San Antonio de Béxar. The year before this peaceful encounter, a Spanish
report listed twenty-two Indian nations in Texas divided into "friendly" and "hostile" camps with Caddos among the former and Comanches and Lipan Apaches
among the latter group.[1] Lost somewhere in the transition period following Mexican independence from Spain are the roots of Tejanos in East Texas among
soldier-settlers who traveled the Camino Real that stretched from Mexico City
into present-day Louisiana at a place called Los Adaes and those with whom they
came into contact with in the "Kingdom of the Tejas."[2] Most telling is that a borderland emerged in the 1730s between Louisiana and Texas that held until the
early 1800s without the bloodshed that scholars describe elsewhere in North
America.[3] Tejanos took advantage of whatever opportunities the borderlands
offered far from Mexico City and so close to the United States that frequently
required "finding the balance" among competing indigenous and Euro-American
interests while negotiating changing identities at the edge of empires.[4]

Forgotten Borderland

The founding of the Spanish fort Nuestra Señora del Pilar de los Adaes
("Los Adaes") and nearby mission in 1721 on the northeastern fringe of Spain's

colonial empire in Mexico was the culmination of historical accident and human misunderstanding. It represented Spain's third, and final, effort to block French expansion from Louisiana. Following La Salle's provocative but disastrous efforts to establish a French outpost on the Gulf coast of Texas in the late seventeenth century, the Spanish Crown imagined Texas primarily as part of a defensive perimeter protecting its mining communities in northern New Spain. Meanwhile, Franciscan missionaries viewed Texas as an opportunity to convert indios bárbaros into Spanish subjects. Yet the mission system of incorporation fizzled under both indigenous and European pressure, leaving the military as the only viable option for colonization, besides defense, in such a distant land.[5] Rather than keeping the "enemy" out, however, the Louisiana-Texas borderlands that emerged at the Arroyo Hondo, a creek located about midway between Los Adaes and the French post at Natchitoches, became an imperial borderland as the Adaeseños (soldiers and residents from Los Adaes) settled onto the countryside and accommodated themselves to their surroundings in order to survive.[6]

Broadly defined, the Louisiana-Texas borderlands is the region from present-day Natchitoches on the lower Red River in northwestern Louisiana, westward across the Sabine River to the lower Trinity and Brazos rivers of East Texas, including the upper Texas Gulf coast east of present-day Houston to southwestern Louisiana. Its natural environment encompasses the western edge of the vast woodlands of North America that extends to the Atlantic coast, and hence a dramatic contrast to the mostly semiarid desert of northern Mexico. The eminent historian, David Weber, describes the borderlands of Louisiana and Texas as one of the "strategic frontiers within the Spanish Empire, areas that faced the possessions of other European powers" and where independent Indians held greater leverage. The Caddos in particular played Spain and France against each other since the region had been their homeland for centuries. Their geographic location on the margins of the woodlands, prairies, and plains, which historian David La Vere explains, essentially "functioned as a door between peoples of the Plains and Southwest and those of the Southeast," positioning the Caddos as a people quintessentially "in between."[7] The Louisiana-Texas borderlands marked the tipping point of military, political, and cultural conquest between Anglo-American expansion from the east and the rising Comanche empire from the west on the Southern Plains.[8]

Tejanos also found themselves "in between" rising pillars of fire like their Caddo neighbors on this crossroads of North America, yet the story of the Adaeseños in particular is overlooked in Texas history for several reasons. Los Adaes was abandoned in the 1770s, and the archaeological site is located across the Sabine River state border in Louisiana near the present-day community of Robeline. Demographically, the Adaeseño community remained very small with no greater than 500 Hispanic residents. [9] Its mostly ranching and subsistence economy remained in the shadows of the more densely settled and agriculturally developed bordertown at Natchitoches with its French and African creole population that lured both Adaeseños and Caddos into the emerging Atlantic market and slave-based economy.[10] Lastly, there are no visible architectural reminders of Spanish missions like those of San Antonio. Descendants of the early Hispanic pioneers, however, are still found in the rural communities of Moral and Chireno near Nacogdoches, Texas, and the Spanish Lake and Ebarb communities near Robeline, Louisiana off the same old, beaten path of the Camino Real that blends into Natchitoches. The significance was not the number of Hispanic settlers or even physical structures, but the fact that they fit into the larger historical process of conquest and negotiating one's identity amid the violence often associated with borderlands, smuggling, and immigration.

During the eighteenth century, the remoteness of the Louisiana-Texas borderlands, from legal ports of entry in Mexico and close proximity to French Natchitoches and Caddo settlements in the backcountry, made Los Adaes a smuggler's paradise. Spanish Bourbon officials could not stamp out the burgeoning contraband trade in hides, horses, captives, cattle, guns, ammunition, tobacco, alcohol, ironware, clothes, and other goods. The nearest source of reliable Spanish goods was approximately 800 miles away at Saltillo in northern Mexico along the Camino Real. Adaeseños, however, more often found themselves smuggling in New Orleans and Natchitoches, where travel down the Red River to its confluence with the Mississippi was faster, and likely safer, than overland routes to the Rio Grande through contested boundaries of Apachería, Comanchería, and Spanish Texas.[11]

For many years the governors at Los Adaes illicitly trafficked deerskins and buffalo hides at Natchitoches with the aid of officers and muleteers. Like their counterparts in New Mexico, the governors of Spanish Texas dominated this economic activity and left no opportunity for the development of a merchant or middle class.[12] Deerskins and tobacco became the effective currency of the Louisiana-Texas borderlands, frequently exchanged for desirable French and British goods similar to other backcountry regions in North America in what historian Dan Usner describes as the frontier exchange economy.[13] Spanish governors at Los Adaes also circulated silver pesos along with livestock into smuggling operations at the expense of withholding salaries or properly equipping the troops, which became the greatest source of soldiers' complaints.[14]

Smuggling, face-to-face bartering, and kinship ties defined commercial relations among the French, Spanish, Caddos, and Africans on the Louisiana-Texas borderlands. According to historian H. Sophie Burton, the Indian trade had been the "only systematic economic activity that linked the region to the

Atlantic World." But the rise of Spanish control over New Orleans in 1769 following the Louisiana transfer to Spain in 1762 increasingly brought the Louisiana-Texas borderlands into the Atlantic economy. Tobacco plantations and commercial livestock ranching in the region played dominant roles in social and economic relations as trade with dwindling Indian populations declined over the late colonial period. Spanish Bourbon economic policy encouraged tobacco cultivation through free seeds, agricultural training, African slaves on credit, and guaranteed markets in Mexico and Spain. Burton eloquently states that the "plantation system revolutionized the remote borderland by replacing the frontier exchange economy as the main framework for cross-cultural relations and encoding more strict and permanent notions of ethnicity and race."[15]

Founding Mothers and Fathers

Three individuals who hailed originally from the Mexican border province of Coahuila and another from Los Adaes help flesh out frontier social development on the Louisiana-Texas borderlands before, during, and after its transitions into imperial and national boundaries. The first is Manuela Sánchez Navarro who was both doña and madame, the Spanish and French terms for a woman of nobility. Doña Manuela was born in 1697 at Monclova to parents originally from Saltillo. In 1716 at Presidio San Juan Bautista, Manuela married Louis Juchereau de St. Denis, a French-Canadian adventurer who became commissary officer and guide in the Ramón expedition that reoccupied East Texas for Spain later that year.[16] The historian Donald Chipman says that St. Denis set events into motion that "would change the course of Texas history."[17] The same may be said about Manuela for she and St. Denis had seven children—five daughters and two sons. The first two were born at Presidio San Juan Bautista where Manuela remained behind for several years before rejoining her husband at the French Natchitoches post where their remaining children were born. Historians Chipman and Denise Joseph note that despite Manuela never having actually resided in Texas, she was "assuredly a high-profile colonial woman of importance to the province."[18]

The newly wed madame Manuela Sánchez Navarro de St. Denis became a political, commercial, and cultural broker with real and fictive kinship connections from northern Mexico to New Orleans. Her story parallels that of a female contemporary named Angelina, a Caddo Indian woman from East Texas who studied at Mission San Juan Bautista on the Río Grande next door to the presidio of the same name. Angelina had served as a guide along with St. Denis for Spanish reoccupation of East Texas. By 1721, Manuela had rejoined St. Denis at French Natchitoches while Angelina disappeared from the written record.[19]

Over the next several decades, St. Denis became the godfather of the region in what Patricia Lémee has called "frontier trade cartels," which made Manuela the godmother since both became godparents to French, Spanish, Indian, and African peoples on the Louisiana-Texas borderlands.[20] Manuela, much like Angelina, helped bridge the often violent encounters between men in Texas.[21]

Manuela outlived her husband, who died in 1744, and did not remarry unlike most widows on the frontier. She belonged to the elite class in French Natchitoches society with tremendous wealth, power, and influence. In 1755 at French Natchitoches, Marie de St. Denis, one of Manuela and St. Denis's many children, married a Spanish deserter from Los Adaes named Manuel Antonio Bermúdez de Soto, and they carried forth their parents' legacy on the Louisiana-Texas borderlands into the next generation. When Manuela passed away in Natchitoches in 1758, she was a landowner, businesswoman, and regional cultural broker. She was a trailblazer from Mexico who became a role model for young women from multiethnic backgrounds on the Louisiana-Texas borderlands.[22] Manuela wielded significant power during the period of the Bourbon reforms that promoted the transformation of society under greater secular and patriarchal control.[23]

The second unheralded person is Lt. Joseph González, a forty-year veteran at Presidio Los Adaes. He was born around the year 1700 in Saltillo and married María Gertrudis de la Cerda in 1720 at Monclova.[24] González and his wife arrived at Los Adaes after General don Pedro Rivera's military inspection in the late 1720s. A military roster of Los Adaes in 1731 listed González as an español (Spaniard) with the rank of Second Lieutenant, evidently a recent promotion following the reorganization of East Texas presidios and missions. This roster was the only one that noted the ethnic and racial backgrounds of the Adaeseños. By the time census figures were recorded in Spanish Texas beginning in the late 1770s, Los Adaes had been abandoned.[25] Nonetheless, other archival records for Los Adaes indicate that most Adaeseños were classified as Spaniards, mestizos, and mulattos.[26]

Lt. González most likely knew madame Manuela because his own fifteen-year-old daughter, Victoria, married at French Natchitoches in 1736 to Jean Baptiste Derbanne, son of a prominent merchant and former business partner of St. Denis. Following mass at the chapel of Los Adaes, Jean Baptiste Derbanne eloped with Victoria González under cover of darkness into the pine forest, allegedly with the help from the De la Cerda family, who were related to Lt. González's own wife, as well as fellow Adaeseños from the Mora family.[27] This marital union occurred during a crucial period in the 1730s when Spanish officials in Mexico City and Madrid were adamant about defining the Texas border with French Louisiana. For Lt. González, his daughter's marriage was an embarrassment in his capacity as interim commandant at Los Adaes while Governor don Manuel de Sandoval attended to Apache raids and recently arrived Canary Islanders at San Antonio de Béxar. The whole purpose of the presidio at Los Adaes, which was designated the capital of Spanish Texas in 1729, was to check French encroachment upon Spanish territory.

Lt. González's letters to Governor Sandoval indicated the troubled state of affairs that also existed at Los Adaes. In one letter, for example, dated April 14, 1735, González explained how St. Denis had prevented the transport of supplies to Los Adaes from the French Natchitoches post. Apparently, the Adaeseños were behind in payments to St. Denis and other French merchants at Natchitoches, which related directly to the problem of Governor Sandoval not having paid the soldiers their salaries that the Royal Regulations had set at 400 pesos annually. By late 1735, González reported among other troubling news: the failure of corn that the Adaeseños had planted, great sickness and death among their people, and repairs needed to the fort. He also asked the governor to send a blacksmith to Los Adaes.[28]

Shortly after his daughter eloped with Derbanne the following spring, Lt. González forewarned Governor Sandoval "of the debts that have been contracted with the French for necessary supplies." He urged the governor to return to Los Adaes and quell the unrest of Adaeseños who tarnished his credibility and nobility because the soldiers were dressed in deerskins while their women and children went about naked, making them ashamed even to attend church.[29] The only immediate relief that Lt. González could provide the Adaeseños was beef from livestock on the ranches that the governor and missionaries controlled. He also referred to the importance of the "salineros" (salt traders) in the Caddo salt trade used for curing meats, as well as hides by which means the soldiers could "cover their nakedness."[30] Perhaps Manuela encouraged her husband to do something for these Adaeseños, many from the same province where she was born in northern Mexico. For whatever reason, St. Denis tried persuading Lt. don Pedro de Sierra, who had helped Marqués de Aguayo establish Los Adaes, into leading a mass desertion of Adaeseños to French Natchitoches where they could have all they ever dreamed.[31]

Ironically, Lt. González was again interim commandant at Presidio Los Adaes years later when the Royal Regulations of 1772 ordered the abandonment and evacuation of the fort and missions in East Texas. The following year he led the government's forced exodus of settlers from Los Adaes to San Antonio de Béxar, but he died at the Nacogdoches mission. His legacy endured, however, through his daughter Victoria, his son-in-law Jean Baptiste, and their son Manuel Berbán [Derbanne], who had served under his grandfather at Los Adaes.[32] Manuel Berbán eventually served on the cabildo at San Antonio de

Béxar as a councilman in 1796 and then as attorney in 1801.[33] Lt. González's lengthy career represented a stabilizing force in the borderlands, both within the Adaeseño community and beyond in an ever-changing environment.

Following the death of Lt. González, the indomitable Antonio Gil Ybarbo assumed leadership of the exiles en route to San Antonio de Béxar, where he and Gil Flores led a petition for their return to East Texas. Born at Los Adaes in 1729, Ybarbo became the best-known Spanish settler from East Texas as founder of Nacogdoches in 1779. His own father, Mateo Ybarbo, had emigrated from Andalusia, Spain and arrived at San Antonio de Béxar sometime during the 1720s. In 1728 at Mission San Antonio de Valero (better known as "The Alamo"), Mateo and his wife, Juana Luzgardea Hérnandez, celebrated the baptism of their daughter, Juana Antonia, before their transfer the following year to Los Adaes.[34] Mateo Ybarbo passed away at Los Adaes in 1744, leaving his fifteen-year-old son, Antonio, to make something of the family name.

Antonio Gil Ybarbo's larger-than-life legacy represented most visibly by the Old Stone Fort on the campus of Stephen F. Austin State University in Nacogdoches, has overshadowed fellow Adaeseños as well, such as Sgt. Domingo Chirino, another longtime resident and veteran at Los Adaes. Domingo, and his brother Manuel, were recruited in 1735 from their hometown of Saltillo. They were in their early twenties, illiterate, and from humble backgrounds.[35] Their father, Lázaro Chirino, was a servant with the Ramón expedition in 1716 that temporarily reestablished the Spanish missions in East Texas before evacuation three years later during the Spanish-Franco War in Europe.[36] In 1720 at Mission San Antonio de Valero, Lázaro and his wife, Teresa Sánchez, celebrated the baptism of their son, Christobal, who became a soldier at San Antonio de Béxar along with Luis Chirino.[37] Another one of Lazaro's children, named Andrés, joined brothers Domingo and Manuel at Los Adaes in 1741 while their parents evidently remained behind at San Antonio de Béxar where they entered into kinship relations with Spanish soldiers from the presidio. While Andrés soon became a troublemaker, the archival records reveal that Domingo was loyal to the governors over the decades and deeply involved in their smuggling operations from northern New Spain to New Orleans.[38]

During the residencia, or official review of governor-commandants, of former Governor Don Jacinto de Barrios y Jáurgeui at Los Adaes in 1761, Adaeseños exposed this wide network of smuggling. Lt. Sierra testified that Sgt. Domingo Chirino and Joseph Arredondo, who was the governor's muleteer, transported between 500 and 600 hides from the storage at Mission Nacogdoches to Saltillo for the barter of supplies.[39] Barrios served as governor-commandant at Los Adaes from 1751 to 1758, a lucrative period of smuggling leading into the critical early phase of the French and Indian War. No other governor ruled Spanish Texas longer than him.

A subsequent investigation further revealed the complicated web of illicit trade with the French and Indians implicating Spanish governors and Franciscan missionaries. In 1766, Sgt. Domingo Chirino, then 52-years old, testified that while on patrol with four other soldiers from Los Adaes he encountered friar Francisco Zedano trafficking goods outside the home of a Bidai Indian named Thomas on the lower Trinity River along the Camino Real to La Bahía. Sergeant Chirino had asked Father Zedano if he possessed an order from the president of the missions for the goods, but the friar responded that he instead received permission from Governor Martos y Navarrete, who succeeded Barrios as governor-commandant at Los Adaes. Perhaps sensing contraband trade, Sergeant Chirino seized the goods and transported the items to Los Adaes, which included 299 bundles of French tobacco, a small barrel of brandy, British-made wares, and other goods. He also delivered the muleteers who assisted Father Zedano and were called to testify against the friar.[40] Although their place of residence was omitted from the investigation, some of Zedano's assistants were from Los Adaes, including Agustín Rodríguez, who later became one of the leaders of former Adaeseños at San Antonio de Béxar.[41]

During the government's investigation against Father Zedano, another Franciscan friar named Francisco Xavier de la Concepción, from Mission Los Ais near present-day San Augustine, Texas, testified that Zedano only hoped to lure apostate Indians back to Mission La Bahía, especially with the French tobacco that "the Indians found most desirable."[42] Whether Governor Martos actually gave Father Zedano permission to sell the goods went undetermined, but the governor became mired in greater controversy when Sgt. Domingo Chirino joined Andres Chirino as his adversaries.

In June 1768, Sgt. Domingo Chirino petitioned the viceroy of New Spain against former Governor Martos after interim Governor don Hugo O'Conor investigated Martos during the military inspection of Marqués de Rubí. Sergeant Chirino's petition included a complaint that Martos had "appropriated" his oxen after he transported artillery to San Antonio de Béxar. Chirino added that the former governor's secretary, Francisco Antonio Solís, did not return his riding gear either and had moved to Mexico City instead of going to Natchitoches as he led the sergeant into believing. Sergeant Chirino eloquently closed his petition to the viceroy by stating that "all these things Your Excellency are of very little value in your country, but in this one are very much esteemed and necessary to serve the King (whom God protects) and that costs half my salary."[43]

By autumn, Sgt. Domingo Chirino appeared before O'Conor at Los Adaes for the residencia of Martos. Chirino testified that the former governor and Solís had overcharged his account, doubling the expense for three oxen, a leather saddle, knapsacks, and saddle pads. Lt. Joseph González testified in Chirino's behalf, stating that the sergeant should be paid his due, which O'Conor ordered. By this time, Sergeant Chirino evidently earned the honorific title of don, signifying a greater social status than when he first entered Los Adaes.[44] In 1770, other soldiers at Los Adaes, emboldened by Chirino's courage, also sued Martos y Navarrete for excessive prices he charged their accounts and back pay for the years 1767, 1768, and 1769.[45] The legacy of the "Chirino" name resonates in present-day Chireno, Texas, located along the Camino Real (Hwy. 21) between Nacogdoches and San Augustine and named after their descendant, José Antonio Chirino, who was born at Presidio Los Adaes in 1755. All of these individual biographies are connected to larger transformations in the contest of empires in North America and speak to social, legal, and cultural development at the local level.

The presence of Hispanic families and devotion to the Virgin Mary on the Louisiana-Texas borderlands also defined relationships and sustained the Adaeseño community. The presence of women and children at Los Adaes after 1721, the secular work of Franciscans beyond the missions at French Natchitoches, and cultural brokers like Manuela Sánchez Navarro de St. Denis helped avert violent conflict often encountered elsewhere in Spanish Texas and northern Mexico. Fortunately for Adaeseños, the international boundary at the Arroyo Hondo could not separate Spanish and French families joined under the same Catholic faith that extended into fictive kinship with Caddos and Africans.

Ironically, the devotion to Our Lady of Pilar, after whom Los Adaes was named together with the small independent Caddo band of Adaes Indians, was most evident in limosnas, or alms, in the war against "hostile" Indians. The soldiers from Los Adaes, assigned duty elsewhere in Texas, offered alms in her name before going into battle against Apaches and Comanches. The Account Book for the year 1771 listing troops from Los Adaes assigned duty at San Antonio de Béxar reveals a number of instances where soldiers donated either pesos or gunpowder in the Virgin's honor. For example, Domingo Diego de Acosta gave two pesos and another two pounds of gunpowder in alms to Our Lady of Pilar and to Our Lady of Concepción. The entry for Joaquín Ruíz's account indicates two pesos "in alms for the Mass of Our Lady of Pilar," and even another peso "to a poor blind man."[46] Other Adaeseño soldiers, including the aged veteran Lt. Joseph González, donated what few pesos they received, and gunpowder, so that Mass could be said in the Virgin's name. Whether or not they were compelled to do so was outweighed by the fear of certain death around San Antonio de Béxar. One Adaeseño in particular, Agustin Murillo, was killed by the Indians and left a widowed wife.[47] Adaeseño soldiers prayed to Our

Lady of Pilar and other religious icons for divine intercession during military campaigns in the wilderness, as thoughts of wives and children remained locked inside their hearts. Just as the Catholic religion served to link various ethnic communities on the Louisiana-Texas borderlands, it also set them apart from Southern Plains Indians.

The Louisiana-Texas borderlands remained a scarcely settled and largely porous region by 1805 when Spanish officials increased Spain's military presence in East Texas with the Trinidad de Salcedo settlement on the Trinity River to check illegal immigration and smuggling from the United States following the Louisiana Purchase two years earlier. Under the Bourbon Reforms, which initially opened Louisiana to "foreigners" after the transfer of Louisiana to Spain in 1762 near the end of the French and Indian War, Spanish officials in Texas became concerned over filibusters like Irish immigrant Philip Nolan, among other North American and European immigrants, who came to Nacogdoches in the 1790s from Natchitoches via the Camino Real. Louisiana's total non-Indian population grew from the majority nonwhite population of 11,000 in 1763 to 50,000 residents by 1800, which included more French, English, American, and German settlers than Spaniards. Meanwhile, Spanish Texas still only had around 4,000 residents by 1800 with the majority at San Antonio de Béxar. Historian David Weber notes that both Anglo-American demographic and economic growth put Spain on the defensive in its North American borderlands as it experienced several decades of decline in colonial trade, public revenue, and challenges to royal authority itself from the French Revolution and the rise of Napoleon Bonaparte.[48] Filibusters, adventurers, and traders sought opportunities in the Louisiana-Texas borderlands whenever possible and came into contact with Tejanos seeking similar advantages under Spanish economic reforms.

Amid increasing tensions between Spain and the United States, many Tejanos grew very familiar with Natchitoches, Louisiana where religious, kinship, and commercial ties had continued since the early eighteenth century.[49] In September 1813, Francisco Treviño, a 58-year-old native of San Antonio de Béxar and husband of Josefa de la Garza, was buried in the cemetery at St. Francis Catholic Church of Natchitoches. Father Francisco Magnes administered the last rites shortly after his reassignment by the Mexican Church from Nacogdoches, Texas to foreign duty at Natchitoches. The following month, Facundo Del Rio, a 16-year-old Spanish native from Nacogdoches, was also buried at this church in Natchitoches. Treviño and Del Rio had succumbed to "fever."[50]

These Tejanos were followed in death at Natchitoches by many other natives from San Antonio de Béxar and other parts of Mexico and Spain. Surnames such as Ramos, Vela, Peña, Borrego, Morales, Soto, Musquiz, and Montoya derived from families who had made Natchitoches, Louisiana, their refuge in 1813–1814 following the Battle of Medina, a river located southwest of San Antonio de Béxar on the boundary between Texas and Coahuila, during the revolt against Spain.[51] Tejanos were also buried in Natchitoches at the dawn of Anglo-American colonization in Texas. In 1820, Ignacio de los Santos Coy, a 27-year-old native from San Antonio de Béxar whose parents were Ignacio de los Santos Coy and Manuela García Falcón, was buried at St. Francis Catholic Church. In January 1821, Francisco Torres, a 45-year-old "Spanish soldier of the Alamo," and María Martínez Navarro, a 20-year-old, unmarried native of San Antonio de Béxar, were also buried at Natchitoches.[52]

Tejanos simultaneously welcomed new life with the baptismal celebrations of future generations to come. In October 1813, the one-month-old daughter of José Prado and María Gertrudis Soto, both residents of San Antonio de Béxar, was baptized. The following month, the infant Luis Ramón Acosta was baptized, and his godparents were Ignacio de los Santos Coy and María Gertrudis Chirino, both natives of Nacogdoches. A few years later, an infant son of Joseph Casanova and María Manuela Sequín, was baptized, and his godparents were J. M. Delgado and M. A. Rodríguez.[53]

The stories of these Tejanos are just some of the examples that collectively reveal the deep connections Hispanic pioneers had on the Louisiana-Texas borderlands and beyond. Although Manuela Sanchez Navarro de St. Denis, Lt. Joseph González, Capt. Antonio Gil Ybarbo, and Sgt. Domingo Chirino were originally from Coahuila and Texas, they and many others were the ancestors of those who came to be known as "Tejanos" after 1821 when Mexico finally achieved independence from Spain. The meeting between Erasmo Seguín and Stephen F. Austin in Natchitoches, Louisiana, in 1821, did not occur in a vacuum following revolutionary and filibustering movements, but had deep roots in the complex relationships among Hispanic, French, Indian, African, and Anglo-American interaction over the preceding century. Tejanos utilized the borderlands in search of opportunity and refuge like anybody else in what amounted to a "middle ground" in the piney woods of East Texas and western Louisiana that increasingly became "divided ground" during the revolutionary movements against Spain.[54] Meanwhile, the origins of Tejanos in the "Land of the Tejas" became lost in translation in what historian Cynthia Radding describes as ethnogenesis, or "ethnic rebirth," on the Spanish frontier in North America.[55]

Notes

[1] Gregg Cantrell, *Stephen F. Austin: Empresario of Texas* (New Haven: Yale U P, 1999), 88, 91–92; Raúl A. Ramos, *Beyond the Alamo: Forging Mexican Ethnicity in San Antonio, 1821–1861* (Chapel Hill: U of North Carolina P, 2008), 60.

[2] William L. Eakin, "The Kingdom of the Tejas: The Hasinai Indians at the Crossroads of Change" (Ph.D. diss, U of Kansas, 1997). The Tejas Indians were one of many Caddo groups that formed the Hasinai Confederacy; see F. Todd Smith, *The Caddo Indians: Tribes at the Convergence of Empires, 1542–1854* (College Station: Texas A&M U P, 1995).

[3] For example, of recent works that emphasize violent encounters in the borderlands, see Pekka Hämäläinen, *The Comanche Empire* (New Haven: Yale U P, 2008); Juliana Barr, *Peace Came in the Form of a Woman: Indians and Spaniards in the Texas Borderlands* (Chapel Hill: U of North Carolina P, 2007); Alan Taylor, *The Divided Ground: Indians, Settlers, and the Northern Borderland of the American Revolution* (New York: Alfred A. Knopf, 2006); James F. Brooks, *Captives & Cousins: Slavery, Kinship, and Community in the Southwest Borderlands* (Chapel Hill: U of North Carolina P, 2002).

[4] Raúl Ramos, "Finding the Balance: Béxar in Mexican/Indian Relations," in *Continental Crossroads: Remapping U.S.-Mexico Borderlands History*, edited by Samuel Truett and Elliot Young (Durham: Duke U P, 2004), 35–65; Andrés Reséndez, *Changing National Identities at the Frontier: Texas and New Mexico, 1800–1850* (New York: Cambridge U P, 2005). The label "Tejano" in the eighteenth century refers to Hispanic residents of Spanish Texas, although the origins of tejano derive from the "Tejas" Caddo Indians of the Hasinai confederacy. Scholars of the nineteenth century define "Tejano" as simply "Texas Mexican;" see Gerald E. Poyo, *Tejano Journey, 1770–1850* (Austin: U of Texas P, 1996), xiii.

[5] Many scholarly works describe the violent, disastrous encounters in late seventeenth- early eighteenth-century Texas. For example, see Robert S. Weddle, *Wilderness Manhunt: The Spanish Search for La Salle* (Austin: U of Texas P, 1973); Donald E. Chipman, *Spanish Texas, 1519–1821* (Austin: U of Texas at Austin, 1992); David J. Weber, *The Spanish Frontier in North America* (New Haven: Yale U P, 1992); and Barr, *Peace Came in the Form of a Woman.*

[6] Francis X. Galán, "Presidio Los Adaes: Worship, Kinship, and Commerce with French Natchitoches on the Spanish-Franco-Caddo Borderlands, 1721–1773," *Louisiana History* 49 (Spring 2008), 191–208. John L. Kessell identifies the Río Hondo (Arroyo Hondo) as the "boundary between French Louisiana and Spanish Texas" in his work, *Spain in the Southwest: A Narrative History of Colonial New Mexico, Arizona, Texas, and California* (Norman: U of Oklahoma P, 2002), 217.

[7] David J. Weber, *Bárbaros: Spaniards and Their Savages in the Age of Enlightenment* (New Haven: Yale U P, 2005), 82 ("strategic frontiers"); La Vere, *The Caddo Chiefdoms: Caddo Economics and Politics, 700–1835* (Lincoln: U of Nebraska P, 1998), 3 ("a door" and "in-between"). For definitions of "frontier" and "borderlands," see Jeremy Adelman and Stephon Aron, "From Borderlands to Borders: Empires, Nation-States, and the Peoples in Between in North American History," *American Historical Review* 104 (June 1999), 815–816, 829–830. For a comparative perspective with the notion of being "in-between," see James H. Merrell, *Into the American Woods: Negotiations on the Pennsylvania Frontier* (New York: W.W. Norton & Company, 1999), 27, 36–38, who argues that the "Long Peace" of the eighteenth century prior to the French & Indian War remained "fragile," and the Indians kept "colonists at arm's length." For other examples of Indians playing off European powers elsewhere in North America, see Richard White, *The Roots of Dependency: Subsistence, Environment, and Social Change among the Choctaws, Pawnees, and Navajos* (Lincoln: U of Nebraska P, 1983).

[8] On the rise of eastern Comanches in eighteenth-century Texas, see Hämäläinen, *The Comanche Empire*, 90–106.

[9] For an estimate of the Hispanic population at Los Adaes, see Francis X. Galán, "The Chirino Boys: Spanish Soldier-Pioneers from Los Adaes on the Louisiana-Texas Borderlands, 1735–1792," *East*

Texas Historical Journal 46 (Fall 2008), 42–58, which contains a census list in 1773 that the author recreated from subsequent Spanish census records for Nacogdoches, San Antonio de Béxar, and La Bahía. For some reason, Spanish officials never recorded a census for Los Adaes during its existence from 1721 to 1773. On the archeological and anthropological investigations of Los Adaes, see George Avery, *Los Adaes Station Archeology Program: 1997 Archaeological Annual Report* (Natchitoches: Department of Social Sciences, Northwestern State U of Louisiana, June 1997) and Hiram F. Gregory, "Eighteenth Century Caddoan Archeology: A Study in Models and Interpretations," (Ph.D. diss., Southern Methodist U, 1973).

¹⁰H. Sophie Burton and F. Todd Smith, *Colonial Natchitoches: A Creole Community on the Louisiana-Texas Frontier* (College Station: Texas A&M U P, 2008).

¹¹Weber, The Spanish Frontier in North America, 173; Juliana Barr, "From Captives to Slaves: Commodifying Indian Women in the Borderlands," *Journal of American History* 92 (June 2005), 19–46.

¹²David J. Weber, *The Taos Trappers: The Fur Trade in the Far Southwest, 1540–1846* (Norman, 1971), 18.

¹³Carl J. Ekberg, *French Roots in the Illinois Country: The Mississippi Frontier in Colonial Times* (Urbana and Chicago, 1998), p. 160; Rhys Isaac, *The Transformation of Virginia, 1740–1790* (Chapel Hill, 1982). On the frontier exchange economy, see Dan Usner, *Indians, Settlers, and Slaves in a Frontier Exchange Economy: The Lower Mississippi Valley Before 1783* (Chapel Hill: U of North Carolina P, 1992), 6–9, who explains that it entailed "substantial intraregional connections" that included a "diverse and dynamic participation of Indians, settlers, and slaves" in relationships marked by fluidity and plenty of common ground for survival in the wilderness. The plantation economy, he argues, increasingly replaced this frontier exchange of livestock, captives, hides, and other goods especially after the Treaty of Paris in 1783 formally concluded the American Revolution.

¹⁴Francis X. Galán, "Last Solders, First Pioneers: The Los Adaes Border Community on the Louisiana-Texas Frontier, 1721–1779," (Ph.D. diss., Southern Methodist U, 2006), chapters 5 and 6.

¹⁵H. Sophie Burton, 'To Establish a Stock Farm for the Raising of Mules, Horses, Horned Cattle, Sheep, and Hogs': The Role of Spanish Bourbon Louisiana in the Establishment of Vacheries along the Louisiana-Texas Borderland, 1766–1803," *Southwestern Historical Quarterly* ("*SWHQ*") 109 (July 2005), 102.

¹⁶Donald E. Chipman and Harriett Denise Joseph, *Notable Men and Women of Spanish Texas* (Austin: U of Texas P, 1999), 259–260; Patricia R. Lemee, "Manuela Sanchez Navarro," *The Natchitoches Genealogist*, 20 (October 1995), 17–19, 21; Debbie S. Cunningham, "The Domingo Ramón Diary of the 1716 Expedition into the Province of the Tejas Indians: An Annotated Translation," *SWHQ* 110 (July, 2006), 39–67.

¹⁷Chipman, *Spanish Texas*, 184.

¹⁸Chipman and Joseph, *Notable Men and Women of Spanish Texas*, p. 261.

¹⁹Teresa Palomo Acosta and Ruthe Winegarten, *Las Tejanas: 300 Years of History* (Austin: U of Texas P, 2003), 4–5.

²⁰Patricia R. Léeme, "Tios and Tantes: Familial and Political Relationships of Natchitoches and the Spanish Colonial Frontier," *SWHQ* 101 (January 1998), 342; see also, Elizabeth Shown Mills, *Natchitoches, 1729–1803: Abstracts of the Catholic Church Registers of the French and Spanish Post of St. Jean Baptiste des Natchitoches in Louisiana* (New Orleans: Polyanthos, 1977).

²¹Juliana Barr, *Peace Came in the Form of a Woman*. For another recent work with discussion of gender on the Louisiana-Texas borderlands, see Burton and Smith, *Colonial Natchitoches*.

²²Galán, "Presidio Los Adaes: Worship, Kinship, and Commerce with French Natchitoches on the Spanish-Franco-Caddo Borderlands, 1721-1773."

²³For a discussion of the importance of gender in eighteenth-century Texas, see Barr, *Peace Came in the Form of a Woman*; see also, Jean Stuntz, *Hers, His, & Theirs: Community Property Law in Spain and Early Texas* (Lubbock: Texas Tech U P, 2005).

²⁴Lemée, "Manuela Sanchez Navarro," 20.

[25]Lista, y relacion, Don Juan Antonio de Bustillo y Zevallos, Governador de esta Provincia de Thexas, Presidio de Nuestra Señora del Pilar de los Adais, 27 de mayo de 1731, Archivo General de México—Provincias Internas, Catholic Archives of Texas, Austin, Box 53.2a, 32–34, transcription. For census data discussion, see Alicia Vidaurreta Tjarks, "Comparative Demographic Analysis of Texas, 1777–1793," *SWHQ* 77 (January, 1974), 291–338.

[26]Relación y Extracto de los Soldados de la Compania de este Real Presidio de Nuestra Señora del Pilar de los Adais, 1734-1736, Archivo General de México—Historia (AGM-Historia), in Catholic Archives of Texas, Box 38, Folder 4c, pp. 176-180, transcription. The only other known military archival record that lists ethnicity at Los Adaes is from 1735, which also notes an actual physical description and place of origin. Other archival documents such as residencias (reviews of governor-commandants) include depositions of soldier-settlers from Los Adaes that also note ethnicity as well as their age, place of residency, and whether they were literate.

[27]Galán, "Last Soldiers, First Pioneers: The Los Adaes Border Community on the Louisiana-Texas Frontier, 1721–1779," 352–355.

[28]Letter, Lt. Joseph González to Governor Sandoval, April 14, 1735, Presidio Los Adaes, Archivo General de la Nación—Historia (AGN-Historia), Vol. 395, Microfilm, Box 5, 230v.–231, in Mission Dolores Historical Manuscript Collection, Mission Dolores Visitors Center, San Augustine, Texas; Letter, Lt. González to Governor Sandoval, November 12, 1735, Presidio Los Adaes, AGN-Historia, 232v.–234v. Father Ignacio Antonio Ciprian, a Franciscan friar from Mission Dolores de los Ais near present-day San Augustine in deep East Texas, also sent the governor dismal reports about the Adaeseño community; Letter, Fray Ignacio Antonio Ciprian to Governor Sandoval, December 4, 1735, Mission Nuestra Señora de los Dolores de los Ais, AGN-Historia, 225.

[29]Letter, Lt. González to Governor Sandoval, April 29, 1736, Presidio Los Adaes, AGN-Historia, Vol. 395, Mf, Box 5, 240v.-243. Author's translation.

[30]Letter, Lt. González to Governor Sandoval, August 29, 1736, Presidio Los Adaes, AGN-Historia, 243–244. Author's translation.

[31]Galán, "Last Soldiers, First Pioneers."

[32]Certification, completion of service for the officers and soldiers, Bexar Archives ("BA"), Mf, 9:0877. The spelling of the French surname d'Herbanne [Derbanne] was changed to Berban in Spanish archival records and also appears as Derban. Among the Chirino boys who appeared on this list were Domingo and Andres; Power of Attorney, granted by officer and soldiers from Los Adaes to Diego Antonio Giraud for the collection of their salaries, December 31, 1751, Presidio Los Adaes, BA, Mf, 9:0287; Power of Attorney, ibid., December 31, 1753, Presidio Los Adaes, BA, Mf, 9:0454. Jean Baptiste Derbanne himself, as Lt. Gonzáles' French son-in-law, was listed among Power of Attorney documents in 1751 and 1753 granted by officers and soldiers at Presidio Los Adaes.

[33]Lemée, "Tios and Tantes: Familial and Political Relationships of Natchitoches and the Spanish Colonial Frontier," 351, n. 40.

[34]Book of Baptisms, Mission San Antonio de Valero, Entry No. 230, July 6, 1728, The Daughters of the Republic of Texas Library at the Alamo ("DRT Library"), translations by John Ogden Leal.

[35]Relación y Extracto de los Soldados de la Compania de este Real Presidio de Nuestra Señora del Pilar de los Adais, 1734–1736, AGM-Historia, Box 38, Folder 4c, 176–180.

[36]Cunningham, "The Domingo Ramón Diary of the 1716 Expedition into the Province of the Tejas Indians: An Annotated Translation," 50.

[37]Book of Baptisms, Mission San Antonio de Valero, Entry No. 56, January 7, 1720, DRT Library; Galán, "The Chirino Boys: Spanish Pioneer-Soldiers from Los Adaes on the Louisiana-Texas Borderlands, 1735–1792," 43.

[38]Book of Baptisms, ibid., Entry No. 315, July 22, 1730, Ana Sosa, legitimate daughter of Juan de Sosa, solider from the Presidio of San Antonio, and María Camacho (Godparents: Lazaro Chirino and his wife, Teresa Sánchez); Galán, *ibid*, 44–45.

[39]Declaration, Lt. Pedro de Sierra, Alférez, from Los Adaes, January 26, 1761, Presidio Los Adaes, Royal investigation into contraband trade, BA, Microfilm, Reel 9, Frame No. 951.

[40]Testimony, Sgt. Domingo Chirino, December 1, 1766, Presidio Los Adaes, Diligencias Practicadas por el Gobernador de Texas sobre el aprehensión de los generos de contrabando que en ellas se expresan, BA, 10:0444-0466. A Texas Historical Commission marker entitled "Don Joaquin Crossing on Bedais Trail," stands near the spot where Father Zedano and many Indians, explorers, and traders traveled. The mission and fort at La Bahía were located near present Goliad, Texas. The Bidai Indians were close allies of the Tejas Caddo Indians.

[41]Agustín Rodríguez led a petition effort in 1778 on behalf of fellow Adaeseños seeking suitable lands for subsistence following their forced removal to San Antonio de Béxar in 1773; see Expediente promovido por los vecinos del extinguido Presidio de los Adaes, Archivo General de Indias—Guadalajara 267, Mf, Reel 2, Doc. 25, Old Spanish Missions Historical Research Library, Our Lady of the Lake U, San Antonio, Texas; see also Jesús F. de la Teja, *San Antonio de Béxar: A Community on New Spain's Northern Frontier* (Albuquerque: U of New Mexico P, 1995), 84–86, who describes the resettlement of remaining Adaeseños onto mission lands.

[42]Testimony, Fr. Francisco Xavier de la Concepción, December 4, 1766, Presidio Los Adaes, BA, 10:0452. Author's translation; see also, Galán, "The Chirino Boys: Spanish Pioneer-Soldiers from Los Adaes on the Louisiana-Texas Borderlands, 1735-1792," 43-44.

[43]Petition, Sgt. Domingo Chirinos to His Most Excellency Sir, viceroy Marqués de Croix, June 15, 1768, Presidio Los Adaes, BA, 10:0579-0580. Author's translation.

[44]Testimony, don Domingo Chirino, sergeant, October 25, 1768, appearing before Governor O'Conor, Presidio Los Adaes, ibid., 10:0582-0583; Testimony, Lt. Joseph Gonzáles, February 1, 1769, ibid., 10:0583-0584; Order, Governor don Hugo O'Conor, February 3, 1769, ibid., 10:0584-0585.

[45]Mediation, don Eliseo Antonio Llana de Vergara, with Power of Attorney for the soldiers from Presidio Los Adaes, appearing before viceroy don Carlos Francisco de Croix, the Marqués de Croix, May 28, 1770, Mexico City, ibid., 10:0723-0725. The "protector mediador" in litigation proceedings among Spanish subjects was similar to the "protector de indios," a crown-appointed official who represented Indians in formal litigation; see Charles R. Cutter, *The Legal Culture of Northern New Spain* (Albuquerque: U of New Mexico P, 1995), 88.

[46]Account Book, Troops from Los Adaes in San Antonio de Béxar, January 1, 1771–December 31, 1771, BA, UT-Austin, Box 2S31, 166-167 (Domingo Diego de Acota); 181 (Joaquín Ruiz), "de limosna p.a, la misa de nstra, Sra., del Pilar," (First Quotation), "aun pobre siego." (Second Quotation). Author's translation.

[47]Account Book [1771], ibid., BA, 210 (Francisco de los Santos); 217v. (Joseph Antonio Gutiérrez); 225 (Pedro de Luna); 241 (soldado Joaquín Mansolo, donated also to Concepción); 241 (soldado Melchor Morin, donated also to Concepción); 244 (soldado Joseph Antonio de Torres); 247 (soldado Prudencio Rodríguez); 252 (Lt. don Joseph Gonzales).

[48]Weber, *The Spanish Frontier in North America*, 274–275; Tina Laurel Meacham, "The Population of Spanish and Mexican Texas, 1716–1836," (Ph.D. dissertation, U of Texas at Austin, 2000), 267. The population of nearby Kentucky alone in 1800 was already 221,000 inhabitants, a dramatic increase from 12,000 in 1783 at the end of the American Revolution.

[49]See, for example, Galán, "Presidio Los Adaes: Worship, Kinship, and Commerce with French Natchitoches on the Spanish-Franco-Caddo Borderlands, 1721–1773"; Burton and Smith, *Colonial Natchitoches*.

[50]Elizabeth Shown Mills, *Natchitoches: Translated Abstracts of Register Number Five of the Catholic Church Parish of St. François des Natchitoches in Louisiana: 1800–1826*, Vol. II (New Orleans: Polyanthos, 1980), Entry No. 864 (Francisco Trevino); Entry No. 871 (Facundo Del Rio).

[51]Mills, ibid., Vol. II, Entry Nos. 865 (Juan Jose Vela) and 866 (Victoriano Ramos), 140; Entry No. 872 (Ignacio Peña); Entry Nos. 876 (Jose Estevan Borrego), 877 (Juan Morales), 880 (María Gertrudis Soto), 142; Entry Nos. 882 (Joaquín Muzquíz), 886 (Jose Pablo Montoya).

[52]Mills, ibid., Vol. II, Entry No. 2700; Entry No. 2716; Entry No. 2719. These Tejanos also died from fever.

[53]Mills, ibid., Vol. II, Entry No. 439 (María Antonia Prado); Entry No. 444 (Luis Ramón Acosta); Entry No. 2839 (Joseph Crisanto Casenave).

[54]Richard White, *The Middle Ground: Indians, Empires, and Republics in the Great Lakes Region, 1650–1815* (New York: Cambridge U P, 1991), x, who explains that the middle ground is a process of accommodation that occurs in a place "in between cultures, peoples, and in between empires and the nonstate world of villages" where new meanings and shared practices arise from initial misunderstanding and violence. By the early nineteenth century, this middle ground ran its course in the pays d'en haut, or Great Lakes, region of the northern borderlands in North America; see also, Taylor, *The Divided Ground*, 11, who plays off the title of White's Middle Ground to reflect "variations in geographic and temporal emphasis, and refers to "common ground" whereby Indians "adapt creatively to the transforming power of intruding empires."

[55]Cynthia Radding, *Wandering Peoples: Colonialism, Ethnic Spaces, and Ecological Frontiers in Northwestern Mexico, 1700–1850* (Durham: Duke U P, 1997), 8; see also, Gary C. Anderson, *The Indian Southwest, 1580–1830: Ethnogenesis and Reinvention* (Norman: U of Oklahoma P, 1999).

"It can be cultivated where nothing but cactus will grow": Local Knowledge and Healing on the Texas Military Frontier

Mark Allan Goldberg
University of Wisconsin-Madison

IN AN 1851 EDITION OF THE NEW YORK JOURNAL OF MEDICINE AND COLLATERAL Sciences, Assistant Surgeon Glover Perin published a paper on the use of maguey as a remedy for scurvy, a nutrition-related illness. Stationed at Fort McIntosh, Texas, the surgeon learned about maguey from a Mexican Catholic priest in the nearby border town of Laredo, who successfully treated himself with the agave plant when he suffered an attack of the disease. Perin then used maguey to treat a few U.S. soldiers after both lime juice and dietary changes did not produce the desired results. Those patients recovered, and Perin wrote: "So convinced was I of the great superiority of the maguey over either of the other remedies employed, that I determined to place all the patients upon that medicine. The result has proved exceedingly gratifying; every case has improved rapidly from that date."[1] Perin was so satisfied that he even suggested that the plant could benefit others in the desert region by transplanting the agave throughout Texas. "As it delights in a dry sandy soil," Perin advocated, "it can be cultivated where nothing but cactus will grow; for this reason, it will be found invaluable to the army at many of the western posts."[2] Doctors stationed in other parts of Texas did not describe the actual cultivation of agave. Nevertheless, the news of Perin's successful results using maguey for scurvy spread to forts in south Texas, and it even reached some posts in west Texas. The Mexican priest and Doctor Perin redefined the contours of local plant knowledge that was situated in northern Mexico; it moved from the border northward, as well as across ethnic lines. Through this transcultural negotiation, army surgeons healed soldiers and sustained the military conquest of the North American West. But even as Anglos targeted Mexican cultures during westward expansion, Mexican peoples reinforced their healing practices by passing on their medical knowledge, which entered the U.S. military infrastructure and the professional medical domain.

The cross-cultural exchange of healing practices occurred within the context of Anglo-American colonization of Texas. Through the language of health, Anglos produced race and gender in the Texas borderlands. Anglo physicians used health to craft images of an American nation in racial terms, which in turn became one basis for the U.S. conquest of the Texas borderlands and furthered the subordination of Mexican and Native peoples in Texas.[3] Following the U.S.-Mexican War, military forts began to dot the landscapes of south and west Texas in the mid-nineteenth century, acting as symbols of the U.S. conquest of the region, and military surgeons treated soldiers stationed at each post. Based primarily on the government's 1856 publication of military medical reports, the "Statistical Report on the Sickness and Mortality in the Army of the United States," this article focuses on Anglo army doctors and their interactions with Mexicans in the south Texas-Mexico border area and Comanches in west Texas. Although stationed in such different landscapes, the physicians in south and west Texas had parallel medical experiences—they encountered diverse healing cultures, and they used race to conceptualize illness. These similarities underscore the broader national and imperial implications of the physicians' medical discourse and practices. Anglos used health to differentiate themselves from and to marginalize Mexican and Native peoples, as the U.S. nation expanded into Texas.

Historian Charles Rosenberg writes that disease has helped to "frame debates about society and social policy . . . [and] has served as both index of and monitory comment on society."[4] Scholars have shown that during debates over westward expansion, politicians, journalists, and boosters east of the Mississippi River promoted the colonization of the West, as they saw the region as land for the taking.[5] They have also highlighted the scientific links to this political rhetoric. From their laboratories, nineteenth-century scientists formulated biological justifications for Anglo-Saxon racial superiority and the conquest of the West and its inhabitants.[6] These scientific theories rendered that Anglos had legitimate access to lands since nonwhites could not establish the necessary "free," "republican" institutions in the West due to their supposed innate inferiority. Moreover, many Anglos claimed that Anglo dominance and the disappearance of the "inferior" peoples were inevitable.[7] This article examines the medical discourse about the West and western peoples from a different perspective. Rather than examine conquest from a safe distance, the cases below show how military surgeons crafted imperialism on site through their medical topographies and their interactions with local populations.

Anglo migrants defined Mexican peoples and their cultural practices as unhealthy and uncivilized, especially those of the poorer classes, who relied on "unorthodox" healers like curandero/as or lived in densely populated jacales. They described Native cultures in similar ways, citing the savagery of Comanche nomadism and Indian spiritual healing. The newcomers sought to impose their own notions of civilization onto Texas inhabitants; however, social interactions among Texas inhabitants undermined Anglo visions of race and nation. Health was a site of differentiation, but it also became a site of interaction between Mexican and Indian residents and Anglo newcomers. At the military posts, Anglo doctors borrowed local plant knowledge and medical practices in order to cure sick soldiers and maintain a healthy military frontier for colonization. Even though medical theory distinguished between white and nonwhite bodies, physicians still used local healing practices on Anglo soldiers —therapies that Mexicans and Indians had been using for generations. By relying on non-Anglo "inferiors," the doctors' actions on the ground exposed the tensions between medical theory and practice.

This article shifts the historiographical focus from political institutions and economies to cultural practice and examines the affects of U.S. conquest on Mexican and Native healing cultures. Through analyses of popular politics, local economies, mapmaking, and social relations, historians have shown that community members shaped the contours of state formation from the ground level.[8] A focus on healing demonstrates that state formation in the nineteenth-century borderlands was not just a political, economic, and social negotiation; it was also a cultural one, as Mexicans and Native peoples shaped the process of colonization through their possession, practice, and transfer of local medical knowledge.[9] The cultural conquest of the West was also a negotiated process, and Anglos could not impose cultural domination.

Disease outbreaks transformed culture clashes between Anglo migrants and Mexican and Native peoples into a process of exchange that facilitated Mexican and Indian cultural continuity. The exchange of healing practices between Mexican and Native residents and Anglo newcomers reinforced local cultures. Through their encounters with locals, military physicians, or surgeons, as they were called at the time, learned about Mexican and Comanche healing practices. When military doctors borrowed local healing practices that Texas residents had been using for centuries, they recognized the power of Mexican and Comanche healing and exposed the limits of their own medical knowledge.[10] Despite Anglo attacks on

Mexican and Comanche cultures, Mexicans and Indians maintained many of their healing practices. Through the exchange of healing knowledge, Mexican and Comanche peoples influenced the course of colonization, as their cures healed U.S. soldiers and also contributed to the U.S. professional medical world.

Military Medicine and U.S. Westward Expansion

Anglo military physicians moved west to help ensure the health of soldiers who went west to protect Anglo migrants and U.S. claims to land. Following the U.S.-Mexican War, the U.S. military established forts in south and west Texas. Each post had a hospital with an army surgeon to minister to sick soldiers. As agents of the nation, these physicians did not solely heal patients, and their service extended far beyond the military. They assessed the "new" lands as fit or unfit for settlement. And the fitness of the land depended on the healthiness of the environment and the character of its inhabitants. In 1852, the U.S. Surgeon General, Thomas Lawson, required that military doctors report on their surroundings to national officials, thereby creating medical topographies. Lawson ordered military surgeons to acquire local knowledge of climate, geological formations, the environment, and causes of disease to test the healthfulness of newly acquired lands for Anglo colonization. Part of the search for disease causation included the observation of "habits and modes of life." When testing the health of a place, Lawson asked physicians to observe the medical experiences of local populations to further understand the health of the region:

> You are also requested to collect together as many facts as possible concerning the vital statistics of the inhabitants in the vicinity of your post, particularly of the Indian tribes; giving a brief but clear account of their several diseases, . . . embracing every matter of information calculated to prove useful or interesting to the [War] department and the medical world.[11]

The medical topographies reflected early nineteenth-century exploration narratives in which the U.S. government also required explorers to document their surroundings as well as local populations. Like the explorers before them, doctors collected knowledge of newly conquered areas and brought these "unknown" regions into the national consciousness. The reports therefore became a tool for the colonial project for the North American West.[12]

Between endemic and epidemic disease in Texas, illness was a daily concern among inhabitants of the region. A number of endemic diseases troubled individuals, especially on the military frontier. Among soldiers, fevers and digestive disorders such as diarrhea and dysentery were a primary concern. In addition, scurvy afflicted many military men as well as neighboring Indians and

Mexicans. Respiratory disease, such as pneumonia and tuberculosis, was found among some soldiers but primarily among Comanches in Texas. Sexually transmitted diseases afflicted residents in the area, including Anglo military men, Mexican locals, and Native peoples. A cholera epidemic hit south Texas in February of 1849, and central and east Texas in May of that year. And yellow fever epidemics ravaged the Gulf Coast in the 1850s.

Daily life for Texas soldiers brought a number of obstacles, exacerbating their bouts with illness. The military stationed in Texas's western frontiers, for example, experienced higher rates of mortality compared to the U.S. army as a whole. Military doctors attributed this discrepancy to longer working hours in a harsher environment. Assistant Surgeon S. Wylie Crawford wrote that in west Texas "the rules of the service impose upon him other and more laborious duties than those belonging to the mere soldier."[13] Moreover, military men often drank alcohol during free moments to cope with the rigorous work schedule.[14] The physicians argued that drinking further exacerbated susceptibility to disease, as it weakened soldiers' physical constitutions. Surgeon S.P. Moore commented on intemperance as a major contributor to illness on the military frontier and "remarked that the drunkard is almost sure to die."[15] Assistant Surgeon W.W. Anderson fought to curb the "nefarious traffic" of alcohol in west Texas because "if continued, this state of things may lead to some unpleasant or fatal consequences."[16] Along with the migration to "new" and "unhealthy" environments and the interactions with locals, the soldiers' everyday routine gave doctors another reason to worry about the health of their patients. These concerns surfaced throughout the physicians' medical reports.

Before physicians were able to pinpoint disease to specific microbes in the late-nineteenth century, they took race and environment into account when diagnosing illness, as the environment was central to pre-germ theories of medical practice. During the 1833 cholera epidemic in northern Mexico, for example, state officials passed a series of initiatives that targeted dirty spaces and sought to maintain cleanliness in order to prevent the spread of the disease.[17] The environment also played a role in the ways that people outside of the medical world understood health. People worried over dirty, impure airs, or miasmas, that emanated from harmful spaces or things because these miasmas produced weakened constitutions.[18] They also believed that illness affected people with different racial backgrounds in different ways. The theory held that people grew fit to their physical surroundings, linking health, race, and the environment.[19] Therefore, migration brought sickness that forced newcomers to become medically acclimated to their new surroundings. In colonial settings such as this one, this form of medical environmentalism was what historian Warwick Anderson calls "a discourse of racial adaptation and colonial settlement."[20]

Newcomers were always concerned with how their surroundings affected their health, and they constantly had to stave off "new" illnesses. For example, Surgeon Moore wrote that the arrival of "unacclimated strangers" at Fort Brown during the 1853 yellow fever epidemic facilitated the spread of the disease.[21] W.W. Anderson felt that because "one-half of the command [at Fort Terrett] is composed of recruits lately arrived, a large majority of whom . . . are unaccustomed to this climate," they were susceptible to illness.[22] Hence, the impetus for the medical topographies: the government had to learn how to approach and inhabit new and potentially unhealthy environments. Health and acclimation, then, determined the success of colonization. And social issues, like race relations, influenced doctors' designation of peoples and places as either healthy or unhealthy. Military surgeons often racialized disease; they often attributed disease causation to race and culture and used health to construct racial difference and "prove" racial superiority and inferiority. Because of the tensions that existed between nineteenth-century medical theory and the actual practice of medicine at the Texas forts, the study of Anglo appropriations of local healing therapies requires a discussion of the social and medical worlds of the West. And since race informed disease diagnosis, the multiracial West offered Anglo physicians a place to explore the connections between race, health, and environment.

Race and Disease Diagnosis on the Military Frontier

Physicians who were new to the region developed a medical discourse that attributed the healthiness of Texas to its climate and environment. In September of 1854, Assistant Surgeon J. Frazier Head, stationed at Fort Merrill along the Nueces River, reported his explanation for a hike in the number of ill soldiers between the months of July and September. He saw that the "rise and fall of the [Nueces] river was followed by an increase of the sick-report" because the sun beat down on the overflowed waters, rendering the water unhealthy.[23] At the end of summer, winds blew the miasma that emanated from the water in the direction of the fort. Assistant Surgeon Israel Moses also noted a "marked increase in the number and intensity of the fever cases immediately after a rainy period" when he was stationed at Fort Merrill.[24] Located near the Gulf Coast, the soldiers at Fort Brown experienced numerous bouts of yellow fever, and Surgeon S.P. Moore attributed the illness to climate. He claimed that the epidemic struck worst in the fall due to sudden temperature changes and after winds carried noxious airs emanating from vegetable and animal decomposition.[25]

Surgeon Moore also reported on living conditions in Brownsville. He emphasized the uncleanliness of Mexican spaces, which certainly had implications for the way he conceptualized the health of the place and the people that inhabited it. His descriptions of the town reflected doctors' concerns over mias-mas. Moore first commented on the streets and drainage system:

> A majority of the inhabitants of Brownsville are Mexicans, living in miser-able hovels, called "jacales;" the streets are not very cleanly, and but par-tially paved; the town contains about 3,500 inhabitants. There is no system of drainage in the town; the water runs off as well as it can, or remains on the ground. The Mexicans are not particular; for it is not uncommon to see the women, after a rain, collecting it from the little puddles around their houses. . . . The men use the river-water. At the season when the river is low, the water is so extremely unpalatable as to render it almost impossible to drink it, being strongly impregnated with sulphur.[26]

The threat of dirty air and water formed a major component of nineteenth-century medical theory. Moore reported that these "miserable" places rendered this predominantly Mexican town unhealthy. He also described the dirtiness within Mexican homes and connected this assessment with his ideas about race. "The Mexicans are a miserable race of beings," he wrote, "existing in squalid wretchedness in their foul cabins, very ignorant and superstitious."[27] For Moore, Mexican spaces both inside and outside the home were filthy environments that produced illness. His report obscured the socioeconomic discrepancies that fos-tered the town's poor drainage systems and the densely populated neighbor-hoods of jacales. Perhaps Moore felt that the town's unhealthy infrastructure "proved" the inability of Mexicans to govern themselves or that the Mexican "race" was too lazy to maintain clean living spaces. These characterizations reflected the Anglo racial ideology of Manifest Destiny that justified conquest in their eyes. In his description of Brownsville and its population, he under-scored the medical dangers that these Mexican spaces, and, by extension, these Mexican peoples, posed.[28]

While they sought out the links between health and the environments in which people lived, Anglo physicians also attributed the healthiness (or unhealthiness) of Mexicans and Indians in the Texas borderlands to their behav-iors and cultural practices. When stationed at the Ringgold arracks located between Laredo and Brownsville, Israel Moses reported that "the Mexicans are remarkably healthy, owing to their simple diet, and being much in the open air." However, Moses also commented on the "immorality" of the Mexican popula-tion in the nearby Mexican town of Camargo, which informed his analysis of their health. He wrote that everyone there gambled, and he particularly cited Mexican women as being "loose in morals, but far superior to the men."[29] Moses elaborated on his position on both Mexican morality and Mexican women in his assessment of sexually transmitted diseases at the Ringgold Barracks. He exclaimed,

> The most extraordinary feature . . . is the complete absence of syphilitic dis-
> ease; the single case of gonorrhea was contracted in the vicinity of Laredo.
> Not a case exists in town, nor among the troops—a fact without precedent!
> That a Mexican town, in which there are about two hundred women, and
> mostly of Mexican morals, should exist without syphilis among them, is a
> wonder.[30]

Despite the actual absence of disease, Moses's assessment revealed the connections that Anglos made among race, morality, and health.

Moses racialized sexually transmitted diseases, as he showed astonishment
at the absence of such illnesses in Mexican towns. Even though it took two to
tango, he ignored the role of soldiers' sexual appetites for Mexican women in
disease transmission and presented the women as the sole cause of venereal disease.[31] Moses cited the role of Mexican women's morality in the spread of
syphilis and linked his conception of the Mexican "race" and "gender" with illness. Unlike those Anglo men who prized Mexican women, Moses saw them as
a threat to the health of American soldiers. Nineteenth-century physicians often
linked morality and health, especially regarding sexually transmitted diseases.
But they rarely expanded on discussions of sex due to the social context of the
period, and Moses is the only doctor in the government publication who commented on sexually transmitted diseases in his report.[32] When S. P. Moore of
Fort Brown declared that "morality is in a very low state, with no sign of
improvement," perhaps he was referring to Mexican women and their so-called
responsibility for sexually transmitted disease around Brownsville.[33]

Similarly, military physicians in west Texas conveyed their ideas about
proper American ways of living through descriptions of healthy and unhealthy
behaviors among Native peoples. Historian Steven Feierman argues that healing
therapies reflected broader social and cultural values, as healers had the "power
to name an illness, to identify its causes, [which] is also the power to say which
elements in the experience of life lead to suffering."[34] Military surgeons argued
that Comanche customs and ways of life caused illness, strengthening the U.S.
government's desire to push Indians onto reservations. In 1853, for example,
Assistant Surgeon S. Wylie Crawford wrote that most of the Comanches who
lived near his post died from respiratory illnesses. He identified a number of
causes for the disease: the cultural practice of smoking; sleeping on the ground
in houses overheated by the west Texas sun; and last, the Native peoples' innate
physical weakness that made them susceptible to any illness.[35] The image of the
sick and weak Comanche helped Crawford define his Indian neighbors as infe-

rior and unhealthy. The issue here is not whether the diagnosis was accurate; rather, it is on the way Crawford used the diagnosis to characterize Comanche culture. The diagnosis highlighted the Native practices that contrasted the "healthy," settled, agrarian life. Comanches slept on the ground in portable dwellings because they were a nomadic tribe. And tobacco smoking was part of numerous Indian rituals. Crawford's writings implied that if the Comanches ceased to live nomadically and altered their cultural practices, then their health could improve, even despite their inherent weakness. Crawford revealed his vision of a proper, civilized way of life through his assessment of Comanche health. This agrarian vision drove U.S. policy toward Indians.

In the mid-1850s, political officials debated over Comanche removal to reservations, especially as violence in the region increased. As a consequence of economic growth, settlers began to expand into west Texas, and they often clashed with the Comanche, who continued to raid settlements. Texas Rangers and settlers mounted attacks on the Indians, who then retaliated.[36] Violence among Comanches, rangers, and settlers engulfed the mid-century west Texas frontier. Historian Gary Anderson shows that during this period, the combination of Anglo settler anxieties and local newspapers' exaggerated reporting created a sense of crisis that blamed Texas Indians, most notably the Comanche, for much of the violence that occurred. Texas Indian agents and military officials argued that anti-Indian Anglo Texans actually caused most of the problems. To keep the peace, General Persifor Smith proposed the allocation of lands for reservations. He also realized that the Comanche were having trouble surviving because dwindling bison populations and droughts reduced the food supply. In addition to fostering peace, then, proponents argued that the reservations could serve to nourish the Indians through farming and the distribution of food.[37] The Secretary of War, Jefferson Davis, named Robert Neighbors as the Texas Indian agent, who emphasized his desire to develop agricultural communities among Native peoples.

In February of 1854, Governor E.M. Pease signed the legislation that established two reservations for Texas Indians located on the upper Brazos River and its tributary, the Clear Fork. Comanche removal onto the reserves did not quell hostilities, however. Seeking the complete removal of Indians from Texas, many Anglos continued attacks on Native peoples. Meanwhile, the Spanish-speaking community in San Antonio supported the reservations and the transformation of Native peoples into sedentary farmers. In the Spanish-language newspaper, El Bejareño, tejanos argued that the government must force Indians to act peacefully, since otherwise, "their behavior will lead to extermination."[38] Like many Anglos, tejanos placed the blame for violence and removal on the Indians themselves. Contrary to Robert Neighbors's expectations, only a few hundred

Comanches relocated onto the reservations, hoping to secure food and other resources.[39] The reserves altered Anglo Texans' approach toward those Native peoples who remained outside the reservations, since Anglos generally believed that the reservations solved what they saw as the "Indian problem." After 1855, many Anglos, including military personnel and the Texas Rangers, did not consider their activities in west Texas an invasion of Indian lands, and they thus felt justified in killing any Indian outside of the reserves.[40] The development of reservations did not pacify the west Texas plains. And on the reservations, the state enacted a policy of cultural violence, seeking to convert Indians into agriculturalists, partly in the interest of Indian health.

Ideas about Comanche health surfaced in the Indian gent's first report to Congress on the status of Native peoples after their first year on the reservation. In the fall of 1856, Robert Neighbors described the physical state of the Comanche to the commissioner of Indian affairs in Washington, D.C. One year after the Indians relocated to the Clear Fork reserve, Neighbors wrote:

> There has been great improvement last year in the moral and physical condition of the Indians now settled. They are gradually falling into the customs and dress of the white man; and by being well clothed, having houses to live in, and relieved from the continued anxieties attending a roving life, their health has greatly improved, and they now, for the first time for several years, begin to raise healthy children.[41]

Neighbors highlighted the advantages of reservation life and the advances that these Comanche "settlers" made as they shifted from a nomadic lifestyle to the practice of subsistence agriculture and as they embraced other Anglo customs. He expressed this sense of progress in the idiom of health.

As Indian agent, Neighbors carried out the U.S. government's vision for Native peoples in the West. The office of Indian affairs ordered Indian agents to encourage Indians "to confine themselves within particular districts of the country . . . and to depend on husbandry for the means of subsistence."[42] This sedentary agrarianism reflected the United States' idea of civilization that informed their visions for the territories that the nation acquired in the 1840s and for the peoples that inhabited them. Robert Neighbors's report shows that the nation's justification for the conquest of the West became manifest in discussions of western health. In their reports on the Comanche, military physicians used the language of health to validate the nation's agrarian vision; the U.S. government translated this vision into practice with the West Texas reservations. In this case, the nineteenth-century discourse of race and health demonstrated its power through Indian policy. At the same time, however, Anglo physicians who adopt-

ed local healing practices in Texas exposed the contradictions within that very
set of ideas.

The Appropriation of Local Healing Practices

In Texas and northern Mexico, a number of therapeutic forms existed
alongside one another. Military surgeons primarily practiced aggressive, or
"heroic," therapies like bleeding and purging, and Mexican and Comanche communities often used efficacious cactus plants and herbs. Thus locals often practiced different therapies than did Anglo doctors. Discussions of this therapeutic
diversity emerged in the military medical reports. For example, Assistant Surgeon Ebenezer Swift reported that a Comanche afflicted with "smallpox,
measles, or any contagious disease, . . . leaves, or is sent out of camp. They have
no medical treatment" for those diseases.[43] Perhaps what Swift called a "lack of
treatment" was actually the practice of letting nature take its course. Healers,
including professional doctors, sometimes avoided drugs or botanics altogether
and relied on the healing power of nature.[44] Swift's report depicted the coexistence of diverse therapies in the region. Although military surgeons did not control the therapeutic process in Texas as a whole, they did control it in the military forts. Occasionally, the surgeons' therapies intersected with local
knowledge about healing and the environment.

When military physicians relocated to Texas forts, they encountered not
only diverse populations, but also new environments. They looked to the environment both to understand illness in their locales, but also to treat sick soldiers.
In the nineteenth century, it was common for doctors to use botanics, such as
herbs, roots, and plant sap, for healing. But success with botanics required local
knowledge to know the proper, effective botanical agents. Since military surgeons were newcomers to the region, they often relied on local, indigenous populations for that knowledge.

In both west and south Texas, doctors and soldiers constantly confronted
scurvy. In the nineteenth century, physicians understood scurvy as a nutrition-
related illness, and therefore prescribed vegetables to treat it. However, surgeons
wrote that they could not procure enough vegetables in west and south Texas,
mainly because they had trouble gardening in the arid frontiers. Lime juice then
became the chosen remedy. Like the vegetables, they also could not obtain sufficient amounts of lime juice to treat the sick soldiers. So surgeons turned to
local botanics and searched their therapeutic potential.

Among some military physicians in south Texas, the use of maguey juice
became the chosen therapy to treat scurvy. As noted above, the military surgeons' "newfound" knowledge about maguey's healing potential originated

with a Mexican priest in the city of Laredo. In the spring of 1851, Assistant Surgeon Perin first used the maguey treatment to treat a soldier with scurvy. On March 25, Private Turby was admitted to Fort McIntosh's hospital. Perin first tried lime juice for nutrients, and he also altered the soldier's overall diet. By April 11, Turby's condition had not improved. Since Private Turby did not respond to the lime juice, Perin decided to try maguey juice, three times a day, while continuing the same diet. Six days later, Perin saw Turby's "general state very much improved; countenance no longer dejected, but bright and cheerful; . . . arose from his bed and walked across the hospital unassisted; medicine continued."[45] After a few weeks, Private Turby returned to his unit. Perin used maguey for twelve more cases of scurvy that month, and all improved. "From observing the effects of the maguey in the cases which have occurred in this command," he wrote, "I am compelled to place [maguey] far above that remedy which, till now, has stood above every other—the lime-juice."[46]

The editor of the physicians' reports noted that other military surgeons in south Texas utilized maguey's healing potential on scurvy patients following Perin's suggestion. J. Frazier Head faced numerous cases of scurvy in June of 1854. Like other military doctors, Head had not received the anti-scurvy supplies that he had requested by the time he confronted the sick soldiers. He had heard that fresh agave juice provided "the most decided benefit" in the treatment of scurvy.[47] So he turned to maguey. At the Ringgold barracks, Israel Moses used maguey for 2 of the 15 cases of scurvy he faced in 1854. But because his patients suffered such negative side effects, he stopped using the plant.[48] All in all, three of the five doctors stationed in south Texas described using maguey for scurvy, even if only sparingly. The other two physicians did not report any cases of scurvy among their soldiers.

Maguey offered medicine, food, and drink to many people throughout Mexico, and the cultivation of the plant required certain skills. Pulque, an alcoholic beverage derived from agave, for example, had been popular in Mexico since ancient times.[49] In the eighteenth and nineteenth century, Mexican landowners grew and marketed the plant. The German naturalist Alexander von Humboldt recorded statistics on the pulque industry in his report on his expedition to the Americas from 1799 to 1804. His data came from the New Spanish viceroy, Juan Vicente de Güemes Padilla Horcasitas, who wrote that in 1791, people in Mexico consumed about 295,000 cargas, or loads, of pulque.[50] In the nineteenth century, the drink generated even greater demand, mainly in urban centers in the Mexican interior.[51] Many Native communities in the countryside also cultivated and consumed maguey; it was "extensively reared as far as the Aztec language extends."[52] One hacienda owner, José Mariano Sánchez Mora, published a guide on the cultivation of maguey in the 1830s that described the history and popularity of the plant. A successful businessman, Sánchez Mora detailed the process of planting, pruning, and transporting maguey to markets in Mexico City. Sánchez Mora and other hacendados hired tlachiqueros, who specialized in cultivation and the extraction of the plant's juices.[53] The complicated process required extensive understanding of the plant and its properties. Cultivation also demanded much maintenance because the "tlachiquero makes a daily pilgrimage to the [maguey] fields."[54] People throughout Mexico had a long-standing knowledge of maguey.

Mexicans used maguey to heal wounds and a variety of ailments, including headaches and a sore throat, fevers, coughs, and bladder infections. In addition to the business aspects of maguey cultivation, Sánchez Mora described some of the agave cures popular in Mexico. He wrote that for women, maguey "served to facilitate menstruation by drinking a sip [of mescal] one hour before eating, uninterrupted for six to eight days." Using maguey sap, or agua miel, Mexican peoples made the alcoholic beverage mescal, which some women drank after delivering babies to sooth the mother's discomfort.[55] The plant could treat symptoms associated with scurvy, such as digestive illnesses and toothaches. Since scurvy caused diarrhea and other stomach-related pains, the sick sipped mescal before eating or at the onset of stomach cramps.[56] With all stomach issues, healers also targeted the blood. They believed that an unbalanced or impure blood flow caused illness, so they practiced therapies that restored the patient's healthy blood balance. Some Mexican healers offered pulque to improve blood flow. Sánchez Mora wrote that the agua miel from maguey "restores and purifies the blood, tempers and cools the liver and blood vessels, undoes hydropsy and obstructions of the stomach, blood vessels, liver, and intestines, as it breaks up and causes continuous excretion of all phlegm and choleras through the urine."[57] Individuals also treated mouth maladies with maguey. When applied to the teeth, for example, small pieces of maguey gum helped mitigate toothaches.[58] Perhaps people also targeted another symptom of scurvy—swollen or bleeding gums—with the cactus.[59] Evidently, maguey's healing power extended to a number of ailments. The efficacy of the cactus for scurvy and its symptoms must have been familiar to the priest in Laredo, who then conveyed his knowledge to Surgeon Perin.

News of Perin's success with maguey even reached forts in west Texas, influencing other doctors to scour the local environment for efficacious plants. For example, Assistant Surgeon Crawford used prickly pear to treat scurvy. Crawford heard from other military surgeons about the healing successes with maguey. Since agave did not grow in his immediate surroundings in the western frontier, Crawford "came to the conclusion, that as the maguey plant had been highly spoken of, the same virtues might be found in a greater or less degree in the whole family of the cacti. He was therefore induced to try the common prickly pear, which was abundant near the fort." After he chose to try the prickly pear, he concluded that the "result was highly satisfactory."[60] The exchange of healing knowledge between the priest at Laredo and Surgeon Perin at Fort McIntosh resulted in successful medical treatments that extended far beyond the Río Grande Valley.

Other western frontier physicians used prickly pear to treat scurvy as well. Assistant Surgeon Ebenezer Swift confronted numerous cases and "recommended . . . cleanliness and a vegetable diet—prickly pear and poke-weed."[61] Swift did not cite the use of maguey for scurvy like Crawford. Perhaps he learned about prickly pear's healing capacity another way. Some forms of prickly pear grew in the U.S. Northeast, so the cactus may not have been entirely new to Swift. But the idea to consume the plant may have. As part of his research for his medical report, he observed Comanche food habits. He wrote that the Comanche ate prickly pear as part of their diet in addition to prairie animals, roots, wild fruits, and "the condemned provisions of military posts."[62] Swift also included a list of diseases that the Comanche suffered from in his medical topography of Camp Johnston. He listed lung diseases as the most common, then fevers, digestive illnesses, syphilis, and gonorrhea. But he did not describe a single case of scurvy among the Comanche. Through his local medical research, he learned that prickly pear was an edible plant that grew abundantly in the area. And since nineteenth-century doctors used botanics for healing purposes and understood scurvy as a nutritional illness, Swift may have learned from the Comanche that prickly pear was an effective therapy.

Conclusion

In the medical topographies, military surgeons often expressed unease about their inability to cure disease and heal their patients. They confronted the issue of vulnerability by seeking out healing practices that required familiarity with the local environment. In their search for this knowledge, they characterized local peoples and places as dirty, inferior, and unhealthy. Surgeon Moore, for example, described the living conditions of Mexicans in Brownsville and emphasized the unhealthiness of poor drainage systems and dirty homes. Some Anglos linked their conception of Mexican morality to health and characterized Mexican women as having "loose morals" and causing sickness among soldiers. This discussion ignored the role of Anglo men in conquest. In west Texas, Surgeon Crawford blamed Comanche battles with respiratory disease on their cultural practices. His diagnosis implied that if the Comanche would shed those practices and embrace a "healthier" agrarian lifestyle, then their health would improve, despite their inherent weakness. This medical narrative paralleled discussions of agrarianism on Indian reservations in west Texas and the U.S. government's goal to "bring civilization" to Native peoples on the reserves.

Yet the construction of locals as inferior racial Others did not prevent doctors from using their healing knowledge to cure sick soldiers. The appropriation of these practices nevertheless revealed a contradiction in the Anglo physicians' racial logic. Nineteenth-century doctors took race into account during diagnosis, as they believed illnesses affected people of different races in different ways. Thus, if physicians understood Anglo bodies as biologically different from Mexican and Indian bodies, how could maguey cure both whites and Mexicans with scurvy, and how could prickly pear cure whites and Comanches? This process undermined the nineteenth-century scientific and medical theories of racial difference. By the mid-nineteenth century, Anglos believed in their innate Anglo superiority and in biological differences among racial bodies, as these ideas appeared in periodicals, literature, and even schoolbooks throughout the United States[6] Mexican and Comanche scurvy cures did not transform these theories, but they exposed the contradictions of white supremacy that was partly based on the idea of inherent racial differences. Anglo use of the medicinal plants also undermined the racialized construction of the U.S. nation. Agents of the nation called on "inferior" Mexican and Comanche cultures to help in a crisis that threatened the "superior" Anglo population in Texas. Struggles over scurvy exposed the cracks in the powerful racial discourse that drove the ideology of Manifest Destiny. The appropriation of Mexican and Native healing practices demonstrated that the success of U.S. colonialism, rooted in ideas of Anglo racial superiority, depended on the very people that Anglos defined as racially inferior and obstacles to progress.

The establishment of a healthy nation proved to be quite challenging, as Anglos relied on Mexican and Comanche healing knowledge to carry out their national visions. In addition to Anglo settlers, surgeons and soldiers aided conquest through their posts in Texas. They worked together to establish U.S. control in the region, helping tomake conquest a reality. Encounters and exchanges among diverse healing cultures affected the course of colonization. Like the medical topographies, the appropriated healing practices became a tool of empire, as physicians used local therapies to maintain a healthy military frontier in places new to soldiers. The transcultural exchange that occurred between doctors who sought healing knowledge and locals who possessed that knowledge, ultimately served the nation and its imperial project. Physicians used local therapies to maintain a healthy military frontier in places new to soldiers and to ensure that the nation's mission in the region could continue. But Anglo reliance on Mexican and Native healing practices also shows that Anglos could not impose cultural domination. Interactions among Texas inhabitants reinforced local cultures, and the exchanges of healing methods strengthened cultural practices that Mexican and Native peoples had been using for generations.

Notes

[1] Glover Perin, "Maguey, or Agave Americana; a Remedy for Scorbutus," *New York Journal of Medicine and Collateral Sciences* 7 (1851): 181.

[2] *Ibid.*, 182.

[3] A similar process of racialization occurred in the twentieth-century U.S. West. California state officials used the languages of health and biological inferiority to justify public health initiatives that marginalized ethnic Mexicans and Asian Americans. Some of the state's projects included sterilization, housing discrimination, and community intervention. In some cases, these communities highlighted the state's racist practices to push for civil rights gains and negotiate some autonomy. See Nayan Shah, *Contagious Divides: Epidemics and Race in San Francisco's Chinatown* (Berkeley: U of California P, 2001); Alexandra Minna Stern, *Eugenic Nation: Faults and Frontiers of Better Breeding in Modern America* (Berkeley: U of California P, 2005); and Natalia Molina, *Fit To Be Citizens?: Public Health and Race in Los Angeles, 1879-1939* (Berkeley: U of California P, 2006).

[4] Charles E. Rosenberg, "Framing Disease: Illness, Society, and History," in *Framing Disease: Studies in Cultural History*, ed. Charles E. Rosenberg and Janet Golden (New Brunswick: Rutgers U P, 1992), xxii.

[5] There are many works that analyze race and white supremacy in the Manifest Destiny era. Some of the best studies are Reginald Horsman, *Race and Manifest Destiny: The Origins of American Racial Anglo-Saxonism* (Cambridge: Harvard U P, 1981); David Montejano, *Anglos and Mexicans in the Making* of Texas*, 1836-1986* (Austin: U of Texas P, 1987); Ronald T. Takaki, Iron Cages: Race and Culture in Nineteenth-Century America, 2nd ed. (New York: Oxford U P, 1990); Tomás Almaguer, *Racial Fault Lines: The Historical Origins of White Supremacy in California* (Berkeley: U of California P, 1994); and Susan Lee Johnson, *Roaring Camp: The Social World of the California Gold Rush* (New York: W.W. Norton, 2000).

[6] For more on scientific racism in the U.S., see Ronald L. Numbers and Todd L. Savitt, "Introduction to Part I: Science in the Old South," in *Science and Medicine in the Old South*, ed. Ronald L. Numbers and Todd L. Savitt, (Baton Rouge: Louisiana State U, 1989), 6; Audrey Smedley, *Race in North America: Origin and Evolution of a Worldview*, 3rd ed. (Boulder, Col.: Westview P, 2007), 235-58.

[7] Horsman, *Race and Manifest Destiny*, 229-230.

[8] For some more recent works that examine state formation in nineteenth-century Mexico, see Florencia E. Mallon, *Peasant and Nation: The Making of Postcolonial Mexico and Peru* (Berkeley: U of California P, 1995); Peter F. Guardino, *Peasants, Politics, and the Formation of Mexico's National State: Guerrero, 1800-1857* (Stanford, Cal.: Stanford U P, 1996); Raymond B. Craib, *Cartographic Mexico: A History of State Fixations and Fugitive Landscapes* (Durham, N.C.: Duke U P, 2004); and Michael T. Ducey, *A Nation of Villages: Riot and Rebellion in the Mexican Huasteca, 1750-1850* (Tucson: U of Arizona P, 2004). For the U.S.-Mexico borderlands, see Andrés Reséndez, *Changing National Identities at the Frontier: Texas and New Mexico, 1800-1850* (Cambrdige: Cambridge U P, 2005); Omar S, Valerio-Jiménez, "Indios Bárbaros, Divorcées, and Flocks of Vampires: Identity and Nation on the Río Grande, 1749-1894," (Ph.D. diss, U of California, Los Angeles, 2001); and Raúl A. Ramos, *Beyond the Alamo: Forging Mexican Ethnicity in San Antonio, 1821-1861* (Chapel Hill: U of North Carolina P, 2008).

[9] For more on the intersection of cultural practices and empire in the borderlands, see Ramón A. Gutiérrez, *When Jesus Came, the Corn Mothers Went Away: Marriage, Sexuality, and Power in New Mexico, 1500-1846* (Stanford: Stanford U P, 1991). Gutiérrez describes local marital practices

and Spanish-Indian relations in his study of gender and sexuality in New Mexico. Another work that explores cultural practices of gender and their role in borderlands diplomacy is Juliana Barr, *Peace Came in the Form of a Woman: Indians and Spaniards in the Texas Borderlands* (Chapel Hill: U of North Carolina P, 2007). For more on material culture in the borderlands, see Andrés Reséndez, "Getting Cured and Getting Drunk: State Versus Market in Texas and New Mexico," *Journal of the Early Republic* 22:1 (Spring 2002), 77-103, and Changing National Identities.

[10]James Sweet's analysis of African religious impacts on Brazilian Catholicism has influenced my arguments here. See Sweet, *Recreating Africa: Culture, Kinship, and Religion in the African-Portuguese World, 1441-1770* (Chapel Hill: U of North Carolina P, 2003), 217-226.

[11]Thomas Lawson circular, in Robert H. Coolidge, ed., *Statistical Report on the Sickness and Mortality in the Army of the United States*, Compiled from the Records of the Surgeon General's Office; Embracing a Period of Sixteen Years, from January, 1839, to January, 1855 (Washington: A.O.P. Nicholson, Printer, 1856), 3-4.

[12]Conevery Bolton Valençius, *The Health of the Country: How American Settlers Understood Themselves and Their Land* (New York: Basic Books, 2002), 159-190.

[13]S. Wylie Crawford, "Medical Topography and Diseases of Fort McKavett," in Coolidge, *Statistical Report*, 392.

[14]James O. Breeden, "Health of Early Texas: The Military Frontier," *Southwestern Historical Quarterly* 80: 4 (April 1977), 385-86.

[15]S.P. Moore, "Medical Topography and Diseases of Fort Brown," in Coolidge, *Statistical Report*, 357.

[16]W.W. Anderson, "Medical Topography and Diseases of Fort Terrett," in Coolidge, *Statistical Report*, 396.

[17]Ayuntamiento of Béxar's proclamation, March 17, 1833, Béxar Archives, Center for American History (CAH), U of Texas at Austin.

[18]Bolton Valençius, *The Health of the Country*, 114-15.

[19]In his work on disease and empire, historian Sheldon Watts describes how the medical discourse of malaria (what he terms "Construct malaria") held that slaves of African descent were biologically different from whites because of their near immunity to the disease. Using this discourse, southern whites argued that because of this biological difference, slaves were fit to work in harsh, unhealthy environments, such as swamps, while whites, who had not built immunity to malaria, were not. The construct, therefore, justified the "economic and social subordination of blacks to whites." See Sheldon J. Watts, *Epidemics and History: Disease, Power, and Imperialism* (New Haven: Yale U P, 1997), 213-256. Quote on page 215-216.

[20]For more on race and medical environmentalism, see Bolton Valençius, *The Health of the Country*, 229-264; and Warwick Anderson, *The Cultivation of Whiteness: Science, Health, and Racial Destiny in Australia* (New York: Basic Books, 2003). Quote from Anderson, *The Cultivation of Whiteness*, 31.

[21]Moore, "Medical Topography and Diseases of Fort Brown," in Coolidge, *Statistical Report*, 357.

[22]Anderson, "Medical Topography and Diseases of Fort Terrett," in Coolidge, *Statistical Report*, 396.

[23]J. Frazier Head quoted in Israel Moses, "Medical Topography and Diseases of Fort Merrill," in Coolidge, *Statistical Report*, 353.

[24]Moses, "Medical Topography and Diseases of Fort Merrill," in Coolidge, *Statistical Report*, 353.

[25]Moore, "Medical Topography and Diseases of Fort Brown," in Coolidge, *Statistical Report*, 355-356. Moore argued that the miasma coming from vegetable and animal decomposition caused the yellow fever epidemics, and he refuted claims that linked yellow fever to mosquitoes and flies. After germ theory, doctors identified the insects as transmitters of yellow fever.

[26]*Ibid.*, 354.

[27]*Ibid.*

[28]Nayan Shah and Natalia Molina's works on race, space, and health in California have influenced my arguments here. Shah and Molina concentrate on the period after germ theory took hold and

examine how public health officials designated certain spaces and peoples as unhealthy, thereby marking immigrant and other ethnic communities as racial others. See Shah, *Contagious Divides*, and Molina, *Fit To Be Citizens?*.

[29]Moses, "Medical Topography and Diseases of Ringgold Barracks," in Coolidge, *Statistical Report*, 358.

[30]*Ibid.*, 360.

[31]For more on the sexual desires of Anglo American men during conquest, see Amy S. Greenberg, *Manifest Manhood and the Antebellum American Empire* (Cambridge: Cambridge U P, 2005), 88-134.

[32]Breeden, "Health of Early Texas," 392.

[33]Moore, "Medical Topography and Diseases of Fort Brown," in Coolidge, *Statistical Report*, 354.

[34]Steven Feierman, "Struggles for Control: The Social Roots of Health and Healing in Modern Africa," *African Studies Review* 28: 2/3 (June/Sept. 1985), 75.

[35]Crawford, "Medical Topography and Diseases of Fort McKavett," in Coolidge, *Statistical Report*, 392.

[36]Pekka Hämäläinen, *The Comanche Empire* (New Haven: Yale U P, 2008), 305-309.

[37]Gary Clayton Anderson, *The Conquest of Texas: Ethnic Cleansing in the Promised Land, 1820-1875* (Norman: U of Oklahoma P, 2005), 246-47.

[38]El Bejareño, "Los Indios de Tejas," March 31, 1855.

[39]Hämäläinen, *The Comanche Empire*, 308.

[40]Anderson, *Conquest of Texas*, 260.

[41]Robert Neighbors to George W. Manypenny, September 18, 1856, in U.S. Office of Indian Affairs, *Report of the Commissioner of Indian Affairs* (A.O.P. Nicholson, Printers, 1857), 173.

[42]L. Lea to John H. Rollins, John A. Rogers, and Jesse Stem, November 25, 1850, in John R. Chenault, ed., *Annual Report of the Commissioner of Indian Affairs* (Gideon and Co., Printers, 1851), 254.

[43]Ebenezer Swift, "Medical Topography and Diseases of Camp J.E. Johnston," in Coolidge, *Statistical Report*, 385.

[44]Even though some physicians valued the theory surrounding this healing method, few doctors actually practiced it. John Harley Warner, *The Therapeutic Perspective: Medical Practice, Knowledge, and Identity in America, 1820-1885* (Cambridge: Harvard U P, 1986), 267-68.

[45]Glover Perin to U.S. Army Surgeon General Thomas Lawson, May 7, 1851, Coolidge, *Statistical Report*, 361-62.

[46]*Ibid.*, 363.

[47]Head, *Statistical Report*, 351.

[48]Israel Moses, "Medical Topography and Diseases of Ringgold Barracks," in Coolidge, *Statistical Report*, 360.

[49]Justin Jennings, Kathleen L. Antrobus, Sam J. Atencio, Erin Glavich, Rebecca Johnson, German Loffler, and Christine Luu, "'Drinking Beer in a Blissful Mood': Alcohol Production, Operational Chains, and Feasting in the Ancient World," *Current Anthropology* 46.2 (April 2005), 275-303.

[50]W. Macgillivray, *The travels and researches of Alexander von Humboldt; being a condensed narrative of his journeys in the equinoctial regions of America, and in Asiatic Russia:—together with analysis of his more important investigations* (New York: Harper and Brothers Publishers, 1869), 313-14.

[51]Mario Ramírez Rancaño, Ignacio *Torres Adalid y la industria pulquera* (Mexico City: Plaza y Valdés, Instituto de Investigaciones Sociales de la UNAM, 2000), 10.

[52]Macgillivray, *The travels and researches of Alexander von Humboldt*, 335.

[53]José Mariano Sánchez Mora, *Memoria Instructiva sobre el Maguey o Agave Mexicano* (Mexico: n.p., 1837), 13.

[54]William Henry Bishop, *Old Mexico and Her Lost Provinces: A Journey in Mexico, Southern California, and Arizona by Way of Cuba* (New York: Harpers & Bros., 1883), 250.

[55]Sánchez Mora, *Memoria Instructiva*, 25-33. Quote on page 25.

[56]Perin to Lawson, May 7, 1851, Coolidge, *Statistical Report*, 362; Swift, "Medical Topography and Diseases of Camp J.E. Johnston," in Coolidge, *Statistical Report*, 381.

[57]Sánchez Mora, *Memoria Instructiva*, 31.

[58]*Ibid.*, 30.

[59]At Fort McIntosh, soldiers with scurvy experienced swollen and bleeding gums. Perin to Lawson, May 7, 1851, Coolidge, *Statistical Report*, 362.

[60]Richard H. Coolidge, "Scorbutus," in Coolidge, *Statistical Report*, 401.

[61]Swift, "Medical Topography and Diseases of Camp J.E. Johnston," in Coolidge, *Statistical Report*, 381.

[62]*Ibid.*, 384.

[63]Horsman, *Race and Manifest Destiny*, 139-157.

Las Escuelas del Centenario in Dolores Hidalgo, Guanajuato Internationalizing Mexican History

Emilio Zamora
University of Texas at Austin

Introduction

THE MEXICAN REVOLUTION REDUCED MEXICO'S CENTENNIAL CELEBRATION
of 1910 to an exaggerated claim by President Porfirio Díaz and his allies
over the emancipatory consequence of the independence movement and
the democratic promise of the new sovereign republic of 1823. The precursory
causes of the Mexican Liberal Party and the Casa del Obrero Mundial anticipated the critique of the celebration by calling for a regeneration of a political
culture that valued and promoted fundamental egalitarian values. Francisco I.
Madero may have offered a narrower "constitutionalist" claim against the Díaz
regime, but he too affirmed a commitment to time-honored democratic values as
he led the first "official" and successful military challenge of the Mexican Revolution, two months after the closing of the festivities in September 1910.[1]

The end of the Mexican Revolution prompted government officials to once
again proclaim national unity and democratic values, this time to consolidate
state power and advance the modernization of Mexico. The rebuilding program
may not have fulfilled its promise of modernizing Mexico, but the effort realized greater unity and forged an invigorated national identity. The new government also ushered in a time of peace that owed as much to the spent energy of
the Revolution as to the strong governing arm of President Alvaro Obregón and
his successor Plutarco Elías Calles. The human suffering and economic devas-

38

tation that the prolonged fighting visited on Mexico gave the appeal for national unity and the modernization of the socio-economy greater urgency, relevance, and importance. Continuing problems like the maldistribution of land, the concentrated power and influence of the Catholic Church, and widespread social inequality also called for an official promise, plan, and vision for a new modern nation. Obregón, the popular general from Sonora, assumed the presidency in December 1920 and introduced a rebuilding program that assumed special regenerative importance in 1921, on the 100-year anniversary of the consummation of Mexico's independence.[2]

This essay examines an extraordinary relationship of cooperation that Mexicans from the United States forged with the residents and officials of Dolores Hidalgo, Guanajuato, the cradle of Mexico's independence and an important site for the centennial celebration of 1921. This relationship involved a highly publicized fundraising campaign in the United States that led to the construction of two elementary schools in Dolores Hidalgo between 1921 and 1923. Las Escuelas del Centenario were named after Miguel Hidalgo y Costilla and Josefa Ortiz de Domínguez, two of the best-known figures initiating the independence movement. Because of the campaign, a large number of Mexicans from the United States participated in the post-revolutionary campaign to rebuild Mexico, especially the effort to reform the nation's educational system under the leadership of José Vasconcelos, the eminent philosopher and head of the Secretaría de Educación during the Obregón administration.[3]

Ignacio E. Lozano, the popular editor of the San Antonio daily *La Prensa* and a leading participant in the transnational world of Mexican politics, led the campaign. He was prepared for the challenge. Lozano had built a newspaper and political career promoting a sentimental attachment to Mexico and a view of immigration as a temporary exodus from la matria, a term coined by the famed historian Luis González Gónzalez to signify the combined sense of the motherland and the fatherland.[4] Under his leadership, the campaign underscored the ties of cooperation between Mexican communities across the international border. It also accentuated the transnational reach of patriotic sentiments and mutualist values among the Mexicans in the United States during the postrevolutionary period.[5]

This essay represents more than an exercise in recovering an important chapter in Mexican history. It also explains how the unfurling of high-sounding words of reconciliation and reconstruction and a vision of a united and more fair-minded Mexican nation in the 1920s caught the attention and imagination of Mexicans in the United States. A diasporic sense of loss and longing as well as a concern for joining in the reconstruction of Mexico disposed them to pay attention and to participate in the Dolores Hidalgo campaign as well as in the larger discourse over the forging of a new nation. Leaders like Obregón and Vasconcelos, on the other hand, welcomed the gesture from afar as if the prodigal sons and daughters had finally returned home.[6]

Lozano negotiated the construction of Las Escuelas del Centenario with federal, state, and local officials. In this way, Lozano gave Mexicans "in the exterior"—as he often referred to the community in the United States—an opportunity to demonstrate their emotional and cultural ties to Mexico and placed them at the center stage of national reconstruction on three occasions at Dolores Hidalgo: during the celebration of Mexican independence on September 15–16, 1921, the inauguration of the construction of the schools during the last week of September 1921, and the official opening of the schools in January 1923.[7]

Beginnings

Lozano may have originated the idea of building Las Escuelas del Centenario, but it was the consultations with Mexican government officials that made the campaign possible. He most probably broached the idea of a San Antonio-based fundraising campaign in June 1920, during a visit with interim President Adolfo de la Huerta and President-elect Obregón, and subsequent meetings with Obregón and Vasconcelos.[8] Obregón, de la Huerta, Vasconcelos, and Lozano no doubt agreed that the campaign and Las Escuelas del Centenario would contribute to the larger process of educational reform. This became obvious after Lozano began to publicize his second visit with Obregón and Vasconcelos in February 1921 and his continuous correspondence with them, as well as with Dolores Hidalgo officials.[9]

Lozano gave credibility to the Dolores Hidalgo campaign by using the pages of *La Prensa* to support Obregón's plan, especially educational reform. De la Huerta, with Obregón's concurrence, had called on Vasconcelos as early as June 1920 to assume the post of rector of the National University and to head the reform effort. Vasconcelos immediately began to rebuild the national educational system with well-publicized policy negotiations, a national literacy campaign, and public commentary. By the end of the year, newspapers were reporting that Vasconcelos had instituted a broad plan of action with the support of leading national figures and El Consejo Universitario, the governing body of the National University of Mexico.[10]

The plan called for constructing new schools, repairing the few that remained after the Revolution, building and equipping public and school libraries, and reforming the public school curriculum. Vasconcelos, the chief architect of the reform initiative, responded to the focus on practical needs in the past educational system with a philosophical turn toward ethics, aesthetics, and religion, as well as an emphasis on Mexico's Spanish heritage over indigeneity. He also spoke about equipping libraries and schools with canonical works—typically, the translated "great works" from Europe—to supplement a nationalistic education with a universal one. Educational reform took a messianic character when Vasconcelos and other leaders declared that the new schools, the new curriculum, and the growing number of young enthusiastic teachers would contribute to the making of a more modern Mexican nation. To promote this view, Vasconcelos took various trips throughout the country, including one in April 1921, to the central part of the country that includes the state of Guanajuato. Although the new federalized system of education did not meet many of its goals, the national leadership considered the reform effort between 1920 and 1924—coinciding with Vasconcelos' term as the Secretary of Education—a significant contribution to reconstruction during the immediate postrevolutionary period. Moreover, leaders like Obregón and Vasconcelos welcomed the Dolores Hidalgo campaign as an important contribution to the building of a new educational system.[11]

Immediately upon returning from his June visit to Mexico City, Lozano began using *La Prensa* to remind the readers of his opposition to President Venustiano Carranza and his association with Obregón. In this way, he underscored his standing as a transnational political actor and the important role that Mexicans in the United States were to play in the national rebuilding project.[12] Obregón, according to Lozano, was a welcomed change from his authoritarian predecessor, Carranza. Carranza had not fully guaranteed freedom of the press, Lozano noted, nor had he officially welcomed back the thousands of Mexicans who had left the country to avoid the violence, political insecurity, and economic instability associated with the Revolution. Carranza, according to Lozano, had also failed to insure a smooth transition in the selection of the next president. Obregón, on the other hand, promised that newspapers outside Mexico could be distributed freely throughout Mexico and that exiles could return home. Obregón also intended to reduce the size of the military, uphold the Constitution of 1917, and once again ensure peace, tranquility, and the rule of law. He had also agreed to lend his support to the Dolores Hidalgo campaign.[13]

The Campaign

Lozano announced the start of the Dolores Hidalgo campaign on June 12, 1921. The occasion was the festive inauguration of a branch of the Comisión Honorífica from Seguín, Texas, a former colonial community situated approximately 745 miles north of the historic Guanajuato town. The Comisiones Ho-

noríficas were public service organizations affiliated with local Mexican con-
sulates, and their installation ceremonies were always important occasions to
affirm local pride, promote self-help, and protest activities on behalf of their
marginalized Mexican communities.[14] Like with other such events, the Seguín
ceremonies included nearby consular representatives, members of other Mexican organizations, and local city officials. This time, however, Mexican consular
officials, the dignitaries who usually presented the principal speeches on these
occasions, deferred the honor to Lozano.[15]

The ceremonies included welcoming remarks by the mayor of Seguín and
the Vice Consul of San Antonio, whose office represented the vast region of
South Texas. Lozano, the main attraction at the event, spoke before an animat-
ed audience of approximately 400 persons. When he finished speaking of "the
patriotism that all of Mexico's good sons keep alive like a sacred flame" and the
need for Mexicans in the United States to join the rebuilding efforts in Mexico
by constructing schools at Dolores Hidalgo, Lozano asked if they would support
the fundraising campaign. According to his biographer, José C. Valadés, the
audience responded with "a loud and resounding yes."[16]

One of Lozano's first reports announced a $50.00 contribution from the
Seguín chapter of the philanthropic organization La Cruz Azul and the use of
the remaining balance from a fundraising campaign for the victims of the 1921
earthquake in Veracruz. Subsequent reports point to an overwhelming response.
The reports included almost daily lists of contributions accompanied with the
names of the donors, their places of origin, reprinted observations and exhorta-
tions from readers, and commentary on the campaign by Lozano and other writers associated with the San Antonio daily.[17]

Although most of the contributions originated in Texas, other parts of the
Southwest, the Midwest, and northern Mexico were also represented among the
donors. The San Antonio paper reported that children contributed small amounts
from their savings, while adults sponsored public events or visited homes in
their neighborhoods with requests for support. Groups of workers, on the other
hand, donated a part of their earnings at their place of work. Also, numerous
community organizations, like mutual aid societies, W.O.W. chapters, independent and affiliated workers' organizations, Comisiones Honoríficas, Cruz Azul
brigades, and Masonic orders sponsored community-wide events and collected
contributions from their members. Contributors also included consular offices,
newspaper editors from Mexico and the United States, and children attending
escuelitas, or private Mexican schools. The donations from the thousands of
donors were typically in small amounts of five or ten cents per person, however, organizations in places like San Antonio, Laredo, and Brownsville sometimes contributed amounts that reached as much as $500. They usually spon-

sored dances, festivals, and other types of public events at local theaters, mutual aid society halls, and Masonic lodges. Eventually, the campaign was able to raise a little over $39,000.[18]

Lozano encouraged the paper's readers with a daily supply of information on the campaign. The newspaper also featured stories that included interviews with performing artists in fundraising activities, correspondence with officers of participating organizations, and reports on the progress of the school construction in Dolores Hidalgo. The enthusiasm expressed early in the campaign seemed infectious. According to Lozano, "[F]rom all the corners of the country where Mexicans live, we have received expressions of support and important donations."[19]

Some organizations, like the Sociedad Hidalgo y Costilla from San Antonio, took a special interest in the seventeen-month campaign with continuous activities that included collections among their members and public events, like the anniversary celebrations of Mexico's independence on the sixteenth of September. Community leaders like Daniel Chávez, the editor of La Revista Semanal from Laredo, also joined in the effort by supporting local activities and giving added legitimacy to the campaign.[20]

The large number of individuals that sent contributions or organized local fundraising activities, however, remained the backbone of the campaign. On numerous occasions, persons like Moisés Morales offered determined observations that the editors dutifully reprinted to encourage added support. Morales assured Lozano that "the town of Valentine will shortly answer the call, just like all good patriots have already responded."[21] An unnamed elderly contributor added a moving note when he urged the younger generation to continue the struggle for Mexican dignity by supporting the Dolores Hidalgo campaign: "I wish that my voice reaches our community so that they can see that their commitment to la matria is an agreement of honor and that they have to fulfill it because it is sacred."[22]

A young woman named Manuela Cortés, from Shiner, Texas, sent $12.20 that she had collected from twenty-nine contributors, but not before adding a sense of wonderment at the way she gave herself to the idea of Las Escuelas del Centenario:

> I truthfully confess that I don't know what came over me when I heard such a wonderful idea; but I do know that I felt the ideal that moves it, and I also felt that despite being Texan-Mexican my heartbeats fully with concern for the much beloved matria that leaves me speechless.[23]

José María Guerra, from Hebbronville, sent his contribution with a proud sense of accomplishment: "All the countrymen from here, as good sons of Mexico, are very interested in completing this great project of the two schools from Dolores Hidalgo."[24]

As the campaign continued to inspire support, Lozano busied himself with the construction plans. Within a month after initiating the campaign at Seguín, he was already visiting Dolores Hidalgo, accompanied by an architect from San Antonio named Poppe. On this occasion, Lozano assured local officials that the campaign was proceeding as planned and discussed with them his participation in the forthcoming patriotic celebration.[25] By August 8, 1921, Lozano was informing Obregón that the architect had prepared the preliminary design and that the construction of the schools would start in September. Obregón had already made available the necessary capital to purchase the properties in the selected site. The state legislature had granted Dolores Hidalgo the right to declare community interests over the privately held properties on the construction site.[26]

Lozano and the architect decided to purchase most of the construction materials and furniture in San Antonio and to transport them by rail through Nuevo Laredo, at which point Mexico's national railroad would assume charge of the transfer to Guanajuato. Some materials were purchased in Mexico, but it was necessary, according to Lozano "to take some of them from this city, including wood for the ceilings and floors, doors and windows, some high-quality bricks, materials for the installation of electricity, etc., aside from the furnishings for the schools."[27] The high cost of transporting the materials led Lozano to request an exemption from the customs duties and a reduction of freight rates on the government-owned railroad. Obregón responded almost immediately. According to the president's personal secretary, he ordered a 50 percent discount on the freight charges from the border and a subsidy equal to the cost of the customs duties. Obregón honored a subsequent request to cover the total cost of transporting the materials to Dolores Hidalgo—which totaled over $4,000 pesos in gold or approximately $2,000 dollars. Once Lozano affirmed Obregón's backing, he reassured his contacts in Dolores Hidalgo that the plans for the inauguration of the construction of the schools could begin in earnest.[28]

The campaign officially ended on February 1922, less than eight months after Lozano had made his public appeal in Seguín, Texas. At least $36,000 was raised in the campaign, although contributions continued to come in during the rest of the year until the construction was completed in January 1923. The amounts contributed by Dolores Hidalgo and the federal government may have increased the total cost of the schools to $50,000 dollars. The workers completed the schools on November 1922, according to a report by Ildefonso Saldaña, the worker who supervised the construction.

Ceremonies and Celebrations

Lozano's first inaugurating act in Dolores Hidalgo occurred on September 16, 1921 when he initiated the celebration of Mexico's independence with the symbolic "Grito de Dolores" that commemorated the famous 1810 call to arms.[29] Dolores Hidalgo officials had invited him to serve as the guest of honor and to make preparations for the official inauguration of the construction of the schools. Vasconcelos joined Lozano in hosting the second celebration between September 24 and 27, 1921. He made his last official visit to Dolores Hidalgo during the first week of January 1923. Joined by an entourage from San Antonio, Lozano presented the finished school to Vasconcelos who acted as the personal representative of President Obregón.

Lozano, along with the architect, departed for Dolores Hidalgo one week before the September 16 festivities to supervise the first building phase of the schools. The "official committee" began the celebration at midday on September 15 by staging "a triumphal parade" through the town's principal streets with a flag from the Hidalgo House and a military band sent by President Obregón at its head. The parade ended at the cathedral where Hidalgo y Costilla issued the first "Grito de Dolores" in 1810. The first set of speeches at the steps of the church lauded the heroes of the independence movement. The major ceremony was staged on the evening of September 15. According to Lozano, the "brilliant ceremony" included speakers who celebrated the heroes of independence and audience members who cheered la matria and the Mexican community from the United States. At the "traditional moment," Lozano stood and gave the "Grito de Dolores" while he waved the Mexican flag on behalf of Mexicans from the United States.[30]

Lozano had previously announced that he would officiate the laying of the cornerstone on September 16, but informed his hosts that this would now occur eleven days later, during the town's centennial celebration of the consummation of Mexico's independence. He had obviously maintained a central role in planning the forthcoming celebration with federal and state officials because he brought the news to Dolores Hidalgo that Vasconcelos, state legislators, and "possibly" Antonio Madrazo, the governor of Guanajuato, would attend. Lozano apparently left word for his staff to make this announcement two days later, along with a report by Teodoro Torres, his correspondent in Dolores Hidalgo.[31]

Lozano's paper announced the forthcoming celebration with prescience and the usual patriotic allusions to the Dolores Hidalgo campaign. For the first time in the history of a people, the paper reported, the Mexican community from the United States had been honored by a "Grito de Dolores" that had been given in its name. It was time, the editors added, for everyone to redouble their efforts to raise the necessary funds for the construction of the schools, the "temples of light." In the end, they concluded,

> We will have demonstrated before the entire nation that despite the distances and all the circumstances that befall us, above all, we have dignity; [we are] the great race that has the strength to honor la matria with the ready tribute and an open heart.[32]

The paper gave full coverage to the next celebration that was to take place during the last week of September.

Lozano, local officials, and other influential members of Dolores Hidalgo society, according to Torres, attended a banquet and dance on Saturday, September 24, where speakers once again paid special tribute to Mexicans in the United States. Vasconcelos, along with the famed artist Diego Rivera, the poet Joaquín Méndez Rivas, and other dignitaries arrived at the local train station the next morning. Mayor Everardo Soto welcomed them on behalf of the town and people of Dolores Hidalgo, many of whom had gathered to receive the visitors. Crescenciano Aguilera, the state representative from Dolores Hidalgo, also accompanied the group as the personal representative of Governor Antonio Madrazo, accompanied by still other notable public figures, including the members of Guanajuato's Supreme Court. Sometime during the day, the state legislature held its regularly scheduled meeting at Hidalgo's former residence, now the town's principal museum. The legislators honored Lozano as their special guest and contributed $300 pesos to the construction of the schools on behalf of the state of Guanajuato. At midday, Mayor Soto hosted a dinner at his home in honor of the town's special guests, especially Vasconcelos. The guests ended the day listening to an evening serenade by the municipal band at the central plaza. It was brightly illuminated, well attended by townspeople, and amply festooned with Mexican flags.[33]

The inauguration ceremonies were held on September 27, two blocks from the town square and the church. Prior to the ceremonies, Vasconcelos donated a public library with 348 tomes to the Hidalgo Museum.[34] He brought a collection of the mostly classic works from Mexico City as part of a national crusade—within the larger educational reform project—to inculcate reading, encourage local initiatives to build or expand libraries, and promote literacy and universal education. The program to lay the schools' cornerstones began at eleven in the morning. Aguilera opened the program by paying tribute to the Mexican community in the United States and Lozano's impressive leadership. Vasconcelos followed with a statement of appreciation and the view that Mexico would be able to offer the children of repatriated Mexican families an education as good as any that they could receive in the United States:

Vasconcelos, Lozano, and other dignitaries laying a cornerstone for Las Escuelas del Centenario, 1921, Photograph hanging on wall of administrative offices of Las Escuelas del Centenario, Dolores Hidalgo, Guanajuato.

> Mr. Lozano, my wish is that you inform the great Mexican colony in the United States that the Mexican government, acting on behalf of the entire nation, deeply appreciates the schools that they have given as a gift to the cradle of independence and that we will seek to honor this gesture, especially if, for some reason, the Mexican residents in the United States do not receive the deserved recognition, that they can be assured that their children will receive it and that when they return to la matria, they will find that their country is at the same educational level of development as the United States.[35]

Lozano responded by promising that the campaign would fulfill its promise and Torres, mindful of the need for continued support, reported to the readers that Mexicans in the United States "were struggling without losing heart for one instant so that they can complete the good deed that will surprise the present generations and receive the adulations of the coming ones."[36]

After Vasconcelos and Aguilera had placed the cornerstones, everyone attended a banquet where they heard even more speeches by Vasconcelos and members of the state legislature. The praise that they extended to the Mexican community from the United States provided Lozano with yet another opportunity to speak. This time, Lozano demonstrated that he was not limited to offering material support for the project of national reconstruction. Lozano also assumed the prerogative of speaking as a statesman when he reportedly made a call for national reconciliation: "that it was urgent that all the parties unite under the flag of la matria to make it strong and respectable." Torres reported that his last words were almost lost in the thunderous applause that followed. It was evident that the event had acquired transnational importance and that Lozano had played a central public role in inserting the Mexican community into the postrevolutionary world of Mexican politics.[37] The day ended with a musical celebration at the plaza and a kermesse at the public market in honor of Vasconcelos and the rest of the special guests. When the festivities ended, Lozano departed for Mexico City for further consultations on the construction of the schools.[38]

Lozano again visited Dolores Hidalgo on January 9, 1923, this time to turn over Las Escuelas del Centenario to Mexico in a ceremony that again included Vasconcelos and delegations representing the state legislature and Mexico's Congress. Lozano arrived on the evening of January 8, accompanied by his wife, Alicia Elizondo de Lozano, and an untold number of "Mexican excursionists" from San Antonio and other parts of the state of Texas. As before, local officials and a large number of townspeople received Lozano with great fanfare and respect. Torres captured the exuberance that resurfaced when the mayor received Lozano with "extraordinary grandiosity."[39] Vasconcelos arrived the next morning to an equally impressive reception at the train station. The group

Vasconcelos and Lozano meeting at the train station in Dolores Hidalgo prior to the inauguration of Las Escuelas del Centenario, 1923, Archivo General de la Nación, Mexico City.

People gathered in front of Escuela Josefa Ortiz de Domínguez to witness inauguration ceremony of Las Escuelas del Centenario, 1923, Archivo General de la Nación, Mexico City.

Close up of audience listening to Lozano during the inauguration ceremony in front of Escuela Josefa Ortiz de Domínguez, 1923, Archivo General de la Nación, Mexico City.

moved to the schools where Lozano delivered "an eloquent speech" and Vasconcelos received the schools on behalf of the government. The ceremonies were held on the portico of the Ortiz de Domínguez school before an audience of officials and townspeople, including some men on horseback. The event ended with a group picture on the steps of the school.[40]

Group picture of participants in the inauguration ceremony of Las Escuelas del Centenario, 1923, Archivo General de la Nación, Mexico City.

More speeches were heard at a banquet hosted by the city of Dolores Hidalgo. Emilio Gandarilla y Romero Ortega, both state representatives, expressed gratitude to the Mexicans from Texas. Two members of the San Antonio group, Amado Gutiérrez and Alicia C. de Longoria, responded on behalf of Mexicans from the United States. The guests were also read a telegram from Obregón that extended a hearty welcome to the Mexicans from the United States and thanked them profusely for their work. Lozano closed the function with a speech that was received with "truly enthusiastic applause."[41] After the banquet, the "excursionists" visited the town's historic sites. Their stop at the Hidalgo museum laid bare the emotions that had motivated them and the thousands of contributors who carried the campaign to fruition. When the visitors entered the site, they were so overtaken by feelings of pride and reverence that they immediately dropped to their knees. Valadés reported that "men and women cried."[42]

Before the day was over, Elizondo de Lozano joined with "prominent" married and single women to host a "merienda," or light evening meal, with 300 children who had been attending the festivities and demonstrating "the greatest of joy."[43] The following day, Lozano and his party departed for Mexico City to meet with Obregón and officials from the Secretaría de Educación who were to honor them once again. They were no doubt pleased that Mexicans from the United States had kept their promise to Dolores Hidalgo and memoralized their magnificent contribution to the cause of educational reform at a moment of high patriotic significance.

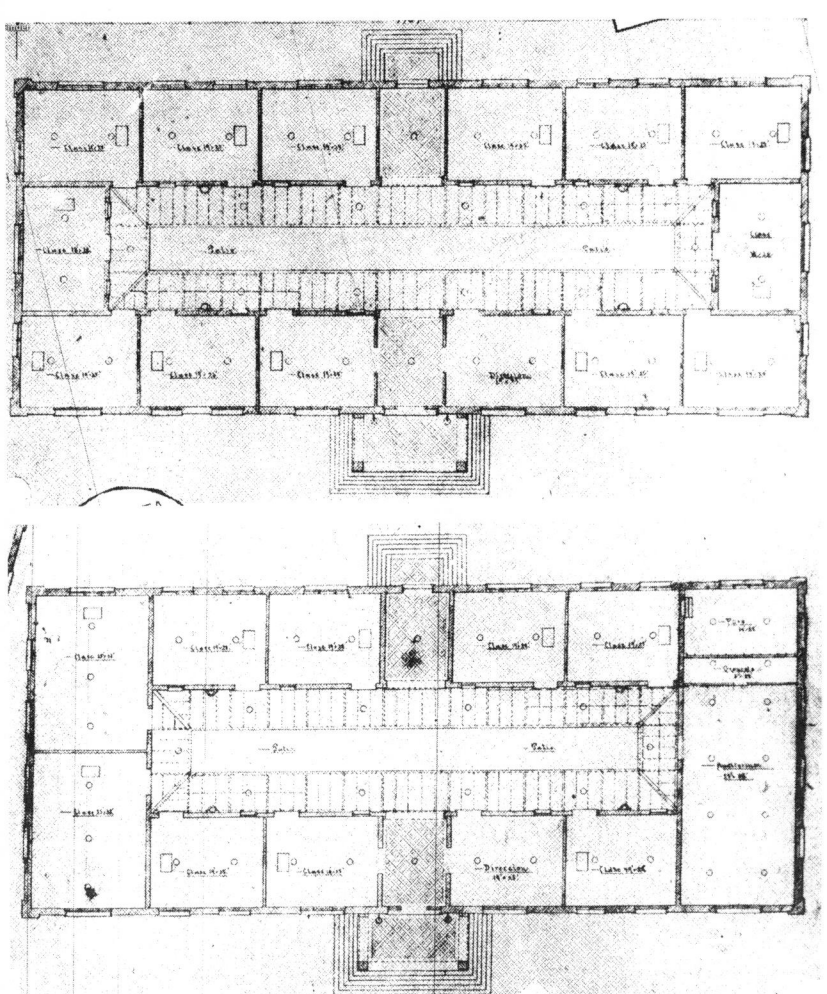

Architectural rendering of schools Ortiz de Domínguez (top) and Hidalgo y Costilla (bottom), "Las Escuelas de Dolores Hidalgo," *La Prensa*, August 28, 1921.

Las Escuelas del Centenario was placed near the center of town on a residential block measuring approximately 112,537 square feet; the structures filled about 32,550 square feet, or 29 percent of the available space. This left a substantial amount of outer space, 80,020 square feet, or 71 percent of the area, to accommodate a basketball court, volleyball courts, sets of swings, an "experimental" section for instructional gardening, decorative gardens in the front of each school, and open playground areas.[44] The Hidalgo y Costilla school had seven classrooms (four for a total of 180 first graders, two for 80 second graders, and three for 104 third, fourth, fifth, and sixth graders) for 364 students, a room for school administrators, and a large auditorium (with stage and back stage areas) that could seat two hundred persons and double as a dining room and a place for community meetings. The Ortiz de Domínguez structure had thirteen classrooms (one for 32 preschoolers, five for 200 first graders, three for 120 second graders, two for 64 third graders, one for 32 fourth graders, and one for 32 fifth and sixth graders) for 448 students and an office for the administration. Together, the two schools could accommodate 900 students, making it the highest capacity school complex in the country.

The buildings reflected a classical style common to U.S. schools of the early 1900s.[45] The signature features that gave the schools a symmetrical look included a base of cement and stone masonry that raised the main floor of the schools approximately four feet above the ground. Numerous curtained windows framed by minimalist lines surrounded the buildings. Staired entrances at the front of each one led to a prominent portico with detailed piers, a frieze, and large wooden doors. Long spacious halls with partial overhanging covers were constructed on an East-West axis in the interior of each building. The shaded and open patio space provided constant and cool ventilation appropriate for the

Drawings of schools Ortiz de Domínguez (top) and Hidalgo y Costilla (bottom), "Las Escuelas de Dolores Hidalgo," *La Prensa*, August 28, 1921.

warm weather of places in the southern and southwestern part of the United States. Although the large windows and the spacious halls provided much sunlight, the buildings were equipped with electrical power to ensure that the children had sufficient lighting. A visitor who entered one of the two main entrances could proceed down a narrow hall that extended in a north-south direction and opened into an outdoor passageway and a smaller structure in the middle containing bathrooms for girls and boys, as well as rooms for a store, a kitchen, and storage space.[46]

The classrooms were spacious and equipped with "modern" desks and chairs, while others served more specialized functions. One of the largest rooms served as an auditorium that seated three hundred persons, while others were workshop spaces dedicated to the teaching of industrial and manual arts like barbering, typing, sewing, and cooking. The size of the auditorium suggests that the schools were meant to convene large numbers of community members to participate in the schooling of their children and in the public life of Dolores Hidalgo. Every room had windows that reached high into the ceiling and overlooked the two large playground areas that almost encircled the schools.[47] In keeping with the promise of federal support for local school reform, Vasconcelos supplied Las Escuelas del Centenario with "a large number of competent teachers" to ensure that the classes began on the day after the ceremonies and celebrations.[48]

The curriculum no doubt reflected the curricular reform ideas of Vasconcelos. A surviving barber's chair in a storage room and references to knitting, cooking, local and regional crafts, and gardening in the documentary record suggests that the teachers adhered to the national emphasis on practical and useful skills that the students could use in their adult lives. An inventory of a school library of approximately nine hundred volumes provides an additional basis for determining the extent to which Vasconcelos influenced learning activities in the schools. A cursory analysis of the library points to a preponderant emphasis on canonical works of the nineteenth century in religion, literature, history, and geography, the greatest number of which were translations of works in French. Other publications addressed the practice of medicine, the history and geography of the Americas, national histories, the structure and functions of governments, agricultural history and practices, poetry, and military histories. The library also contained general reference materials like dictionaries, encyclopedias, biographies, and collections of government decrees and laws as well as a few readings for children, including *The Child's Book of Nature* (1870) and *Tablas Aritméticas* (1761). The lack of materials for children and the preponderance of readings that required knowledge of foreign languages like French and English suggest that the library was primarily intended for the teachers and administrators and possibly reflected the "teacher-centered" focus that Vasconcelos gave the elementary school curriculum.[49]

Lozano

The importance of Lozano to the Dolores Hidalgo campaign requires some attention to his biography and work. He was born in Mapimí, Durango in 1886. Political instability, hard times, and the death of his father drove the twenty-two-year-old Lozano and his family to San Antonio, one of the most popular destination points for political exiles and economic refugees during the Revolution. Life was fraught with difficulties for Lozano as he became the head of a household with a mother and several sisters. While the sisters worked as clerks or at service jobs, Lozano established a modest bookstore and worked with the eminent exile and anti-Diaz writer Adolfo Duclos Salinas on two newspapers, La Revista Mensual and El Noticiero. He also managed and edited the daily El Imparcial de Texas, owned by Francisco A. Chapa, a pharmacist and member of the staff of Governor Oscar B. Colquitt in the 1910s. His early earnings were meager but they improved, and he remained determined to succeed as a businessman and journalist. In 1913, at a time when Spanish-language newspapers appeared briefly and intermittently, Lozano decided to launch *La Prensa*. Hard work and astute business practices earned him much success in his newspaper, as well as with his bookstore, a publishing house, and a printing company.[50]

Lozano's *La Prensa* became a daily and reached a circulation of 10,000 within its first year of operation. The paper's early success owed much to its "independent" or even-handed coverage that its editors claimed to give political developments in Mexico. It was also due to Lozano's reputation as an effective and trusted leader who often took initiatives of public service and completed them successfully. A case in point was the highly publicized program for poor children that he and his staff regularly organized during Christmas. The program staged at the local Teatro Nacional distributed candy and toys to the poor Mexican children of San Antonio. Most of the Mexican organizations in the city, hundreds of mostly Mexican volunteers, and thousands of children and their parents participated in what became one of the major social events in the city. The local press, including *La Prensa*, gave full coverage to the annual function and thus promoted the idea that Lozano was one of the major exponents of self-help and goodwill in the Mexican community in the United States.

Lozano also used his newspaper to regularly render aid to needy Mexicans in other parts of the state. Between September and October 1919, for instance, he led a campaign through *La Prensa* that raised $3,000 for hundreds of Mexican families who suffered losses after a major hurricane hit the Texas coast.

Although the details of the 1919 effort are not known, the experience no doubt allowed him to develop his technique of utilizing popular nationalistic and humanitarian concerns in his journalistic appeals for financial support. This occurred again, two months later, when Lozano drew on the generosity of the Mexican community to support the residents of Veracruz, Mexico after a destructive earthquake hit the state in January 2, 1920, primarily south of the city of Xalapa, in the nearby towns of Coatepec, Xico, Teocelo, and Cosautlán.[51]

The newspaper reported that children gave generously of their savings, while representatives of local organizations, in most cases women, went house to house requesting donations. Workers, on the other hand, donated parts of their limited earnings to the campaign with contributions to their organizations or to the volunteers who visited their homes. Lozano delivered to the officials and organizations from Veracruz the money they had raised. According to Valadés, the Veracruz campaign raised $46,000 in two months. "After this effort," Valadés noted, "the man and his newspaper could rest knowing that they had reached the greatest Mexicanist [patriotic] achievement."[52]

One of the most striking aspects of the fundraising campaigns is that Lozano appealed to all Mexicans, regardless of their station in life. Moreover, the general enthusiastic response by large numbers of Mexicans demonstrated that the thought of la matria in need could, if only for the duration of the enterprise, encourage everyone to put aside class, nativity, and ideological differences within the Mexican community. This does not mean that these differences were not evident or that the effort may not have accentuated them. The campaign, after all, was directed primarily at the recent arrivals whose memories of the homeland were most fresh. Also, the mostly small contributions and the articles in *La Prensa* that acknowledged the poverty among the donors underscored the largely marginalized status of the Mexican community. Some fundraising activities, like the theatre productions that catered to "higher status" members of the community, were also stark reminders that the Mexican community was stratified and that Lozano's language often reflected and possibly reinforced class bias, especially among the better-placed political exiles.[53]

When Lozano spoke on behalf of Mexicans "in the exterior," he often called them sojourners, but he and his growing stable of writers also spoke broadly and vehemently against discrimination and in favor of the Mexican cause for equal rights in the United States. Lozano certainly rejected leftist ideas by organizations like the anarcho-syndicalist Mexican Liberal Party exiled in Central Texas during the first decade. His moderate appeal for equal rights in the United States and peace in Mexico, however, struck a responsive chord among his readers.[54] Lozano's popularity as a successful journalist and businessman no doubt gave him the opportunity and authority to advocate for the rights of Mexicans in the

United States and to promote public service activities, including initiatives like the Dolores Hidalgo campaign.

The overwhelming response to the Dolores Hidalgo campaign also owed much to Lozano's appeals to the nationalistic sensibilities of the readers of *La Prensa*. Lozano was especially adept at giving expression to popular sentiments of loss and longing among the refugees and exiles who wished to return home. The numerous articles that appeared during the campaign, however, most often expressed the notion of recovering a natural process of progressive evolution in the history of the Mexican nation that the Revolution had disrupted. The editors of *La Prensa* acknowledged that distance from la matria strengthened a sense of belonging, but their focus on this attachment and a form of political impartiality that the distance had supposedly fostered most often led them to emphasize a special patriotism of generosity and caring. Apparently, Lozano was less interested in lamenting a loss than in motivating his readers to join a lofty purpose, to support a campaign on behalf of a reconstructed nation.

The campaign, according to Lozano, "has been the best proof of solidarity" and a "beautiful patriotic gesture" by the Mexican community from the United States. Participating in such a laudable national purpose had the added benefit of demonstrating a generous and caring spirit. The beginning of the construction of the schools provided Lozano occasion for reflection on this point. "The great Mexican community that lives far from la matria," he noted, "reserves for her the most wholesome and temperate heart." The schools represented "the highest tribute of love that the community placed with reverence at the same place where one century ago the first word of liberty was heard."[55]

To further motivate his readers, Lozano made use of nostalgic views of Mexico as home—a place of care, beauty, and fulfillment. When Lozano returned from his June 1920 visit with de la Huerta and Obregón, for instance, he recounted the pain and pleasure of once again experiencing Mexico in all its beauty and need:

> To visit la matria after a long period of ostracism; to be there to contemplate the beauty of our country; to feel from close range the pain that our people have suffered during the ten years of civil war; to place myself in contact with men and events and to again admire—after a forced and prolonged absence from Mexico—the elegance of our mountains, the charm of our historic cities, the exuberance of our countryside, of our gardens, of our ancient forests; to see things closely and to study carefully the men who struggle and live within our borders, some in the world of politics, others in the sciences and the arts, and the rest in the world of everyday work that calls for one's labor and minds.[56]

Lozano also expressed confidence in leaders who were rebuilding the country and suggested that the rest of the population should support them:

> Mexico has taken a major step towards tranquility which is the force that generates noble activities and all the patriotic undertakings. There is a grand and immense desire for peace—and leaving aside the political opportunists, the persons who spend their time in the wings of the different government agencies seeking properties or lucrative posts—the good elements in society are willing to cooperate in whatever way to insure that order is once again established in Mexico. There are good people, who doubts this! And it is necessary that they be given free rein, that no one undermines their initiatives, that we wish them well and not get in their way.[57]

The patriotic and sentimental language that Lozano used to draw support for the Dolores Hidalgo campaign explains much of its success, but this does not mean that the caring and concern that he expressed did not also grow out of a collective experience that, according to García Naranjo, yielded "a love that was purified by distance."[58] Speaking for Mexicans in the exterior, an unnamed writer for *La Prensa* pointed out that Mexicans in the United States had remained above the divisions of the Revolution and only wished to work on behalf of the country that they loved: "We live outside of Mexico and because of that, we do not share in the passions that divide our compatriots. We only see the nation's problems broadly. . . . We love our country above all and we shall be with whomsoever saves her."[59] Querido Moheno, a political exile and frequent contributor to *La Prensa*, offered a similar observation on unity:

> The mere crossing of the border has been enough to make us agreeable with each other. If we were still there we would be fighting each other. But since we are here, in this land where the remains of our grandfathers rest, all of us raise our hearts to bless la matria.[60]

Torres added that Mexicans were attached to Mexico as "a divine obsession" and that newspapers simply nurtured this passion by always speaking out for la matria, "of pleasant things that they welcome in their isolation like rays of hope and like blessings." Years later, Federico Allen Hinojosa observed the same kind of attachment among the millions of Mexicans and U.S.-born Mexicans who were "reconquering" the lost territory of 1846–1848 with "a firm, resolute, and unshakeable nationalist spirit."[61]

Conclusion

Las Escuelas del Centenario stands as the monuments they were intended to be, as a testament to the generosity of Mexicans in the United States. Their expression of goodwill was especially important because the majority of the people who contributed to the campaign were poor and, in some cases, destitute. Also, they supported the construction of the schools that neither they nor their children had ever had the opportunity to attend in Mexico. They faced similar situations in places like Texas, especially north of the border region where Mexicans predominated. Their children usually attended separate and unequal facilities that were a far cry from the modern structures they had built in Dolores Hidalgo. The construction of the schools, consequently, appears as a selfless act, a decision to forego personal wants and desires to satisfy national needs. Other motivations, however, were also present.

The sense of loss that accompanied the immigrants as they left family and country behind, coupled with their longing to return to la matria, no doubt, mitigated feelings of personal and even group sacrifice, especially since it was obvious that reconstruction required national unity, cooperation, and reconciliation. The long years of fighting and the devastation of the Revolution led to a national resolve for peace and renewal that Spanish-language newspapers like *La Prensa* and transnational leaders like Lozano broadcast throughout the United States and parts of Mexico. It also helped that popular and respected leaders like Lozano influenced the readers of *La Prensa* to accept the grand commission to put aside personal interests and political divisions and contribute to the building of a new modern nation. The emphasis on a national identity and on rebuilding the country, in other words, gripped a nation and its people "in the exterior."

The enthusiastic response to Lozano's appeals for unity in support of fellow Mexicans in need may have also reflected and reinforced the longstanding value of mutuality (or reciprocity) and the moralistic impulse that set it in motion.[62] An artisan tradition of cooperation coupled with a working-class mutualist strategy to survive and protest difficult living and working left a distinct documentary mark in the history of organizational life during the early 1900s. The Mexican Revolution, the understandable immigrant and exiled gaze toward Mexico, and the Dolores Hidalgo campaign encouraged Mexicans in the United States to join the national project of reconciliation and reconstruction, but the seeds of cooperation had long been sown outside of Mexico. Cooperation for the common good, however, was no longer confined to its immediate surrounding; it was now practiced on a larger, transnational scale and with greater nationalist force.

Observers like García Naranjo, Moheno, Torres, and Lozano acknowledged, sometimes in amazement, that Mexicans in the United States exhibited a high degree of unity despite Americanization and political differences that exiles and their allies accentuated with the diverse political programs of the first three decades of the twentieth century. These influences, particularly the invidious side of Americanization that questioned the worth of being Mexican and the highly partisan calls for change in Mexico, however, may also have energized political activity. This no doubt increased the numbers of Mexicans entering public life and their vigorous calls for equal rights in the United States and peace and reconstruction in Mexico. Lozano brought this civic culture to transnational light, and he did it with a masterful touch.

Lozano had established a transnational reputation as a successful businessman, journalist, and civic leader when the Revolution ended and Mexico began the process of reconstruction. His calls for peace in Mexico and critiques of discrimination and inequality at home added to his stature as a leader who truly cared about la matria and the Mexican community in the United States. His crowning transnational achievement was the successful Dolores Hidalgo campaign and the construction of Las Escuelas del Centenario. His organizing genius was evident in timing the campaign and the construction of the schools with the start of the educational reform movement and the celebration of the consummation of Mexico's independence. Moreover, he did this with the distinct patriotic style of a seemingly selfless leader who placed la matria above all.

Vasconcelos, Dolores Hidalgo officials, and the numerous donors who commented on the campaign,,directed most of their praise on Lozano. Lozano, on the other hand, always turned the public's attention to the extraordinary outpouring of support for the campaign. Although the congratulations and credits were well deserved, underlying tensions were also present. Subtle, yet noticeable, class distinctions appeared in the pages of *La Prensa* as well as in the writings of García Naranjo, Torres, and Lozano. Federal officials also failed to publicly acknowledge the campaign and the construction of the schools in its major reform periodical, El Boletín de la Universidad. Vasconcelos himself made no note of them in his numerous writings. One could even say that Lozano's transnational business ventures benefited from the campaign and that he may have pursued it with this in mind. His larger contribution, however, eclipses this possible and understandable interest.

Now that Mexicans begin the preparations for the celebration of independence from colonial rule, they would do well to recognize past commemorations. Our understanding of the independence movement, its consummation, and the very idea of independence has been influenced by the way that we have commemorated them in the past. This memory—always in the process of recovery—should be incorporated into the way we celebrate today. These relations with our past call on us to increase our knowledge of history so that we can recognize and appreciate the singular efforts made by Mexicans "in the exterior" between 1921 and 1923. Aside from its account of a historically significant case of cooperation across the international divide, this essay has sought to demonstrate that the decision to take to the road in search of better opportunities, then as now, blurs the borders and creates an extraterritorial space from which Mexicans elaborate their patrias chicas, or discrete cultural regions, and assert their own sense of national purpose, identity, and responsibility.

Notes

[1] See the following recent publication for an examination of the Mexican Revolution: Héctor Aguilar Camín and Lorenzo Meyer, *In the Shadow of the Mexican Revolution: Contemporary Mexican History, 1910-1989,* Translated by Luis Alberto Fierro, an imprint of the Institute of Latin American Studies, U of Texas at Austin (Austin: U of Texas P, 1993). For studies on independence-day celebrations in Mexico, see: Mauricio Tenorio Trillo, *Mexico at the World's Fairs: Crafting a Modern Nation* (Berkeley: U of California P, 1996); William H. Beezley and David Lorey, eds., *Viva México! Viva la Independencia, Celebrations of September 16* (Wilmington, Del.: Scholarly Resources, 2001). Neither the centennial celebration in Dolores Hidalgo nor the history of Las Escuelas del Centenario have drawn the interest of researchers. The following local histories demonstrate these failings in the literature: Pedro González, *Apuntes Históricos de la Ciudad de Dolores Hidalgo* (Guanajuato: Instituto Estatal de la Cultura de Guanajuato, Ediciones La Rana, 2001); J. Zacarías Barrón, *Inspector Honorario de Monumentos Nacionales, Lugares Históricos Edificios Notables, Dolores Hidalgo, Cuna de la independencia* Nacional (Guanajuato, Guanajuato: Talleres de la Imprenta Universitaria, 1951).

[2] The following selective works examine the Obregón administration, including efforts at reconstructing Mexico in the post-revolutionary era: Mario Mena, *Figuras y Episodios de la Historia de México, Álvaro Obregón, Historia Militar y Política, 1912-1929* (México, D.F.: Editorial Jus, 1960); Linda B. Hall, *Alvaro Obregón: Power and Revolution in Mexico, 1911-1920* (College Station: Texas A&M U P, 1981); Jaime Tamayo, *El Obregonismo y los Movimientos Sociales: La Conformación del Estado Moderno en México (1920-1924)* (Guadalajara: Universidad de Guadalajara, 2008).

[3] Educational reform during the Alvaro Obregón administration represented a key component in the overall effort to create national unity, consolidate state power, and address social ills like social inequality. Consult the following, for a basic synthesis of the history of educational reform during the postrevolutionary period: Ernesto Meneses Morales, *Tendencias Educativas Oficiales en México, 1911-1934; La Problemática de la Educación Mexicana Durante la Revolución y Los Primero Lustros de la Época Posrevolucionaria* (México, D.F.: Centro de Estudios Educativos, Universidad Iberoamericana, 1998). I have also consulted the following regularly scheduled bulletin for accounts of political initiatives, policies, administrative activities, and the leadership of important figures, especially José Vasconcelos, the president of the National University and director of the Secretaría de Educación Pública, during the early 1920s: Universidad Nacional de México, Boletín de la Universidad (México, D.F.: Departamento Universitario y de Bellas Artes, 1921-1922).

[4] González y González, *Pueblo en Vilo; Microhistoria de San José de Gracia* (México: Fondo de Cultura Económica, 1984).

[5] Historians have not yet written an extended study of Lozano or the newspapers that he founded, *La Prensa* (San Antonio: 1913-1957) and *La Opinión* (Los Angeles: 1926-Present). This paper draws heavily from a biography of Lozano by historian José C. Valades that appeared in the 25-year anniversary issue of *La Prensa*: Valadés, "Un hombre y un periódico," *La Prensa,* 13 de febrero, 1938. Other notable works include: Onofre di Stefano, "'Venimos a luchar': A Brief History of *La Prensa*'s Founding," *Aztlán* 16.1-2 (1985), 95-118; Nora Ríos McMillan, "A Biography of a Man and His Newspaper," *The Americas Review,* 17.3-4 (Fall, Winter 1989), pp. 136-49; Ríos McMillan, "Ignacio E. Lozano," *Handbook of Texas Online,* http://www.tshaonline.org/handbook/

online/articles/LL/flo47.html>. (Accessed April 5, 2009). Nicolás Kanellos, "A Socio-Historic Study of Hispanic Newspapers in the United States," In *Handbook of Hispanic Cultures in the United States, Sociology*, Edited by Félix Padilla, General Editors: Nicolás Kanellos and Claudio Esteva-Fabregat (Houston: Arte Público P, 1994), pp. 239-54.

[6] The previously noted works on Lozano and *La Prensa* agree that the San Antonio daily represented a popular diasporic mentality characterized by a nostalgic view of Mexico. The novel, *La Patria Perdida*, by Teodoro Torres, may have been the major exponent of the sense of loss and longing that some historians have found in *La Prensa*, although the novelist added a different resolution to this view, that is, one can never return home because of constant change in place and person. Torres, *La Patria Perdida* (México, D.F.: Ediciones Botas, 1935). See the following to situate Torres' novel within the larger corpus of Latino literature: Nicolás Kanellos, "Recovering and Reconstructing Early Twentieth-Century Hispanic Immigrant Print Culture in the US" *American Literary History*, 21.2 (Summer 2007), 438-55.

[7] The Dolores Hidalgo campaign was known as a prominent phase in Lozano's life. His biographer, José C. Valadés, and a fellow journalist from San Antonio, Federico Allen Hinojosa, kept this memory alive. Valadés published Lozano's biography in the 25th anniversary issue of *La Prensa* and Allen Hinojosa included a short biographical statement that recognized Lozano's role in constructing Las Escuelas del Centenario. Valadés, Un Hombre Y Un Periódico," February 13, 1938; Allen Hinojosa, *El México de Afuera y Su Reintegración a la Patria* (San Antonio: Artes Gráficas, 1940), p. 51. The editors of *La Opinión*, a paper that Lozano founded in 1926, reprinted the biography as a series in the paper's Sunday supplement, "La Comunidad," between September 1982 and January 1983.

[8] Lozano's opposition to the Carranza administration on the pages of *La Prensa* no doubt gained him favor with Obregón and may explain why the president agreed to meet with him and cooperate on the Dolores Hidalgo campaign. Lozano had also met Vasconcelos during the latter's stay in San Antonio in 1919. Vasconcelos and Antonio Villarreal established a pro-Obregón newspaper to promote his presidency among Mexicans in the United States. Lozano's appearance on the pages of the official publication of the national university suggests that he had integrated himself into the circle of educational reformers by March 1921. He appeared as the registered owner of several works published by his publishing house, Editorial Lozano. "Se fundará en San Antonio un Gran Diario," *El Imparcial de Texas*, December 18, 1919, p. 12; "Noticia de las Propiedades Artísticas, Literarias y Musicales, que se han registrado en la Oficina de la Universidad Nacional," *Boletín de la Universidad*, Época IV, II.5 (Julio de 1921), pp. 154-55. See the following, for publications by Editorial Lozano: Ernest Richard Moore, *Bibliografía de Novelistas de la Revolución Mexicana* (New York: Lenox Hill Publishing and Distribution Company, 1972).

[9] "La colonia mexicana de los estados unidos construirá dos escuelas en Dolores Hidalgo, GTO," *La Prensa*, 13 de junio, 1921, pg. 1. Lozano's first visit corresponded with the interim presidency of de la Huerta, between June 1 and December 1, 1920. Vasconcelos was already an important political figure since de la Huerta had appointed him the head of the National University soon after assuming the presidency. Obregón was elected president in September, 1920, and assumed the nation's top office on December 1, 1920. This means that Lozano's second visit to Mexico City in February 1921 included Obregón as president. Unless otherwise noted, all cited newspaper articles originate in *La Prensa*.

[10] Consult the following for accounts of Vasconcelos the writer and educational reformer, as well as the educational reform movement that he directed during the postrevolutionary period: Edgar Llinás Álvarez, *Revolución, Educación y Mexicanidad, La Búsqueda de la Identidad Nacional en el Pensamiento Educativo Mexicano* (México, D.F.: Universidad Autónoma de México, 1978); Ricardo Navas Ruiz, *José Vasconcelos y la Educación en México* (Salamanca: Publicaciones del Colegio de España, 1984); Ernesto Meneses Morales, *Tendencias Educativas Oficiales en México, 1911-1934; La Problemática de la Educación Mexicana Durante la Revolución y Los Primeros Lustaros de la Época Posrevolucionaria* (Mexico, D.F.: Centro de Estudios Educativos,

Universidad Iberoamericana, 1998); Luis A. Marentes, *José Vasconcelos and the Writing of the Mexican Revolution* (New York: Twayne Publishers, 2000).

[11]For an examination of Vasconcelos' philosophy in light of the comparable ideas in education of John Dewey and the positivists who preceded him in Mexico, see the following standard essay on the subject of educational reform: Stanley D. Ivie, "A Comparison in Educational Philosophy: José Vasconcelos and John Dewey," *Comparative Education Review*, 10.3 (October 1966), pp. 404-17.

[12]Other authors cited in this study have demonstrated that Lozano was a notable transnational figure by virtue of his work as the editor of one of the most successful Spanish-language newspapers with wide circulation in the United States and Mexico. His editorial condemnation of President Calles during the Cristero rebellion of the 1920s is a case in point. His publishing house, Editorial Lozano, also influenced the world of letters beyond the borders of the United States. We know less of his direct involvement in political causes, although scattered information about his partisan political activity does exist. On April 5, 1920, for instance, while Carranza was serving his last days as president, the San Antonio Consul reported to the Foreign Affairs office that Lozano and a group of at least five political exiles had conspired against his administration at a meeting at Encinal, Texas, about fifty miles north of Laredo. In 1929, Lozano lent his assistance to Vasconcelos by secretly publishing his Plan de Guaymas, where he accused Calles of committing fraud and denying him the presidency. Gonzalo G. de la Mata to Oficial Mayor de Relaciones Exteriores, Encargado del Despacho, April 22, 1920, Archivo Histórico Genaro Estrada, Archivo de la Secretaría de Relaciones Exteriores; José Vasconcelos, *Memorias; El Preconsulado* (México, D.F.: Fondo de Cultura Económica, 1982), pp. 891-92.

[13]According to Nemesio García Naranjo, Lozano made his first trip to Mexico "to get a close view" of the Obregón administration. De la Huerta had already allowed exiles to return and Spanish-language newspapers from the United States to be distributed in Mexico. After a six-year banishment, *La Prensa* began appearing in the border towns of Matamoros, Nuevo Laredo, Piedras Negras and Ciudad Juárez. Once he returned to San Antonio, Lozano instructed his writers to rein in their acerbic pens. García Naranjo suggested that the conciliatory policies of de la Huerta and Obregón had led him to end his "aggressive posture", but it was obvious that a friendlier view of Obregón also made good business sense. Prior to joining *La Prensa* as one of its most distinguished essayists, García Naranjo had served as the Secretary of Education under President Victoriano Huerta and had published *La Revista Mexicana*, the very popular anti-Carranza newspaper from San Antonio. García Naranjo, *Memorias de Nemesio García Naranjo; Nueve Años de Destierro, Octavo Tomo* (Monterrey, Nuevo León: Talleres de 'El Porvenir', n.d.), pp. 341-42; Antimaco Sax, *Los Mexicanos en el Destierro* (San Antonio: International Printing Company, 1916), pp. 58-59; Nora E. Ríos McMillan, "Nemesio García Naranjo," *Handbook of Texas Online*, http://www.tsha online.org/handbook/online/articles/GG/fga94.html, Accessed June 27, 2009.

[14]Cynthia E. Orozco, "Comisión Honorífica Mexicana," *Handbook of Texas Online*, http://www.tshaonline.org/handbook/online/articles/CC/pqc1.html. Accessed May 15, 2009. According to Orozco, "the general consulate office of San Antonio had jurisdiction over Division 1, with approximately 163 chapters of comisiones in East, Central, and South Texas and Oklahoma, Kansas and Nebraska in 1927. It was also responsible for about 203 groups of the Cruz Azul Mexicana, a charitable women's organization. The organizations were prominent in the early 1920s and its members were "respected members of the community."

[15]"La colonia mexicana de los estados unidos construirá dos escuelas en Dolores Hidalgo, GTO," June 13, 1921, p. 1.

[16]Valadés, "Un hombre y un periódico."

[17]"Siguen los representantes consulares cooperando para las escuelas en Dolores," August 26, 1921, p. 1, "hermoso gesto patriótico de la colonia."

[18]Unless otherwise noted, the observations regarding the list of donors, fund-raising activities, and commentary by the editors of the paper and their readers are based on almost daily news, reports, and editorials that appeared in *La Prensa* during the life of the campaign, between June 1921 and January 1923.

[19]"La colonia mexicana de los estados unidos construirá dos escuelas en Dolores Hidalgo, GTO.";
"de todos los rincones del pais donde existen mexicanos, han llegado voces de aliento y donativos
de importancia."

[20]"Con \$516.77 contribuyó Laredo, Texas para Las Escuelas del Centenario," June 28, 1921, p. 1

[21]"La colonia debe hacer un esfuerzo más, para que las escuelas sean grandiosas," August 24, 1921,
p. 5; "el pueblo de Valentine sabrá responder dentro de poco al llamamiento, como han respondido
todos los buenos patriotas."

[22]"La voz de un anciano patriota habla a todos los mexicanos residents en Estados Unidos,"
September 15, 1921, p.1. "Yo quiero que llegue mi voz a la colonia, para hacerle ver que es un
compromiso de honor el que han contraído con la patria, y que ese compromiso tienen que
cumplirlo porque es sagrado."

[23]"La colonia debe hacer un esfuerzo más, para que las escuelas sean grandiosas," August 24, 1921,
p. 5. "Le confieso sinceramente que no sé lo que por mi pasó cuando me enteré de tan bella idea;
pero si sé que sentí el ideal que la anima, y sentí también, aunque soy méxico-tejana, que mi
corazón palpitaba lleno de interés por esa patria tan querida de la que no tengo palabras con que
expresarme."

[24]"No sólo los mexicanos contribuyen para las escuelas; también lo hacen extranjeros," August 23,
1921, p. 5. "Todos los compatriotas de este lugar, como buenos hijos de México, estamos
interesadísimos por ver terminada la gran obra de las dos escuelas de Dolores Hidalgo."

[25]The preparations in Guanajuato included a decree by the state legislature that acknowledged the
importance of Dolores Hidalgo in the planned celebration. "Decreto número 147 previniendo que
para celebrar el Primer Centenario de la Consumación de la Independencia Nacional, el H.
Congreso Local celebrará una sesión solemne en la Casa del Padre de la Patria, Don Miguel
Hidalgo y Costilla, en Dolores Hidalgo," *Periódico Oficial del Gobierno del Estado de
Guanajuato*, Año VII, Tomo XI (June 12, 1921), p. 370, Archivo de la Legislatura del Estado de
Guanajuato, Guanajuato, México.

[26]Ignacio E. Lozano to Sr. Gral. D. Álvaro Obregón, August 8, 1921, Archivo Álvaro Obregón,
Plutarco Elías Calles Collection, Archivo de la Nación, México, D. F. [hereafter cited as Obregón
Calles Collection]. The Obregón Calles Collection contains numerous letters between Lozano and
Obregón, most of which pertain to the assistance that the president gave the Dolores Hidalgo campaign.

[27]*Ibid.* "llevar algunos desde esta ciudad, tales como maderas para cielos y pesos, puertas y ventanas,
algo de ladrillo fino, materiales para la instalacion de luz electrica, etc., aparte del mobiliario todo
con que se dotara a las escuelas."

[28]Secretario Particular to Ignacio E. Lozano, August 27, 1921, Obregón Calles Collection;
Secretario Particular to C. Senador Carlos B. Zetina, H. Cámara de Senadores, June 10, 1922,
Obregón Calles Collection. According to Lozano, senator Zetina, represented the Mexican community in the United States and was responsible for coordinating the assistance from Obregón's
office.

[29]The "Grito de Dolores" symbolically represents the call to arms that Hidalgo y Costilla made on
the steps of the church in Dolores Hidalgo on September 15, 1810. The battle cry is supposed to
have been "Viva México, Viva la Independencia," the exhortation that is often repeated by guests
of honor like Lozano on the eve of the independence movement.

[30]Lozano, "El director de '*La Prensa*' dio el grito en la ciudad de Dolores Hidalgo, GTO,"
September 17, 1921, p. 1.

[31]*Ibid.* "La colocación de la primera piedra de Las Escuelas del Centenario será una ceremonia
brillante y muy significativa," September 18, 1921, pp. 1, 13.

[32]"La colocación de la primera piedra de Las Escuelas del Centenario será una ceremonia brillante
y muy significativa."

[33]The following articles provide a full account of the festivities: "Grandes fiestas en Dolores
Hidalgo, GTO," September 27, 1921, pp. 1, 10; "El gobierno, en nombre de toda la nación
agradece con ternura el obsequio de las escuelas que se hace a Dolores Hidalgo," September 29,

1921, p. 1; "Los diputados contribuyen para las escuelas," September 29, 1921, p. 1. "Lo mas granado de la sociedad hidalguense."

[34]"El Gobierno, en nombre de toda la nación agradece con ternura el obsequio de las escuelas que se hace a Dolores Hidalgo," p. 1; "Resúmen de las obras repartidas por la Universidad Nacional de México, durante el mes de Septiembre de 1921," Universidad Nacional de México, *Boletín de la Universidad*, Época IV, Tomo III, Número 7 (Diciembre de 1921), p. 203.

[35]"El gobierno, en nombre de toda la nación agradece con ternura el obsequio de las escuelas que se hace a Dolores Hidalgo," September 29, 1921, p. 1.; "Quiero, señor Lozano, que diga usted a la gran colonia mexicana residente en los Estados Unidos, que el gobierno de la república, a nombre de toda la Nación, agradece con ternura el obsequio de las escuelas que se hace a la cuna de la Independencia, y que procuraremos corresponder a este tributo de manera que, si por circunstancias especiales, los actuales mexicanos residentes en los Estados Unidos no reciben la recompensa a que son acreedores, sí pueden contar con que sus hijos la recibirán, y que cuando ellos regresen a su patria, encontrarán que ella se encuentra a igual altura y civilización escolar que los Estados Unidos."

[36]"El gobierno, en nombre de toda la nación agradece con ternura el obsequio de las escuelas que se hace a Dolores Hidalgo"; "se encontraba luchando sin desmayar un solo instante, para dar cima a la obra que ha de sorprender a las generaciones presentes, y ha de ser la veneración de las futuras."

[37]*Ibid.* "que era urgente la fusión de todos los partidos bajo la bandera de la patria, para hacer a esta fuerte y respectable."

[38]"Los diputados contribuyen para las escuelas." Alberto Gloria Zavala, "Las Escuelas del Centenario son la piedra angular de nuestra cultura y desarrollo," *El Grito* (Dolores Hidalgo), July 5, 1998, pp. 8-9.

[39]"Las escuelas del centenario serán inauguradas hoy con toda solemnidad en Dolores Hidalgo," January 9, 1923, p. 1; "grandiosidad extraordinaria."

[40]"Dolores Hidalgo vibra de entusiasmo con la inauguración de las escuelas," January 10, 1923, p. 1.

[41]"En medio de un regocijo general el Director de 'La Prensa' hizo entrega de los monumentos al Secretario de Educación Pública, Lic. Vasconcelos," January 10, 19231, p. 1, 5.

[42]Valadés, "Un hombre y un periódico." Torres also reported on the emotional scene at Hidalgo's home. "En medio de un regocijo general el Director de 'La Prensa' hizo entrega de los monumentos al Secretario de Educación Pública, Lic. Vasconcelos."

[43]*Ibid.* "la más grande alegría."

[44]Most of the information on the school structures originates in *La Prensa*. A more recent architectural rendering available at the schools, however, points to additional information regarding the playground space, the small middle structure connecting the main buildings, and changes in the use of some of the rooms. Regarding the changes, the administration office in the Ortiz de Domínguez school was eventually converted into an office for area school inspectors and a classroom across from the administration offices in the Hidalgo y Costilla school became a library. The library, possibly the one donated by Vasconcelos to the city in 1923, was moved into its present location, the office of the school's director, Maestra Marisa Victoria Ramírez González and her secretary, Ms. Alma Delia García. Profesor Eusebio Guerrero C., "Plano de la Escuela Urbana Federal Centenario," 1965, Framed document at Las Escuelas del Centenario, Dolores Hidalgo, Guanajuato. According to Ramírez González, the original plan was lost and a new one was drawn to meet federal regulations. I wish to thank Maria Esther Artiaga Rodríguez, an architect from Guanajuato, Guanajuato, who reproduced the plan from a digital photograph so that I could have a clearer understanding of the design of the entire site design.

[45]The description of the architectural features of the schools are based primarily on my observations of the architectural drawings, my observations of the building, and some clarifications from Professor Richard Cleary, School of Architecture, University of Texas at Austin.

[46]The following translations that correspond to terms in the recent architectural plan are based on common usage and conversations by the author with school officials and former elementary students in Dolores Hidalgo and Guanajuato, Guanajuato: Jardín—Decorative Garden; Columpios—

Swings; Cancha de Vólibol—Volleyball Court; Campo de Experimentación—Vegetable and Herbal Garden; Cancha de Básketbol—Basketball Court; Inspección—Office for Area School Inspectors; Corredor—Spacious Hall; Pasillos—Narrow Hall; Tienda de Artículos Escolares —Store for School Materials; Baños Para Niñas y Niños—Bathrooms for Girls and Boys; Cocina —Kitchen; Bodega—Storage Space.

[47]*Ibid.*

[48]*Ibid.* "un numeroso cuerpo de profesores competentes."

[49]Secretaría de Educación de Guanajuato, "Levantamiento Físico de Inventarios de Acervo Bibliográfico," Twenty-seven page inventory of library at Escuela Primaria "Centenario," 11DPR1754G, July 19, 2005. Copy in possession of the author. Original in the offices of the Secretaría de Educación de Guanajuato, Guanajuato, Mexico.

[50]di Stefano, "'Venimos a luchar': A Brief History of *La Prensa*'s Founding"; Ríos McMillan, "Ignacio E. Lozano" and "*La Prensa*," *Handbook of Texas Online*, http://www.tshaonline.org/handbook/online/articles/LL/eel3.html. Accessed June 27, 2009; Teresa Palomo Acosta, "Francisco A. Chapa," *Handbook of Texas Online,* http://www.tshaonline.org/handbook/online/articles/CC/fch50.html. (Accessed June 27, 2009). The literature on the exiled community in the United States includes the following: Fernando Sául Alanis Enciso, "De factores de inestabilidad nacional a elementos de consolidación del Estado posrevolucionario: los exiliados mexicanos en Estados Unidos, 1929-1933," *Historia Mexicana*, 54, No. 4 (April, June 2005), pp. 1155-1205; Victoria Sigal Lerner, "De la Época de la Revolución, El Caso Huertista Frente al Villista (1914-1915), *Estudios de Historia Moderna y Contemporánea de México*, 19 (1999), 85-114; Sax, *Los Mexicanos en el Destierro*; W. Dirk Raat, *Revoltosos: Mexico's rebels in the United States, 1903-1923* (College Station, Texas A & M U P, 1981); Peter V. N. Henderson, *Mexican Exiles in the Borderlands, 1910-1913*, Southwest Studies, Monograph, 58 (El Paso: Texas Western P, U of Texas at El Paso, 1979).

[51]The earthquake, registering a force of 6.7 degrees, left at least 3,000 persons dead. Its effect was primarily felt fifty kilometers outside of Jalapa. Ricardo Luna, "Estudia centro de ciencias de la tierra posibles sismos en el centro de Veracruz," *Gaceta; Universidad Veracrazana*, No. 61 (Enero 2003), 1-3.

[52]Valadés, "Un hombre y un periódico," p. 8.

[53]See the following for an examination of the stratified Mexican community of San Antonio: Richard García, *Rise of the Mexican American middle class; San Antonio, 1929-1941* (College Station: Texas A&M U P, 1991). The city built a reputation during the Mexican Revolution for drawing the largest numbers of political exiles and economic refugees of the upper class. Members of this sector constituted an important part of *La Prensa*'s audience, since Lozano himself minimized internal and nativity differences with his focus on Mexico and "los mexicanos de afuera." This focus was especially acute during the Mexican Revolution and the period of reconstruction when an undetermined but significant number of Mexicans returned to Mexico, as émigrés as well as deportees.

[54]For information on the split between the Mexican Liberal Party and Lozano, consult the following: Emilio Zamora, *The World of the Mexican Worker in Texas* (College Station: Texas A&M U P, 1993), pp. 139-53.

[55]"La construcción de las escuelas va a comenzar y la colonia mexicana debe estar orgullosa del homenaje," September 17, 1921, p. 1; "ha sido la mejor prueba de solidaridad"; "La gran colonia mexicana que lejos de la patria conserva para ella el corazón más sano y más templado"; "el homenaje altísimo de amor que la colonia depositaría con reverencia en el mismo lugar en donde un siglo atrás se escuchara la primera palabra de libertad"; "Siguen los representantes consulares cooperando para las escuelas en Dolores"; "hermoso gesto patriótico de la colonia."

[56]Valadés, "Un hombre y un periódico." "Hacer un viaje a la patria después de largos años de ostracismo; ir a contemplar las bellezas de nuestro suelo; palpar de cerca los dolores de nuestro pueblo que ha sufrido dos lustros los horrorers de la guerra civil; ponerme en contacto con hombres y acontecimientos y admirar nuevamente, tras de obligada y rologadísima ausencia de la

patria, las gallardías de nuestras montañas, el encanto de nuestras viejas ciudades, la exuberancia de nuestros campos, de nuestros jardines, de nuestros bosques milenarios; ver de cerca las cosas y de cerca estudiar a los hombres que luchan y que viven dentro de nuestras fronteras, los unos en el campo de la política, los otros en el de las ciencias y las artes, los de más allá en el trabajo fecundo que pide brazos y que pide cerebros."

[57]*Ibid.* "Hay un grande, un inmenso deseo de paz, y fuera de los 'buscones' de la política, de los que se pasan la vida en las antesalas de las diferentes dependencias del gobierno, a caza de granjerías o de puestos lucrativos, los elementos buenos de la sociedad están deseosos de cooperar en cualquier forma para lograr que se restablezca el equilibrio en el país. Hay buenos elementos, ¡quién lo duda!, y es preciso que se les abra camino, que no se entorpezcan sus iniciativas, que se les demuestre buena voluntad para no atajarles el paso."

[58]García Naranjo, "El gran discurso del Licenciado Nemesio García Naranjo," February 20, 1938, p. 3.; "un amor purificado por la lejanía."

[59]Valadés, "Un hombre y un periódico." "Nosotros vivimos fuera de México y por lo mismo, ajenos a las pasiones políticas que dividen a nuestros compatriotas, sólo vemos al problema nacional en su conjunto. . . Amamos la patria sobre todas las cosas y estamos y estaremos con quien la salve."

[60]Querido Moheno, *Sobre el Ara Sangrienta* (México: Andrés Botas é Hijo, 1922), pp. 263-64. Cited in Zamora, *The World of the Mexican Worker in Texas*, p. 91.

[61]Torres, "La Tristeza del Emigrante; El Secreto de Muchas Desazones," January 9, 1921, p. 8. "una obsesión divina." Allen Hinojosa, *El México de Afuera* (San Antonio, Texas: Artes Gráficas, 1940), p. 8. "Un firme, decidido e inquebrantable espíritu nacionalista." Allen Hinojosa had travelled to Texas earlier as a political exile and stayed to work as a journalist.

[62]See the following for a fuller account of the value of mutuality and its moralistic orientation to explain Mexican political behavior during the early 1900s: Zamora, *The World of the Mexican Worker in Texas*, pp. 86-109.

RACIALIZED IDENTITIES

Enriching *Rodríguez*: Alberta Zepeda Snid of Edgewood

Virginia Raymond
Texas After Violence Project

TODAY, AS FOR OVER A CENTURY, MEXICAN-AMERICAN PARENTS, TEACHERS, students, community and religious leaders, and other advocates protest, organize, litigate, lobby, create new institutions and transform existing ones—all to ensure that children and young adults will be able to educate themselves in preparation for ever-changing circumstances. This article explores the story of one woman, Alberta Zepeda Snid,[1] who played a key role at one critical moment in the enduring struggle: the 1968 rebellion at Edgewood High School and the Edgewood community's subsequent challenge of the Texas school finance system in *Rodríguez v. San Antonio ISD* (the case that reached the U.S. Supreme Court as *San Antonio ISD v. Rodríguez.*). It will argue that the Edgewood community was more multiracial and politically diverse than often recognized and the reasons for the poor conditions at Edgewood schools were multiple and interrelated.

Edgewood Rises

On May 16, 1968, beginning at 10:25 a.m., about four hundred students at Edgewood High School in San Antonio walked out of school.[2] [3] Their demonstration followed several months of activity by Edgewood students who were upset about the conditions and programs at their high school. One floor of the high school was infested with bats,[4] parts of the building were crumbling, and the science labs contained outdated and broken equipment. Perhaps even more alarming, many teachers were uncertified and unqualified, and worst of all many (but not all) believed that Mexican-American students did not need to be educated.[5]

Meeting with the student councils of two other San Antonio high schools, Edgewood students discussed and shared strategies for addressing these problems.[6] They came up with lists of demands that they presented to school administrators. Anger with the school superintendent, Bennie Steinhauser, had been building in the community for many months. When he did not respond to the students, hundreds of them walked out marching to the district's headquarters. They did not walk alone. Many parents and the civics teacher, Albert Sabater, walked with them, and other teachers openly supported the protest as well.

Father Henry Casso, a priest who would later help found Padres Asociados para Derechos Religiosos, Educativos, y Sociales (PADRES), supported the students, as did "the MAYO kids" (members of the Mexican American Youth Association) and at least one of the school board members, Manuel Garza told me that Judge Albert Peña, then a county commissioner, acted as a mentor to the students. A young Willie Velasquez, then a graduate student, urged the students to boycott classes if the district didn't meet their demands, telling them "with the education you get at Edgewood, most of you are going either to Vietnam or wind up as a ditchdigger."[7]

The Edgewood High School walkout, although the product of local conditions and organizing in San Antonio, is best understood in a broader context. It was one instance of Chicana/o activism across the Southwestern United States in which students demanded "an end to a multitude of discriminatory practices in the public schools" and protested the Viet Nam war that was claiming the lives of a disproportionate number of young Mexican-American men. For instance, as the Edgewood ISD newspaper later claimed, "out of all districts in Texas, Edgewood ISD lost the most men in Viet Nam," somewhere between 52 (as the district newspaper reports)[8] and 57 men (as one participant at an informal reunion in 2008 told me). Those who died were mostly from the classes of 1968, 1969, and 1970, and the current high school is named Memorial in their honor. These Chicana/o mobilizations took place during a period characterized by cries for fundamental change across the United States (Memphis, Washington, D.C., Atlantic City, New York, and Chicago), Latin America (Mexico City, Santiago), and Europe (Paris and Prague).

In East Los Angeles, students staged "blow-outs" to protest the "obvious lack of action on the part of the L.A. school board in bringing their schools up to par with those in other areas of the city."[9] Chicana/os in East Los Angeles wanted schools of equal quality, smaller class sizes, and for paid employees, rather than students, to perform janitorial work. The L.A. youth also wanted Spanish-speaking teachers who lived in their neighborhoods and who understood "the history, traditions and contributions of the Mexican culture," revised textbooks, an end to prejudice and discrimination, and freedom of speech and assembly. The Crusade for Justice led school walkouts in Denver in November 1968.[10] In Texas, one of the most significant walkouts took place in November 1968, at the Edcouch-Elsa High School in the Rio Grande Valley.[11] Severita Lara and her peers walked out of the Crystal City schools in 1969.[12] Students also walked out of schools in Abilene and Lamesa.[13]

The Edgewood Concerned Parents Association was comprised primarily of mothers, according to Cynthia Orozco,[14] but included fathers as well. Demetrio Rodríguez acknowledges that the primary parent organizer was "a very active lady named Mrs. Alberta Sneed."[15] Alberta Zepeda Snid was a newly widowed mother with five children, one son who was a soldier and four children at home. At the time of the walkout, only one of Mrs. Snid's children, José, attended the high school. He was an athlete[16] who paid attention to administrators' warnings and threats and did not participate in the walkout. But Alberta Snid was a life-long activist, deeply committed to her community and an unending quest for justice. She threw herself into the fight. By October of 1968, Snid was a paid organizer for the association, working out of its headquarters at 1162 General McMullen Drive.[17]

Alberta Zepeda Snid at home.
Copyright Alan Pogue, 1978.
Used with permission.

As an organizer, member, and staffer of the parent group, and, with four of her children, a plaintiff, Snid made possible the filing of *Rodríguez v. San Antonio ISD,* the lawsuit that forced the State of Texas to defend its school finance scheme in the federal courts. Although the written historical record has accorded Alberta Zepeda Snid little mention, in the Edgewood community, she is still a hero. Diana Briseño Herrera, Edgewood High School alumna (Class of 1969), participant in the spring 1968 walkout, teacher in the Edgewood district for thirty years, union member, and advocate recalls, "Mrs. Sneed was the spark for our fight in the struggle for equity in the state of Texas."[18]

The case, all the work supporting and surrounding the lawsuit, the subsequent challenges to Texas's school finance system in the state courts, and decades of agitating and lobbying demonstrate the discipline and determination of an organized community to sustain a social movement over the very long haul. We can not exhaust the meaning of these narratives until we examine the role played by Alberta Zepeda Snid. Her life reveals the rich complexity of communities and struggles of the people of San Antonio and of the gaps, for better and worse, between the law and lived experience.

The Life and Times of Alberta Méndez Zepeda Snid

Alberta Méndez Zepeda was born in San Antonio on April 8, 1919, to Cirilia Méndez and Pedro Zepeda,[19] Mexican immigrants from Mier y Noriega, Nuevo León and San Luis Potosí, respectively.[20] Cirilia, Pedro, and their children migrated from San Antonio south to the Río Grande Valley and as far north as Michigan and Illinois picking cotton, corn, strawberries, sugar beets, and other crops.[21] In San Antonio, they lived in the West Side of San Antonio. "West Side" here means an older, primarily Mexican and Mexican-American neighborhood settled in the early twentieth century with Mexican immigrants as opposed to the broader area that is also sometimes called "the West Side."

Alberta Snid's son, José Alberto Snid, guided me on a tour of both the Edgewood school district and the "old" or "original" West Side, a neighborhood that included Tampico and Zarzamora Streets and Guadalupe Church. Snid told me that his mother was born on or near Colima Street, but the family moved to Tampico Street and lived in a house that remains in the family today.[22] José thinks that his mother attended school up to the sixth or seventh grade, attending the David Barclay School on South Zarzamora and Vera Cruz. Not having had the opportunity to continue in school, Alberta Snid valued education very highly and would later read to her children frequently and encourage them in their studies.

With their mother and occasionally their father, the Zepeda girls worked as pecan shellers at the Zarzamora Street plant in San Antonio.[23] Pedro, Cirilia, and two of their five daughters, Concepción and Alberta, participated in the three-

Glenn Scott and María Flores (wearing Texas Farm Workers Union T-shirt) of People's History in Texas interview Alberta Zepeda Snid about her experiences in the San Antonio pecan shellers strike of 1938, but not about her role in the Edgewood Concerned Parents Association. *The San Antonio Light* headline on May 16, 1977 reads, "Lulacs Attack Carter Policy." The story reported on a resolution passed at the LULAC state convention which, according to Ruben Bonilla, "condemned the Carter administration for complete insensitivity, indifference and breach of faith with Hispanics." Copyright Alan Pogue, 1978. Used with permission.

month pecan sheller strike that began on January 31, 1938. José Snid remembers his mother telling her children that when she, her father, and her sisters were jailed, they sang the whole time.

Forty years after the pecan shellers' strike, labor historians María Flores and Glenn Scott asked Alberta Zepeda Snid if the strike had been worthwhile. She answered,

> Yes it did some good at the time because I think we learned . . . we learned that through organization we could do something . . . we learned that being united is power, regardless it is power. A single person cannot do anything,

alone we cannot do anything. People are power. Yes, I think we learned a whole lot. I think we learned how to even defend ourselves more. I think we forgot a little bit of the fear that we had because before we couldn't say nothing, we couldn't talk, period. Afterwards it was entirely different.[24]

Later events would prove that Snid was not afraid to speak out.

Alberta Zepeda gave birth in 1941 to a son, Lawrence or Lorenzo, with Santos Adame, but the relationship with Adame did not last. Sometime in the 1940s or early 1950s, Alberta Zepeda met the man who would become her second husband. Joseph Emmanuel Sneed (later Joe or José Snid) was born on August 23, 1915, to Joseph Sneed and Roxana Barifiell.[25] He worked at different points in his life for the U.S. Treasury Department and on his own as a television repairman. He was also a musician, playing guitar and piano with jazz and blues ensembles in local clubs as well as on tour. Sneed also performed popular Mexican songs. Joseph E. Sneed had been married once before, to a woman named Eunice, but the couple had no children. Sneed was a Black man and had grown up in what was then a predominantly Black neighborhood (it no longer exists).[26]

Had they stayed in their designated places, Zepeda on the West Side and Sneed on the East Side, Alberta and Joseph might never have met. However, as in many other places in the United States, the racial segregation in San Antonio was not complete. Fort Sam Houston, Kelly Field, Lackland, Randolph, and Brooks Air Force Bases fueled the San Antonio economy for the first two-thirds of the twentieth century. Besides money, these bases brought men, including Black men, to the city. (During World War II, the military economy also drew women.) Outside of counties that had been part of the original Confederacy, especially where slavery had given way to prison labor and tenant farming, the only Texas cities with significant Black populations were those with forts (in the nineteenth century) or military bases (in the twentieth). That San Antonio has a recognizable Black population is due in large part, both directly and indirectly, to its military economic base.[27]

In the 1940s, the Black population in San Antonio grew at a rate faster than the "white" population.[28] Moreover, life on military bases was more likely to be desegregated than elsewhere, thanks primarily to the work of A. Phillip Randolph and the Brotherhood of Sleeping Car Porters. The all-Black union, built in the 1930s, pressured President Franklin Delano Roosevelt to open jobs to African Americans, and they pressured President Harry Truman to desegregate the military forces.[29] As a consequence, the large military presence in the San Antonio region exerted a relatively progressive influence in race relations.

Although their stays may have been short, servicemen far from home possessed at least some leisure time and money to spend, thus developing a market for entertainment. In the 1930s, as Christopher Wilkinson describes in *Jazz on the Road: Don Albert's Musical Life,* racially mixed audiences in San Antonio could hear Black bands at Shadowland and Danceland.[30] While there were relatively few opportunities for interracial mixing or socializing,[31] musical venues provided the space and bands the reason for people to gather, at least when the police were not shutting down these venues. The number of clubs where people of different "races" could enjoy music and each other grew throughout the 1940s: Famous Door, Woodlake Country Club, Carver Library Auditorium, Kelly Field, Municipal Auditorium, and Don's Keyhole.[32] The clubs, particularly, were "centers of social interaction between the races."[33]

According to Texas law, Alberta Zepeda and Joseph Sneed should not have had much to do with each other. They certainly should not have married. Alberta Zepeda was "Latin American" and Joseph Sneed was "Negro."[34] In the 1940s, Texas law classified "Latin Americans" as "white," following a line of reasoning that began with the Treaty of Guadalupe;[35] it continued with *In Re: Rodríguez,* in which a federal district proclaimed that although Mexicans were "anthropologically" brown, they were legally "white."[36] This was reinforced by the forty-eighth Texas legislature that passed a resolution in 1943 mandating "equal privileges" for all people of "the Caucasian Race."[37] Mexican Americans in Texas were, in Ian Haney-López's term, "white by law."[38] (Not until the U.S. Supreme Court's decision in *Hernández v. Texas* did the federal courts recognize the gulf between legal terminology and actual practice.) If there were any doubt remaining about the legality of interracial unions, a Texas antimiscegenation statute banned the marriage of any Caucasian person, including Alberta Méndez Zepeda, with any person of African descent, such as Joseph Sneed.[39]

Social changes preceded legal ones. Joseph Sneed and Alberta Zepeda met at some event where Joseph Sneed was performing. To marry, the couple had to leave Texas. They went to Mexico, where they married in a civil ceremony in Nuevo Laredo, Tamaulipas; years later they were married in a Catholic ceremony in Texas. Marriage certificates from both ceremonies render the family name as "Snid." Alberta and Joseph, who on paper, at least, more frequently went by "José," lived together on the West Side of San Antonio, but moved further west than Alberta's parents' home in the "original" west side. José and Alberta had four children together: José Alberto, Catalina, Angelina, and Selina.

The couple lived in a constant state of "illegality," as the law not only did not recognize their marriage, but it also forbade their union. Yet "the state" is not a single thing; its disparate parts and agents reflected ambivalence about the couple's status. On José Alberto's birth certificate (the only one I have seen), the father, thirty-seven-year-old "Jose" Sneed, laborer and musician, is identified as "Negro," and the mother, thirty-three-year-old Alberta Zepeda, a housewife, is identified as "Latin American." Yet to the question of whether the child was legitimate, the registrar answered "yes," thus committing a small but significant act of civil disobedience and effectively rendering the antimiscegenation statute illegitimate. Similarly, in the humble recording of real estate and building trans-actions,[40] the participants acknowledged that, in fact, the Alberta and José Snid were married; if they had not been spouses, a lien against one would not have constituted a lien against the other. The facts "on the ground" were proving that "the law [was] an ass—an idiot."[41]

José Alberto Snid recalls that his mother was always active in the Parent-Teacher Associations (PTA) at whatever schools her children were attending, his Cub Scout activities, and in St. Gabriel's Church. Evelyn Jasso shared warm memories of plays that took place in Mrs. Snid's yard; José thought she might have been talking about plays that the kids performed while they were in reli-gious schools. Before the parish built classrooms, St. Gabriel's children received religious lessons in the Snids' large, shady yard. She made her chil-dren's clothes out of flour sacks.

José Emmanuel Snid died on June 16, 1967. He drowned, possibly after being beaten,[42] but no investigation took place. Bexar County recorded the death of a "Joe Snid" and identified him as "single." José Alberto Snid remembers that officials initially refused to release his father's remains to his mother. Were these simple errors or misunderstandings, or were they deliberate acts of county offi-cials who refused to recognize the marriage of José and Alberta? Their son sees the official rebuff of his mother as an instance of the prejudice of the day. Indeed, the U.S. Supreme Court had struck the Virginia antimiscegenation statute only a few days earlier, on June 12, 1967, in the case of *Loving v. Vir-ginia*.[43] [44] *Loving* deemed all antimiscegenation statutes constitutionally void, but Bexar County apparently hadn't caught up with the news. The Court's rul-ing in *Loving v. Virginia* failed to prevent these final odious insults to the Snid family.

Only a year after her husband's death, Alberta Snid found herself embroiled in the protests at Edgewood High School and became the prime parent organiz-er. After the parent group, Snid went to work for the Mexican American Unity Council (MAUC), as a mental health outreach worker at a moment when social work had not yet been taken over by degreed professionals. Snid continued to work for MAUC through the 1970s,[45] although she was disappointed when the organization abandoned its commitment to social justice issues to focus on eco-nomic development. When employees called a strike against MAUC—a rare occurrence in a "movement organization" during that period—Snid supported the strikers and brought food to the family of at least one worker who was fired for participating in the strike.[46] Although Snid did not strike herself, she spoke up. She also protested MAUC's treatment of its women employees.

Alberta Méndez Zepeda Snid spent her last years in retirement, cared for by her son. She died on November 22, 1994[47] and is buried with her husband, José Emmanuel Snid, in the San Fernando Cemetery #2.

The Lawsuit

Why were the physical conditions at the Edgewood High School so poor? What could account for the bat infestation, the crumbling building, and the missing, outdated, or broken equipment in the science lab?[48] Why were teachers uncertified, Alberta Snid wanted to know.[49] And why were too many teachers at Edgewood apathetic; why did they discourage their students? Why did the faculty—like José Snid's ninth grade P.E. teacher who told the Mexican-American students, "You don't have to worry about anything, you'll be working"— believe and act as if Mexican Americans didn't need to be educated?

No one factor could account for the multiple failures of the poorest school district in San Antonio. Yes, the district was underfunded. Edgewood homeowners paid taxes at a higher rate than did their counterparts in neighboring districts and, most dramatically, in Alamo Heights. The district was property-poor and its people low-income. To point to poverty only, though, was to beg the question: why were people so poor, and why were so many poor people concentrated in Edgewood? Why was the value of the land so low?

The plaintiffs, through their lawyer, Arthur Gochman, alleged that

> a pattern of discrimination against Mexican-Americans in the Southwestern United States . . . has resulted in a generally poorer education, more substandard housing, limited job opportunities, smaller incomes, and more deprivation of civil and political rights.

In arguing that inextricably connected racial and class discrimination consigned their children to inferior schools, the Edgewood parents echoed the complaint of Black residents of Washington, D.C., who had similarly argued that neither race discrimination alone nor poverty alone accounted for the inadequate education. In this case, *Hobson v. Hansen,* a federal district court ruled that a combination of racial and economic discrimination violated the Fourteenth Amendment rights of low-income Black school children to equal protection of the laws and so ruled in favor of the plaintiffs in 1967.[50] Arthur Gochman argued that a "nexus of race and poverty" in San Antonio resulted in an unconstitutional denial of decent education to the Edgewood students. (The argument would have been more precise had it alleged a nexus of racism and poverty.)

At first, the strategy worked for both the Black plaintiffs in Washington, D.C. and Mexican-American plaintiffs in San Antonio. In 1969, the Court of Appeals for the District of Columbia upheld *Hobson v. Hansen* by a two-to-one vote. In 1971, the three-judge panel that heard *Rodríguez v. San Antonio*[51] ruled the Texas system of school finance unconstitutional, in what one letter writer described as "one of the most momentous decisions that had ever happened to public education in our state and I hope to our whole country."[52]

The initial *Rodríguez* decision was, in fact, far too momentous for the privileged and powerful to swallow. The State of Texas appealed to the U.S. Supreme Court, and state governments rushed to join Texas in its plea to overrule *Rodríguez*. As outrage mounted at the socialist idea that all children should have equal access to education and as foes of the Edgewood plaintiffs mobilized their forces, two quieter but critical changes took place.[53] President Richard Nixon promoted Warren Burger to the Supreme Court, naming Burger Chief Justice. Second, new lawyers offered to assist Gochman represent his clients in the U.S. Supreme Court.

The Neighborhood

In the early 1950s, José and Alberta Snid moved to a neighborhood that was, in the late 1940s and early 1950s, on the western edge of San Antonio. They lived first at a house on Southwest 35th Street and later on Southwest 39th Street, where Alberta Snid spent the rest of her life and where her son still lives. The Snids came to the Edgewood area not long after the establishment of the Edgewood Independent School District on January 21, 1950.[54] The district includes the physical territory of what was originally Kelly Field, then Kelly Air Force Base, and now Kelly USA, and the district's greatest period of growth took place during World War II and in the immediate postwar period, as families moved to the area to be close to jobs on the base. District-wide student enrollment leaped from 1,911 in 1943, to 5,140 in 1950, and 13,416 by 1959.[55]

The rapid population growth that resulted in the creation of a new independent school district also created the need for new churches. St. Gabriel's parish was established on April 9, 1958.[56] The Missionhurst Missionaries came to San Antonio in 1947 at the request of Archbishop Robert Lucey,[57] who was particularly interested in Mexican immigrants and Mexican Americans and who had established the Committee for the Spanish Speaking two years earlier.[58] (The name of the committee later changed to the Bishop's Committee for Hispanic Affairs.)

The plaintiffs spent reams of paper establishing the poverty of people in the Edgewood School District, the low property values, the high rate at which people taxed themselves, and the low per-pupil expenditures. These facts have been rehearsed many times in the last four decades. The heterogeneity of the Edgewood populace is less well known. The district had a small Black population, but significant enough to be noticed, and significant because most African Americans, in the 1950s and 1960s, lived on the East Side of San Antonio. The Black community owes its existence on the West Side to the presence of Kelly, as does indeed the existence of the Edgewood community as a whole. Educators in what would later become the Edgewood Independent School District took the first steps to educate Black children in 1942 when it hired a teacher for a segregated class. In 1942, it dedicated George Washington Carver Elementary School, exclusively for "Colored" students, at 216 Purcell Street.[59] Later, Lincoln served as both an elementary and junior high school for Black children only, who joined Mexican-American and Anglo students only when they made it to high school, which was Edgewood (and thus integrated). The first class of Lincoln first-graders graduated from Edgewood High School in 1969; by then the district had closed Carver following a desegregation order. In 1960, 90 percent of the residents of Edgewood were counted as Mexican American and about 10 percent identified as Negro.[60] In 1967, Edgewood Superintendent Bennie Steinhauser figured that about "800 Anglos, almost 12,000 Negroes, and almost 20,000 Mexican American" students attended schools in the district.[61] These numbers doubtless mislead us because these "racial" categories appear as fixed and certain when they could not have been.

In 1975, the Texas legislature adopted a law barring school districts from admitting undocumented children, unless they paid tuition. Although numerous districts argued in favor of the restrictive law on the grounds that student needs already overwhelmed the limited funds and other resources at hand, Edgewood ISD filed an amicus brief urging the U.S. Supreme Court to overturn the law.

Deracinating *Rodríguez*

The new lawyers almost completely deracinated *Rodríguez v. San Antonio ISD*. That is, they shifted from an argument about the "nexus of race in class" to an argument based solely on economic discrimination. This change in argument had several different effects. The most obvious one, and the one I will discuss at some length below, was on the legal outcome of the case. There was a second, subtle but palpable, shift that has received less attention. This has to do with the place of race or ethnicity in the discussion.

From 1971, lawyers for plaintiffs (and then appellees) mentioned the Mexican-American identity of their clients without alleging discrimination against those clients on the basis of race, color, or national origin. The lawyers complained of income discrimination against children who attended a "poor and overwhelmingly Mexican-American school district." Thus, the Edgewood lawyers insinuated that "race is a factor" without saying how and why race mattered, or what role it played, in causing West San Antonio schools to be underfunded. It was as if the lawyers knew that something was not quite right, but either did not understand the nature of the discrimination against Mexican Americans in Texas or were afraid to name race discrimination. This weak and sloppy form of argumentation failed.

In this revised formulation, the role of race changed. The lawyers no longer alleged that the State of Texas discriminated against schoolchildren on the basis of race or ethnicity. Rather, the lawyers simply used "poor and overwhelmingly Mexican American" as attributes of the Edgewood Independent School District community, and, by extension, a defining feature of the plaintiff/appellee class.

Worse, "overwhelmingly Mexican American" carries a negative connotation, as if to be "overwhelmingly Mexican American" is a pitiable condition. It is the Mexican-American-ness that overwhelms, not poverty, and not racial discrimination. Two different adjectives applied to people and schools—poor and Mexican American—are read as "poor, Mexican American," with further slippage to "poor Mexican American" as if the very condition of being Mexican American was piteous. The phrase "overwhelmingly Mexican American" comes perilously close to implying "bad" or "inadequate"—as though the fault lay with the "overwhelming" Mexican American-ness of the place or the people, or as if the poor and "overwhelmingly Mexican-American" people were pitiable with or without a decent school system.

There is a huge gap between saying that the State of Texas discriminates against kids who are poor and Mexican American and equating "Mexican American" schools and people with inferiority. The first formulation places the responsibility on the state funding system, the other emphasizes the characteristics of those injured. The latter rhetoric either harshly blames the targets of discrimination for their misfortunate or condescendingly faults characteristics that Mexicans or other minorities "cannot help."

Thirty-five years after the fact, it is difficult to understand why the Edgewood parents' lawyers made the radical decision to drop the argument of racial discrimination. Between 1968 and 1973, there was no doubt that government actions based on race would be judged by strict scrutiny (even though the requirements for proving racial discrimination were about to change). Mexican

Americans specifically were protected under the strict scrutiny standard (*Hernández v. Texas*, 1954; *Cisneros v. Corpus Christi Independent School District*, 1971) and would continue to be so protected in *White v. Regester,* the voter districting case[62] that was pending as *Rodríguez* was argued, considered, and decided.

Apparently, the lawyers believed that "the problem . . . [with the plaintiff/appellees' original claim] was that there had not been any legislated segregation of Mexican Americans in Texas."[63] It is painful to come across a comment that reveals such dangerous ignorance. In its 1954 ruling in *Hernández v. Texas,* the U.S. Supreme Court had explicitly recognized the particular nature of anti-Mexican American and anti-Mexican discrimination in Texas.[64] The Supreme Court, as constituted in 1954 and early 1973, was not fooled by the absence of Jim Crow laws or other de jure racial or ethnic discrimination. It was fully capable of recognizing the racist practices even in the absence of explicitly racist laws.

Neither the courts nor anyone else aware of Mexican-Anglo relations in Texas believed that the absence of codified discrimination made Anglo discrimination against Mexican Americans any less pervasive, historically based, deepseated, intractable, or real. Unfortunately, it seems that the Edgewood parents' lawyers had never read *Hernández v. Texas* or given much thought to the particular ways in which Anglo-dominated power structures subordinated Mexican Americans in the U.S. Southwest. Their belief that there was no way to prove anti-Mexican discrimination without de jure segregation reveals the results of a lamentably widespread inadequacy in legal education. This education failed to teach the history of Mexicans and Mexican Americans in the Southwestern United States, the history of Mexican-American struggles for education, and even Supreme Court jurisprudence.[65] An education fails when it fails to demonstrate that racism manifests itself in varying ways at different places and at particular historical moments.

The *Rodríguez* lawyers' lack of faith in a race claim is also painfully frustrating, because it could have been alleviated had they attended to the work the Mexican American Legal Defense and Education Fund (MALDEF) was doing at the same time in *White v. Regester. White v. Regester* initially challenged the 1970 Texas redistricting plan for essentially disenfranchising Black voters in Dallas. MALDEF intervened because the same redistricting plan disenfranchised Mexican-American voters in San Antonio and in the same way. While the *Rodríguez* attorneys fretted that they could not prove racial discrimination against Edgewood residents without facially discriminatory laws, MALDEF attorney Ed Idar, Jr., was busy assembling the evidence that proved that racial discrimination. Idar represented Mexican Americans who lived in the barrio, twenty-eight contiguous census tracts, where Mexican Americans constituted the majority of the population that were mostly on the West or South Side of San Antonio. This area included the Edgewood school district, and, in fact, both ethnic Mexicans and poor people were more concentrated in the Edgewood area than in the barrio as a whole.

The U.S. Supreme Court's consideration of *San Antonio ISD v. Rodríguez* overlapped with its consideration of *White v. Regester*.[66] The lack of explicitly anti-Mexican-American statutes did not prevent either the trial court or the Supreme Court finding racial discrimination against Mexican Americans in *White v. Regester*, because MALDEF had proven the existence, in practice, of such racial discrimination. Private individuals, corporations, and the state had all discriminated against Mexicans and Mexican Americans. While the Texas Legislature had not enacted laws that called for poor treatment of Mexican Americans, the state did enforce restrictive covenants that created and maintained racially and ethnically segregated neighborhoods.[67] The Supreme Court found that the enforcement of racially discriminatory restrictive covenants constituted unlawful discrimination against Mexican Americans who had effectively been restrained to the barrio for decades. Racial discrimination robbed Mexican-American residents of the West Side of San Antonio voting rights and thus political power, with extremely detrimental effects.

In other words, neither God nor nature decreed that Mexican Americans would live in West and South San Antonio, that Black people would live mostly in East San Antonio, and that Anglos would live in Alamo Heights. The demographic map of San Antonio was the result of human decisions and actions. The Supreme Court ordered single-member districts in both Bexar County and Dallas County. This *White v. Regester* ruling came just three months after it had failed to find racial discrimination or a violation of equal protection for Edgewood ISD. The Supreme Court was clearly capable of finding discrimination against Mexican Americans in San Antonio, but they had to be asked to do so. The MALDEF interveners, Bernal et al., in *White v. Regester* asked, but the lawyers representing Demetrio Rodríguez and his cohorts failed to make the argument.

In 1973, the U.S. Supreme Court upheld the Texas school finance system in a five-to-four decision, despite the incontrovertible facts that children in low-income school districts did not receive the same quality of education as did schoolchildren in wealthy districts. The Court held that the equal protection clause of the Fourteenth Amendment did not require a state to provide the same education to children living in different neighborhoods or to rich and poor. In order to sustain the Texas system, the Court had to rule both that education was not a fundamental right and that discrimination against the poor was not unconstitutional. The Court's decision dealt a fatal blow to educational equity litigation under the U.S. Constitution. It also marked the end of the era in which the Fourteenth Amendment equal protection clause began to fill its long-dormant promise. *San Antonio ISD v. Rodríguez,* an unmitigated disaster, marked the outer limit of equal protection: economic class. The dismissal of education as a fundamental right came as a shock to many advocates; the refusal to extend equal protection to the poor should not have been a surprise. A country with a capitalist economy cannot ban discrimination on the basis of income. The entire economic system is predicated on the existence of different economic classes. If everyone had equal access to resources, there would be no such thing as competition or "getting ahead."

Moreover, Chief Justice Burger had been the one judge on the D.C. Court of Appeals who had dissented in *Hobson v. Hansen.* It was the Burger Supreme Court that read the pleadings, heard the oral argument, and issued the fateful ruling in *San Antonio Independent School District v. Rodríguez.* The Burger court was not disposed to expand rights; it grudgingly recognized that the U.S. Constitution prevented racial discrimination (at least obvious racial discrimination for which a specific person or action could be blamed) but did not see a constitutional problem with discrimination against poor people.

The Supreme Court's 1973 ruling in *San Antonio ISD v. Rodríguez* was bad news for equal protection, bad news for education, and a disaster for low-income children who live in poor school districts. The decision appeared to signal to Texas lawmakers that it would be constitutionally permissible to bar undocumented immigrant children from public schools. Knowing that the Supreme Court did not see education as a fundamental right, Texas legislators took the next opportunity—the 64th legislative session in 1975—to pass a law excluding these children from public schools.[68]

The Court's decision did not, however, end the fight for equity. Rather, the decision provoked a rededicated and intensified fight at the state legislature and in the state courts with the support of the Intercultural Development Research Association (IDRA), MALDEF, the Southwest Industrial Areas Foundation, and many other individual and organizational advocates. Sixteen years after the U.S. Supreme Court refused to find the Texas school finance system unconstitutional, the Texas Supreme Court did so in *Edgewood ISD v. State of Texas.* Attempts to enforce the court's rulings have faltered; the struggle continues unabated.

What's In A Name?

The Edgewood Concerned Parents Association brought their complaints to Arthur Gochman, and some of them decided to serve as plaintiffs. They numbered twenty-two: seven adults and fifteen children. They were listed in the following order:

- Demetrio P. Rodríguez, his wife, Helen M. Rodríguez, and Alexander Rodríguez[69]
- Mrs. Alberta Z. Snid, a widow, and her children José Snid, Catalina Snid, Angelina Snid, and Selina Snid.
- Joe Hernández, his wife, Carmen D. Hernández, and children Yolanda Hernández, Irma Hernández, Richard Hernández
- Martín R. Cantú, Sr. and children Linda Cantú, Brenda Cantú, and Blanche Cantú
- Reynaldo F. Castaño and children James Castaño, Robert Castaño, and Steve Castaño.[70]

Only one of the original twenty-two named plaintiffs came to publicly represent the parents, the district, and their story. This is normal. Few individual people who act collectively in any grand social movement will receive recognition even at the time of their action, much less decades later. For Edgewood, the case is titled *Rodríguez v. San Antonio ISD,*[71] and the public face of the struggle is Demetrio Rodríguez.

The rhetorical—and often visual—reduction of a complex collective movement to a single figure is the norm, but that does not mean we should take the norm for granted or accept the particular consequences of a specific representation as preordained or natural. What is in a name? Did it matter, and does it matter, that the Edgewood community's struggle was—for many years—symbolized by one person? What are the effects of Demetrio Rodríguez as a symbol?

First, the format of the case name pits a single person against a government agency. This arrangement is not inherent to the legal process; corporations or other entities frequently precede the names of individual plaintiffs or defendants. The choice of what names to put first—because people almost never refer to a case by its full name—has the effect of personalizing or depersonalizing the name. A legal challenge in the name of a single person, especially when that person becomes the primary or even sole public symbol of a larger public, as it necessarily reduces and distorts the nature of a collective struggle to an individual one. Alberta Snid, who had played a key role in organizing the parents, is all but obscured in legal history; the Hernández, Cantú, and Castaño families also fade from view, as do other Edgewood community members who are never named at all. Such a reduction of a collective struggle to individual heroes is easier to write, but it is not accurate.[72]

Second, *Rodríguez v. San Antonio ISD* announces itself as a conflict involving Mexican Americans and the public education system. Not all cases involving racial or ethnic oppression announce themselves quite as clearly as

Rodríguez v. San Antonio ISD does. The name *White v. Regester,* 412 U.S. 755 (1974), does not reveal that it is a challenge to legislative districting or that the complainants are African American and the interveners Mexican American; *Plyler v. Doe,* 457 U.S. 202, does not clue the uninitiated into the xenophobic and anti-Mexican racism that provoked the statute in question; *Katzenbach v. Morgan,* 384 U.S. 641 (1966), does not hint at discrimination against Spanish-speaking voters in Puerto Rico. There are also case names with Latina/o roots that are sometimes Anglicized to the degree that the circumstances that produced the conflict and the identities of the people concerned are pushed into the background and (almost) forgotten. The "Mee–rahn–duh" of *Miranda v. Arizona,* 84 U.S. 436 (1966), becomes "Mih–ran–duh." Rodríguez, however awkwardly pronounced, remains Mexican. The case name serves as a mnemonic device. A case named *Snid v. San Antonio ISD* would not have produced an automatic identification with the cause and Mexican Americans.

Third, Rodríguez's prominence—to the exclusion of Snid—has the effect of pushing female leadership into the background. In the pleadings, each woman plaintiff—except for Alberta Snid—is identified by her marital status, but there is no corresponding identification for the men. Additionally, neither the mother of the Cantú children nor the mother of the Castaño children appear as plaintiffs. It is possible that these women were either absent or did not approve of the lawsuit, but it is also possible that the active women's names dropped out when the controversy moved from the school and neighborhood to the more formal realm of the courts.

Finally, that Rodríguez was the first and therefore most prominent plaintiff obscures the contributions of the left in the cause of education. Rodríguez, a member of LULAC and the GI Forum, was active in organizations that took pains to emphasize their patriotism, desire for assimilation and respectability, and mainstream goals. Snid was a labor activist from her first years as a paid worker to her last, and recognition of her role would highlight the inextricably linked nature of struggles for decent pay and working conditions, education, and racial justice. Demetrio Rodríguez was legible, comforting, and unthreatening as a patriotic patriarch, while Alberta Zepeda Snid would have been too confusing.

Legal Hostility to Mixture

The law does not deal well with ambiguity or mixtures. As Neil Foley has noted, "the United States has repudiated the idea of racial hybridity for most of its history, and consequently has no cultural or legal context for understanding the racial place of Mestizo people."[73] What is true of people has also been true of causes: courts have a difficult time with multiple causes and mixed causes. This difficulty, and outright hostility, is not universally shared and was the subject of contention between "classical" and "realist" legal scholars in tort law and contracts before the emergence of "civil rights" as we have known it. Jurists in the "classical" legal tradition who want single causes belong to an intellectual tradition of objectivism and positivism, seek universals, yearn for predictability and consistency, and tend to value freedom over equality. These jurists follow Emile Durkheim in asserting that every effect must have only one cause, and that if it appears that you have found more than one cause you are in actuality dealing with entirely different things or phenomena.

Although there has been a consistent strain in civil rights movements to pursue equality on multiple fronts, "civil rights" litigation—until *Rodriguez v. San Antonio ISD*—primarily meant challenges to race discrimination to the exclusion of class. The addition of income discrimination was a welcome development. But in focusing on income discrimination, excluding racism as a cause, and leaving in "race" and ethnicity only as descriptors, the *Rodriguez* lawyers committed a grave error with disastrous consequences. You might say that it was the opposite error that civil rights lawyers had been making since the late 1940s, which was to focus on race to the exclusion of class.

On another level of analysis, you might say that the school finance error was precisely the same error that legal structures frequently force advocates to make, which is to oversimplify and to force complex fact situations into artificial and too-neat categories. Perhaps this act of remembering Alberta Zepeda Snid and her husband José Snid (or Joseph Sneed) can serve as a partial corrective. Just as the many aspects of systematic injustice are deeply rooted in complex and contradictory history, so too are the movements for social justice, and the people who challenge them.

I am indebted to José Alberto Snid, for talking to me for hours, showing me around Edgewood, the West Side neighborhood where his mother grew up, and the former site of the East Side neighborhood where his father grew up. I also thank him for taking me to the informal reunion of Edgewood walkout participants, and for allowing me to read and make copies of family records. Alan Pogue generously allowed me to use his 1978 photographs of Mrs. Snid. Thanks, also, to Monica Perales for her patience, to Emilio Zamora for his encouragement, and to my family for everything. This article contains material that I have published previously in Virginia Raymond. "Mexican Americans Write Toward Justice in Texas, 1973-1982." (Ph.D. Dissertation, University of Texas at Austin, 2007); "Alberta Zepeda Snid: Activist Parent," *La Voz de Esperanza* (San Antonio: Esperanza Peace and Justice Center, May 2008); and "Alberta Zepeda Snid." *Handbook of Texas Online*. Texas State Historical Association <http://www.tshaonline.org/handbook/online/articles/SS/fsn12.html>. Accessed December 15, 2008.

Notes

[1] Alberta Zepeda Snid's last name is spelled "Sneed" in some accounts, after the initial spelling of her husband 's name. When Joe Sneed married Alberta Zepeda, it seems that they mostly spelled the family name as "Snid," which is how Spanish language speakers would render the sound that English would render as "Sneed." Joe Snid also was sometimes rendered as José. The spelling, however, was not always consistent. "Snid" is a Hispanicized version of "Sneed"; at least one of the descendants of Alberta and Joe/José spells his name as "Snid" while others use "Sneed." Variation in the spelling of family names is neither unusual nor necessarily of great import in itself, but this discrepancy is significant because related to the family's ambiguous "racial" status. To test this idea, I reviewed a set of church records, real estate transactions, and government-issued documents to see what spelling appeared under what circumstances, noting also minute clues (lines left blank, boxes empty, different officials applying different rules). The enterprise takes too many pages to include in this article. I use "Sneed" for events taking place before the couple's marriage, and "Snid" afterwards, unless I am directly quoting a document that uses "Sneed" after the couple's marriage.

[2] The fight for educational and school finance equity in Texas is a long one that has been told in many ways and with many different starting points, especially by Guadalupe San Miguel, *"Let All of Them Take Heed": Mexican Americans and the Campaign for Educational Equality in Texas, 1910-1981* (Austin: U of Texas P, 1987); José A. Cárdenas, *Texas School Finance Reform: An IDRA Perspective* (San Antonio: Intercultural Development Research Association, 1997); and Rubén Donato, *The Other Struggle for Equal Schools: Mexican Americans during the Civil Rights Era* (Albany: State U. of New York, 1997). In beginning the chronological story at the Edgewood High School student walkout, I am following Cynthia E. Orozco's article, *"Rodríguez* v. San Antonio ISD," *Handbook of Texas Online*, Texas State Historical Association, <http://www.tsha online.org/handbook/online/articles/RR/jrrht.html>. Accessed December 15, 2008; Richard Lavine "School Finance Reform in Texas, 1983-1995," in Robert H. Wilson, ed., *Public Policy and Community: Activism and Governance in Texas* (Austin: U of Texas P, 1997), 121; and Paul A. Sracic, *San Antonio v. Rodríguez and the Pursuit of Equal Education: The Debate over Discrimination and School Funding* (Lawrence: U P of Kansas, 2006).

[3] Ron White, "School Chief Insists It's Classes 'As Usual'," *The San Antonio Light*, May 17, 1968, 6.

[4] Scracic, 20.

[5] José A. Snid credits his former teacher and counselor, Marlene Simon for encouraging him and for helping him get into St. Mary's U. Mr. Snid earned a Master's degree and taught for several years in the 1970s; he also served in the military.

[6] This paragraph is drawn from the recollections and conversations of Edgewood High School Alumnae as they gathered on April 1, 2008, at their alma mater in the late afternoon. The informal gathering was prompted by the upcoming forty-year anniversary of the walkout. In preparation for a story for the *San Antonio Express*, a reporter had asked people to gather for a photograph. Serendipitously, I was in San Antonio to meet and interview José Alberto Snid when a friend came by Mr. Snid's house to remind him of the gathering. Mr. Snid allowed me to accompany him to the high school, where I took notes as people reminisced about the events leading up to the walkout, the protest itself, and the aftermath.

[7] White, 6.

[8] "Fallen Comrades Honored at Memorial Day Ceremony," *The Edgewood ISD Historian*, 1.3, (Summer 2005), 5.

[9] Chicana/o Student Movement News, reproduced in F. Arturo Rosales, *Testimonio: A Documentary History of the Mexican American Struggle for Civil Rights* (Houston: Arte Publico P, 2000), 353-354.

[10]Rosales, 360.

[11]B. James Barrera. "The 1968 Edcouch-Elsa High School Walkout: Chicano Student Activism in a South Texas Community," *Aztlán* 29:2 (Fall 2004): 93-122.

[12]Severita Lara, oral history with José Angel Gutiérrez, July 18, 1996, CMAS 13, Special Collections, U of Texas at Arlington Libraries, Tejano Voices, <http://libraries.uta.edu/tejanovoices/interview.asp?CMASNo=013#>. Accessed August 2, 2009.

[13]Nephtalí DeLeón, "Chicanos Walk Out in Abilene," *Texas Observer*, December 5, 1969, 4-5; "Young Chicanos' Unrest Spreads to Lamesa," *Texas Observer*, January 23, 1970, 6.

[14]Cynthia Orozco, "*Rodríguez v. San Antonio ISD*," *Handbook of Texas Online*. Orozco spells Alberta Zepeda's last name as "Sneed."

[15]Demetrio Rodríguez, in Peter Irons, ed., *The Courage of Their Convictions: Sixteen Americans Who Fought Their Way to the Supreme Court* (New York: Free P/Macmillan, 1988), 258. Paul Scracic, at 20, also credits Alberta Snid as the primary organizer.

[16]José Alberto Snid told me he played football in 9th grade, and then basketball for three years.

[17]Edgewood Group Opens Offices." *San Antonio Light*, October 27, 1968, 9-B. According to George Maldonado, who is quoted in the article, the office and Mrs. Sneed's position was made possible by a $4,000 grant from the Mexican-American Unity Council, headed by Willie Velasquez, which in turn received its money from the Ford Foundation. In 1968, the Ford Foundation also made a large grant to the brand-new Mexican American Legal Defense and Education Fund (MALDEF); Gochman sought MALDEF's involvement in the Rodríguez case but MALDEF did not initially agree to participate.

[18]Diana Briseño Herrera to Virginia Raymond, July 22, 2009, personal communication by e-mail.

[19]Certificate of Birth Registration of Alberta Zepeda, City of San Antonio Health Department, No. 11621, Register No. 814 ½, September 20, 1946. This document is in the possession of José Alberto Snid.

[20]Alberta Snid oral history interview with María Flores and Glenn Scott.

[21]Author telephone interview with José Alberto Snid, March 25, 2008, and in-person interview in San Antonio on April 1, 2008.

[22]Interview with José Alberto Snid and guided tour, April 1, 2008.

[23]Alberta Snid oral history interview with María Flores and Glenn Scott; José A. Snid interview with Virginia Raymond on April 1, 2008.

[24]Alberta Snid oral history interview with María Flores and Glenn Scott.

[25]In her later years, Roxana Barifiell Sneed achieved hero status when she saved a life. According to one account, "An 80-year-old woman who wouldn't leave her small home despite five fires in the last five years was rescued from her flaming home Wednesday by a 68-year-old neighbor." The article further reported that "Officers said Mrs. Mariz (sic) Garza, 219 Victoria, was asleep in her home when Mrs. Joseph Sneed, 223 Victoria, pulled her from the blaze." "80-Year-Old Rescued from Flames," *San Antonio Express*, January 11, 1962, 1.

[26]José A. Snid has a certificate of his parents' first, secular marriage certificate. Issued by the municipality of Nuevo Laredo, the certificate is in Spanish. José E. Sneed, 36, single, a musician lived at 1024 E. Commerce, San Antonio, and José E. Sneed's mother, Roxana Sneed, lived at 223 Victoria St., San Antonio. José Sneed's father had already passed away by the time of José and Alberta's marriage.

[27]U.S. Bureau of the Census, *Sixteenth Census of the United States Population, 1940, Volume II, Characteristics of the Population. Part 6: Pennsylvania—Texas*. Table 21: "Composition of the Population of the Counties: 1940," (Washington, DC: GPO, 1943), 792—806; U.S. Bureau of the Census, *Sixteenth Census of the United States Population, 1940, Volume II, Characteristics of the Population. Part 6: Pennsylvania—Texas*. Table 22: "Age, Race, and Sex, by Counties, 1940 and 1930," (Washington, DC: GPO, 1943), 807 -857. <http://www.census.gov/prod/www/abs/decennial/1940.htm.>. Accessed July 17, 2009.

[28]Christopher Wilkinson, *Jazz on the Road: Don Albert's Musical Life* (Berkeley: U of California P, 2001), 235.

[29]Karin Chenoweth, "Taking Jim Crow out of Uniform: A Philip Randolph and the Desegregation of the U.S. Military." *Black Issues in Higher Education*, 14.13, (August 21, 1997), 30.

[30]Wilkinson, 100.

[31]William S. Taylor, "Some Observations of Marginal Man in the United States," *Journal of Negro Education*, 9.4 (October 1940): 604-609.

[32]Wilkinson, 206-212.

[33]Wilkinson, 235.

[34]These are their designated "races" on their son, Jose's, birth certificate.

[35]Treaty of Guadalupe, <http://avalon.law.yale.edu/19th_century/guadhida.asp>. Accessed July 17, 2009.

[36]*In re: Rodríguez*, 81 F. 337 (W.D. Texas 1897).

[37]H.C.R. No. 105, *General and Special Laws of the State of Texas Passed by the Regular Session of the Forty-Eighth Legislature* (48th Legislature), Austin, January 12, 1943 to May 11, 1943, 1119; Neil Foley, *The White Scourge: Mexicans, Blacks, and Poor Whites in Texas Cotton Culture* (Berkeley: U of California P, 1997), 206.

[38]Ian F. Haney-López, *White by Law: The Legal Construction of Race* (New York and London: NYU P, 1996).

[39]Title 75 of the Texas Civil Statutes, Article 4607. "Certain intermarriages prohibited.—It shall not be lawful for any person of Caucasian blood or their descendants to intermarry with Africans or the descendants of Africans. If any person shall violate any provision of this article, such marriage shall be null and void."

[40]The online Index to Bexar County Historical Records lists several documents regarding Jose Snid and others regarding Alberta Snid in 1959 and 1964. The transactions recorded are a mechanic's lien against Alberta Snid, grantor to the U.S. Building Materials Company grantee, on December 23, 1959; correction for the same mechanic's lien on December 28, 1959; the same transactions are also listed for José Snid, grantor. The online index also references a deed by José Snid, grantor, to the State of Texas on March 30, 1964; a deed of trust by José Snid, grantor, to Charles D. Lum on April 4, 1964; and the release of a mechanics lien by Richard Gill to José Snid, grantee, on April 13, 1964. Index to Bexar County Historical Records, Bexar County, Gerry Rickoff, County Clerk, <hittp://www.countyclerk.bexar.landata.com.default/asp>. Accessed November 14, 2006. The Bexar County Clerk online index also references lien transactions in 1976 and 1978, and an affidavit of heirship signed by Alberta Snid in 1987 and filed in 1988 <http://www.countyclerk.bexar.landata.com/Default.aspx>. Accessed August 1, 2009.

[41]Mr. Bumble's words in Chapter 51 of Charles Dickens' *Oliver Twist*.

[42]Interview with José Alberto Snid, April 1, 2008; "SA Musician Drowns in Swim Pool," *San Antonio Light*, June 16, 1967, 4.

[43]*Loving v. Virginia*, 388 U.S. 1 (1967)

[44]Almost two decades earlier, in *Perez v. Lippold* (initially *Perez v. Sharp*), the California Supreme Court ordered the County Clerk of Los Angeles County to issue petitioners Andrea D. Perez and Sylvester Davis a marriage license. This case, decided in 1948 at roughly the same time that Alberta Zepeda and José Sneed went to Tamaulipas to marry, challenged the California anti-miscegenation statute partly on the grounds that the law prevented the free exercise of their religion. "They maintain[ed] that since the [Catholic Church] has no rule forbidding marriages between Negroes and Caucasians, they are entitled to receive the sacrament of matrimony" (J. Traynor for the majority). In a powerful, passionate opinion, the majority voided the California statute as unconstitutional under the Equal Protection clause of the Fourteenth Amendment. But there was more. The racial distinctions were not only odious but also unconstitutionally vague and uncertain. Exactly how much "Negro," "white," "Malay," "mulatto" and "Mongol" ancestry determines a person's racial classification? Who is what "race" based on how much of which ancestries? 32 Cal. 2d 711, 198 P.2d 17 (1948).

[45]José A. Snid, personal conversations. Alberta Snid was working for MAUC by 1972, when she was described as "a mental health worker with the Mexican-American Unity Council" who was 52 years old, who had completed the fifth grade at David Barkley School, and who had three children attending Edgewood High School. Aziz Shihab, "The People Behind the School Funding Ruling," *San Antonio Express and News*, January 23, 1972, p.85.

[46]These recollections of Alberta Zepeda Snid's activism within MAUC, her support of her coworkers, and the controversies at MAUC in the early 1970s come from Evelyn Jasso García and Pancho García (personal conversation, May 24, 2007, San Antonio) as well as Rodolfo Rosales (Rosales e-mail to Virginia Raymond, December 14, 2006).

[47]Certificate of Death, San Antonio Metropolitan Health District, in the possession of José Alberto Snid.

[48]Scracic, 20.

[49]José Alberto Snid remembers that his mother was particularly upset about unqualified teachers (personal interview, April 1, 2008).

[50]*Hobson v. Hansen*, 265 F. Supp. 902 (1967)

[51]The published opinion gives the date of the opinion as December 23, 1971, with the additional note "As Clarified Jan. 26, 1982." The full citation is *Demetrio P. Rodríguez, et al. v. San Antonio Independent School District at al.*, 337 F. Supp. 280 (W.D. Texas—San Antonio Div. 1971). The style of cases always names the moving party — here, the plaintiff, later, the appellant – first. Thus, the case began as *Rodríguez v. San Antonio ISD*, but since the lower courts ruled for the plaintiffs and the defendants appealed, went to the U.S. Supreme Court as *San Antonio Independent School District v. Rodríguez.*

[52]Luis Fortuna, Letter to the Editor, "Edgewood Parents Hailed," *San Antonio Express*, January 5, 1972, 6-B.

[53]This observation is from Paul Scracic's account.

[54]History of Edgewood," Edgewood Independent School District, <http://www.eisd.net/history.htm>. Accessed July 20, 2009.

[55]"History of Edgewood," Edgewood Independent School District.

[56]Parish Information, Archdiocese of San Antonio, <http://www.archdiosa.org/ParishLocator/ParishInfo.asp?ID=4147>. Accessed July 18, 2009.

[57]Missionhurst Missionaries, "Our Ministry Among Hispanics in the U.S.," <http://www.missionhurst.org/texas/index.shtml>. Accessed July 20, 2009.

[58]Teresa Palomo Acosta, "Bishops' Committee for Hispanic Affairs," *Handbook of Texas Online*, Texas State Historical Association, <http://www.tshaonline.org/handbook/online/articles/BB/icb5.html>. Accessed July 22, 2009.

[59]A historical marker at the site reads, in part: "The birth of a school for Black children in Edgewood Common District 41 began in 1942 . . . The school was founded because Black and White students were not permitted to attend the same school before the mandate to integrate in 1955. . . . In 1953, Edgewood's superintendent told school board members he was investigating sites for future Black schools to handle increasing enrollment. . . On July 21, 1955, Edgewood Independent School District received word from the State Board of Education to desegregate. In 1957, Carver Elementary School closed."

[60]This data is included in the Appendix to record sent "up" to the U.S. Supreme Court.

[61]"6 Area School Districts Unafraid of Desegregation," *San Antonio Express and News*, October 5, 1968, 10-D.

[62]*White v. Regester*, 412 U.S. 755 (1973) and 422 U.S. 935 (1975).

[63]Scracic, 81.

[64]*Hernández v. Texas*, 347 U.S. 475; Michael A. Olivas, ed. *"Colored Men" and "Hombres Aquí": Hernández v. Texas and the Emergence of Mexican American Lawyering* (Houston: Arte Público P, 2006).

[65]Few—if any—constitutional law classes assigned *Hernández v. Texas*, never mind state court and lower federal court decisions dealing with Mexican Americans as Mexican Americans. In fact, *Hernández* had not made it into standard constitutional law reference books such as Erwin Chemerinksy' s *Constitutional Law: Principles and Policies*, 2d Edition, by 2002.

[66]*White v. Regester*, 412 U.S. 755 (1973), 422 U.S. 935.

[67]The U.S. Supreme Court deemed enforcement of restrictive covenants state action in *Shelley v. Kramer*, 334 U.S. 1 (1948).

[68]Texas Education Code § 21.031.

[69]Demetrio Rodríguez had several children, according to Carlos R. Soltero, but only one was a plaintiff in the original lawsuit. Carlos R. Soltero, *Latinos and American Law: Landmark Supreme Court Cases* (Austin: U of Texas P, 2006), 79.

[70]Plaintiffs' Third Amended Complaint and Pre-trial Order, 58.

[71]The case was originally filed as *Demetrio Rodríguez, et al., v. San Antonio Independent School District, et al.*, but because it won at the lower courts, the former defendants became the moving parties, or the appellants. Thus the name of the case at the Supreme Court level is reversed: *San Antonio Independent School Dis., v. Rodríguez*, 411 U.S. 1 (1973).

[72]The later chapters of the school finance struggle—Edgewood I, Edgewood II - are closer to the truth, but "Robin Hood," perhaps the most popular or most-used term, is a radical oversimplification.

[73]Neil Foley, "Over the Rainbow: Hernández v. Texas, Brown v. Board of Education, and Black v. Brown." *Chicana/o-Latino Law Review*, UCLA, vol. 25 (Spring 2005), 139-152.

The Schools of Crystal City
A Chicano Experiment in Change

Dennis J. Bixler-Márquez
The University of Texas at El Paso

THE DATE WAS JANUARY 1, 1975—JUST PAST THE HEIGHT OF THE CHICANO Civil Rights Movement—and history was in the making in Crystal City, Texas. In a moving ceremony in front of the courthouse, José Angel Gutiérrez was sworn in as judge of Zavala County. Reflecting the nationalism and sense of ethnic accomplishment that marked his election, he took the oath of office, expanding it to include his promise "and I further do solemnly swear, to faithfully and diligently preserve, protect, and advance, the ideals, causes, and goals of the Raza Unida Party (RUP) and its beautiful people, so help me God." Judge Gutiérrez reminded his supporters in Spanish that the courthouse was now in the hands of the people, and it was their duty to defend it. With a mariachi group playing in the background, he welcomed the citizens to an open house celebration of the political and cultural change that had come to Crystal City with yet one more victory for the RUP.

While those celebrating the occasion savored the moment as it unfolded, cameras captured the event for posterity. Judge Gutiérrez' swearing-in ceremony would become the opening scene for the documentary film, *The Schools of Crystal City*, a visual depiction of an experiment in social change. The film recounts the dynamics—and success—of a South Texas rural community that fought for political and educational reform. It also reveals the social turmoil and political conditions under which an American minority community attempted to craft nonviolent strategies to effectively overcome social injustice. More specifically, the half-hour documentary shows how the schools of Crystal City

92

changed as a result of both the RUP's gaining control of local politics and the involvement of citizens of all walks of life. It also demonstrates a very distinct and effective model for the education of Chicanos and Chicanas, one that was based on Chicano nationalism, social justice, and the emancipation of its citizenry.

The documentary was produced in 1975 by the Urban/Rural School Development Program (U/R) Leadership Training Institute (LTI) at Stanford University. The setting for the film—Crystal City, Texas—was a predominantly Chicano community of approximately 10,000 inhabitants whose livelihoods depended mainly on agriculture, oil and gas wells, cattle, and a Del Monte factory that canned vegetables. Hank S. Resnik and Marene Compton directed the film; Roger Williams edited their work. Back at Stanford University, site service coordinators and other staff members of the Stanford LTI consulted on the film's production.

As a member of the Stanford LTI, I had more than a passing interest in the production of *The Schools of Crystal City*. I worked as a site service coordinator attending to the U/R projects in San Juan, Puerto Rico; San Luis, Colorado; San Antonio, Texas; and Crystal City during the second stage of the Urban/Rural School Development Program. During this stage, which started in 1973, we brought the experiment in educational reform to fruition and documented its outcomes. I was later associate director in charge of promoting the institutionalization of the school-community councils in their respective school districts. My involvement with the film was twofold. Initially, I consulted on the production of the documentary; later, I became the documentary's guardian when opponents of the RUP's educational reform efforts in Texas attempted to seize it and hide it from the public.

In order to fully appreciate the film as it unfolds, it is necessary to understand the circumstances and events that by 1975 led to a complete change in the closely linked political and educational institutions of Zavala County, Texas. The educational condition of Chicanos in South Texas prior to the RUP's presence in the region was deplorable, a situation that was recognized by Mexican American civil rights organizations as early as the 1920s (San Miguel, 1987: 67). While it privileged the more stable and affluent Anglo and Chicano youth, the community's education system held out little hope of opportunity or advancement for the rest of its Chicano population, many of whom were migrant farmworkers living below the poverty line. Segregation, sub-par educational attainment, and minimal representation of Chicanos and Chicanas as teachers and administrators were often the norm. The education of Chicanos, particularly those of low income, was designed to supply a menial labor force to the major industries in the state. In the urban areas, domestic service and manufacturing requiring low-skill and low-wage labor were the principal economic avenues for their sustenance. In rural areas like Zavala County, cattle and agriculture, much of it seasonal, were the primary sources of employment for the Mexican origin population.

After World War II, civic organizations, such as the League of United Latin American Citizens (LULAC) and its offshoot, the G.I. Forum, began to demand and even propose alternative educational approaches that would address the unique cultural, linguistic, and class needs of Chicano students. These organizations won important legal and political battles that challenged segregationist policies and practices in Texas. San Miguel (1987: 78) indicates that in 1930 "LULAC made its initial legal challenge to segregation in *Independent School District et al v. Salvatierra et al*," a class action suit against school officials in Del Rio, a border community in Valverde County, not far from Crystal City. This case, notes San Miguel, tested the constitutionality of judicial review of educational practice concerning Mexican Americans and laid the foundation for future challenges to educational segregation in Texas. However, it allowed segregation for academic reasons, like a student's limited English proficiency, to stand. Building on the Salvatierra case, the 1948 *Delgado v. Independent School District* ruling enjoined school districts from segregating Spanish-speaking children, seriously undermining "the rigid segregation of the Texas school system" (González, 1990: 155–156).

Nonetheless, the educational status of Chicanos in the period preceding President Lyndon Baines Johnson's War on Poverty was that of a subordinate population marginally benefiting from public education. The 1957 Texas Education Agency's *Report of Pupils in Texas Public Schools Having Spanish Surnames, 1955–1956* reveals a profile of low academic achievement, particularly in the number of school years completed. Very few programs had been developed that successfully addressed the unique educational needs of Chicanos by the mid-1960s. The 1972 report by the U.S. Civil Rights Commission on Civil Rights, *Mexican American Education in Texas: A Function of Wealth* concluded that reliance on property taxes for public education had a deleterious effect on the education of Chicanos in Texas, a practice which, though modified over the years, still prevailed in 2009.

By the mid-1960s, federal sources of financial support were increasingly used to address the educational needs of Chicanos. The Education and Secondary Education Act of 1965 (ESEA) and other federal educational legislative mandates began funding educational reform measures that could be tailored to ethnic and linguistic groups (Carter & Segura, 1979: 20–28). Political activists had long advocated greater measures of empowerment for disenfranchised minorities in the educational arena as integral to their overall socioeconomic empowerment and integration into American society. The War on Poverty held out such hope and promise to the underprivileged across the nation by virtue of the community participation requirements made by the federal government in the planning and implementation of its social development programs. The Chicano Civil Rights Movement that flourished in South Texas under the aegis of RUP was also influenced by the 1969 Plan Espiritual de Aztlán, a manifesto advocating Chicano nationalism. One of its goals was the creation of an educational system that would be effective and "relevant to our people." Having endured severe discriminatory practices for generations, historically affected South Texas communities found RUP's political platform for educating Chicanos attractive. Not surprisingly, in Crystal City the schools became the first political target of the RUP, as Chicano public support for change—particularly student and parental support—was palpable by the late 1960s.

In 1968, the U.S. Office of Education (USOE) began to conceptualize a national experiment in the decentralization of decision-making in public education, the Urban/Rural School Development Program (U/R). John Lindia (1974), former deputy commissioner in the USOE's Office of Career Education, remarked that the U/R Program's success and potential impact hinged on its ability to achieve change at the school-building level by meaningfully involving community members in school governance and educational endeavors. The U/R Program's architects recognized the need for a collaborative approach to school governance that could enable the principal actors in a child's education—parents, community members, teachers, and administrators—to forge instructional strategies politically supportable by all concerned parties. This would be a radical departure from the top-down administrative model; it would require a new civic engagement paradigm.

Mesa (1975) in the Urban/Rural Story stresses that the civil rights movement influenced the formation of the U/R program tremendously. Various communities across the nation felt disenfranchised and alienated from their governance structures and leaders. The 1968 Kerner Commission on urban disturbances recommended a massive investment in the human and socioeconomic infrastructure of affected communities and, as a preventive strategy, those likely to experience similar upheaval (Tibaldo-Bongiorno, 2007). The War on Poverty brought governance to the grass roots by funding community development programs like the Model Cities and Career Opportunities Programs that required citizen participation in their planning and implementation.

Tyack (2003:14) indicates that the educational programs that emerged in response to the civil unrest had to come to grips with the tension between the centralized governance preferred by state agencies and schools and the radical decentralization demanded by protest groups. Detractors of the decentralization trend claimed that providing greater autonomy to actors in the lower rungs of schools usurped the legal power of duly elected school boards and their designated administrators. Cárdenas (1980: 432) illustrates that school districts in the 1960s and 1970s found the concept of neighborhood control and power sharing alien. For example, Fantini (1974: 3–4) relates how the Ocean-Hill Brownsville experimental district in Bedford-Stuyvesant was in deep turmoil as a result of school-community conflict, in which parents openly manifested their dissatisfaction with teachers and schools. The structural decentralization of New York City schools into various districts did not result in a political decentralization, i.e., substantive access by parents to the formulation of policy and educational strategies at the school-site level. However, this community unrest was emblematic of the societal tensions that were to provoke change in future federal policy and strategies espoused by the educational arm of the War on Poverty.

Mesa (1975: 2; 1976: 52–70) reveals how in May of 1968 all sixty-five proposals for the Trainers of Teacher Trainers (TTT) were rejected by a national advisory council "because their community involvement components did not respond strongly enough to the demands of the time." With university support and guidance, the TTT program trained cadres of teacher trainers in school districts to nurture and guide subsequent generations of teachers to be sensitive to the cultural and pedagogical needs of minority students. In spite of the program's orientation and intent, the rejection of all the individual project proposals was a clear signal from the federal government that future staff development programs would be required to have substantial and meaningful community participation in their conceptualization and implementation in order to be funded. Therefore, the U/R planning task force proceeded to visit the Ocean-Hill Brownsville schools, an experience that was to influence the architecture and direction of the national U/R program.

The resulting U/R program was designed to improve schools by implementing staff development programs after school-community councils, composed of teachers, parents, administrators, and even students in some instances, conducted a needs assessment of their school. Based on the results, the aforementioned councils planned a staff development program to be negotiated with the school and district administration. This level of parity in the decision-making process represented, to some administrators and local and state elected officials, an intrusion into the prerogatives and fiscal responsibilities of the school district administration and school board. To the disenfranchised, it represented access to the active management of the educational process in their community. The USOE wanted to test the hypothesis that this innovative approach would produce a more relevant, community sensitive, and effective means of educational innovation, one that would produce stakeholders and reduce the racial and political turmoil of the late 1960s.

To implement this strategy at the national level, USOE funded the Urban/Rural Leadership Training Institute (U/R LTI) at Stanford University's Center for Educational Research and Development in Teaching. Twenty-six school districts across the nation received planning and later operational grants, as they demonstrated progress toward achieving operational status. The sites were 50 percent urban and 50 percent rural, hence the program label of Urban/Rural. The sites also represented a cross-section of the nation's major ethnic groups: Whites, Chicanos, Puerto Ricans, Native Americans, and African Americans. The goals of the national Urban/Rural program and the ethnic and regional composition would accurately reflect the Kerner Commission's belief that it was "time to make good the promises of American democracy to all citizens—urban and rural, White and Black, Spanish-surnamed, American Indian and every minority group" (Eisenhower Foundation, 2008: 2).

In this grand experiment, the role of the Stanford U/R LTI, as it was commonly known, was to provide developmental and technical assistance to the school-community councils via national and regional conferences, workshops, and onsite training. A concomitant responsibility was the documentation of the individual site efforts and the aggregate results. The U/R program was in operation from 1970 to 1976, at the same time as other federal in-service educational training efforts, such as the National Teacher Corps, with which it cooperated in comparative evaluation and documentation projects.

In the fall of 1973, the U/R LTI learned that Crystal City had been added to the U/R program somewhat later than other projects. Díaz de León (1973) and Galicia (2008), site service coordinators with the first cadre of the U/R LTI, 1970–1973, indicated that originally, the Ysleta Independent School District in El Paso, Texas, was selected to receive a U/R project. However, school officials, particularly those concerned with the implementation of the project, were apprehensive about the requirements for community participation in the governance of the project. This concern emanated from their firsthand experience with the 6th Cycle of the National Teacher Corps, for which, coincidentally, I was an intern from 1971–1973. Given the autocratic nature of the school district administration at the time and the conflict it experienced with interns politicized by the Chicano movement, the rejection of the U/R project in El Paso is not surprising.

As graduate interns at the University of Texas at El Paso, we were trained in a TTT-influenced master's program that mandated active participation by interns in school and community affairs. Our curriculum, aside from the traditional courses in education, had a strong sociocultural education component that we used to analyze extant political and educational issues, often with the guidance of national Chicano experts and local community leaders. Furthermore, the program required that we reside in the communities of the elementary schools where we underwent field-based training. We became conversant with the leading socio-educational issues in our schools and communities, and we worked with parents to deliver cultural and instructional programs relevant to a predominantly Chicano student population. Our close proximity to parents and our desire to jointly bring about cultural and instructional change to some schools generated friction with the educational establishment in the two major school districts in El Paso. This friction led to the sudden assignation of some interns to different schools and dismissal for others. Our experience is representative of the school-community conflict that Cárdenas recalled and the resistance to the labor of educational and political activists by Texas schools in the civil rights era.

From a variety of sources, I learned that Dr. José A. Cárdenas, at that time superintendent of the Edgewood School District, was instrumental in Crystal City receiving the allocation that was originally destined for the Ysleta Independent School District. An official visit by a three-person team from the U/R LTI, led by Angela García, the late Isabel Hernández, and me, took place in the fall of 1973. It was obvious to us that, under the tutelage of the Raza Unida Party (RUP), a shared and dynamic governance was thriving in the Crystal City Independent School District, not to mention its proactive U/R school-community council. Furthermore, the district's curriculum and instruction were being transformed to address the matrix of the society the schools served (Urban/Rural, 1973). The U/R program was a major agent of faculty, staff, and community development for a school district engaged in a massive retooling and certification of its personnel.

For several reasons, successful reform made the Crystal City Independent School District a prime candidate for a major documentation effort. The school district had met the U/R goals for community participation in the educational process. The democratic and nonviolent takeover of the school district, the city government, and, eventually, the Zavala County government by the RUP had generated positive national publicity. Crystal City parents, students, and faculty were active in U/R local, regional, and national training efforts (Resnik, 1975: 13–15). Crystal City hosted a national conference in 1975, showcasing its schools for other U/R projects and federal officials. Thus the Stanford LTI decided to film a documentary on this site, along with other key U/R sites like Bayfield, Wisconsin, a Native American community. The medium of film was deemed appropriate to record and evaluate the outcome of the national experiment to determine whether actors closest to the educational process could bring about effective school reform. However, the story of each individual U/R school effort could only be told in the context of its historical and socioeconomic dynamics. *The Schools of Crystal City* would tell a story of the struggles unique to that South Texas rural community.

It was against this backdrop of social and political turmoil and educational renewal that Hank Resnik began filming *The Schools of Crystal City*. From the initial scene, the swearing-in ceremony of Judge José Angel Gutiérrez described in the introduction of this essay, the documentary reverts chronologically to the politics of the student walkout in 1969 that led to the capitulation of the Crystal City school board to RUP, which would subsequently have its candidates duly elected to a new school board. The filmmakers skillfully included historical footage from San Antonio television stations on the student walkout that had thrust Crystal City into the limelight of the Chicano civil rights movement. This segment provided the historical platform for understanding the causes of change and educational aspirations of Chicanos in Crystal City.

The documentary superbly captures how the schools of Crystal City had changed and were changing for the better by 1975, as a direct result of citizen participation in school governance. Amancio Cantú, who succeeded Angel Noé González as superintendent of the Crystal City Independent School District, relates how a personnel crisis ensued after the departure of the previous regime. A capitulation of the board and a concomitant mass departure of teachers and staff were supposed to bring about a collapse of the emergent RUP school board. An opposition coalition of conservative Mexican Americans and Anglos, who either benefitted from the status quo or felt negatively impacted by the ascendance of RUP to power, devised a strategy to undermine the operational success of RUP. The opposition's strategy was predicated on history repeating itself, for in 1965 the victorious Mexican-American City Council of Crystal City, Los Cinco (the Five), was unable to respond effectively to a similar crisis. However, the strategy failed to bring about the collapse of RUP governance of the schools. Amancio Cantú explains in the film how the district effectively juggled a multitude of federal grants to address faculty and staff shortages and training needs. He goes on to defend the political participation by school employees in a dramatic fashion. He proclaims that school and political participation go hand in hand and that "in Cristal we're shouting it to the world!" "There is no job more political than that of superintendent," he concluded.

Amancio Cantú emphasized that bilingual education is the most important program in the district. It was clear to outside observers like me in 1973–1977 that bilingual education K-12 was not only an emancipatory educational strategy in Crystal City, but a nationalistic one, as well. It positioned the Spanish language and Chicano culture on a par with English and American culture, challenging the educational status quo in Texas that had traditionally excluded the former. The film showcases some of the instructional materials, in print and video, produced by Crystal City educators to fill the void of Chicano culture, history, and Spanish language materials appropriate for schools, some of which were disseminated to other Texas schools. The film reveals a high school course in visual media production, unusual for that time, with political propaganda potential; high school students were producing and broadcasting news and cultural programs. The ability to enculturate through the airwaves and compete with American media was not lost on viewers, particularly the educational establishment in Texas.

Viewers saw Crystal City projected as a fountain of innovation in language and cultural production and education. *The Schools of Crystal City* reveals the extent to which a cultural and political transformation of the district was taking place. Viewers at screenings who completed their K-12 education in the United States marveled at the cultural curriculum that stood in sharp contrast to their own formative educational experience. For example, the rendition of the Mexican revolution ballad "Valentín de La Sierra," which opens and closes the film, provoked emotion then as it still does today. That Chicano musical repertoire was not typically found in American schools. The dance class performed a Mexican folklore number, not quite the American modern or traditional dance curriculum either.

The film mentions, in interviews with parents in opposition to RUP, that this cultural and political transformation spilled over to the entertainment portion in school sports events and was a contributing factor to their children withdrawing from Crystal City schools. These critics of RUP charge that the cultural content was frequently associated, in curricular and extracurricular activities, with the politics of the student walkout that led to the resignation of the school board. Bobby McVoy, a former member of the marching band booster club and principal of the alternative school in Crystal City, at the time of his interview, claims that "each week at the football game the half-time activity got more and more political, all the politics, of course, referring to the big walkout and the subsequent political undertakings. We really didn't feel that the school was the proper forum for this." The film features important historical footage of the aforementioned 1969 student walkout that was emulated at the half-time productions with the clenched-fist salute, reminiscent of the controversial protest by the Black athletes John Carlos and Tommie Smith during the award ceremony of the 1968 Olympics in Mexico City (ESPNC, 2005). Conversely, individual interviews with selected Chicano high school students revealed a positive sentiment for RUP changes in the schools. Griselda Flores, for example, expresses her dissatisfaction as a student with the previous segregationist behavior in her community and her support for the changes brought about by RUP, stating "Now I'm really happy. I think that now that we've taken over and every-thing we're doing just fine." Not unexpectedly, the film portrays how opposite backgrounds and experiences with RUP produced divergent views among the citizenry of Crystal City.

It is not surprising that one of the most controversial dimensions of the new educational paradigm was the Chicano Studies curriculum that often made ref-erences to the student walkout. Amancio Cantú casually informs the viewer that a high school Chicano Studies course is required for graduation; it is not just an elective course. This graduation requirement portends the district's intent to privilege the Chicano curricular perspective and ensure that official cultural and civic transmission in schools adheres to the goals of the Raza Unida Party. The instructional and faculty development sessions depicted in the film also reveal the ubiquitous presence of Chicano culture. In addition, the screening in the Chicano Studies course of films, like *Memoirs of Underdevelopment*, a Cuban film, is discussed in *The Schools of Crystal City*. Its inclusion signals the pres-ence of a curriculum aligned with third-world political manifestations, which, coupled with a visit by RUP officials to Cuba, generated the label of Little Cuba for Crystal City by conservative elements in both major political parties and the generally conservative press in Texas. According to Gutiérrez (1998: 239–240), it was a classic case of red baiting. Again, nearby schools, the state education agency, and opposition parents found this radical departure from established norms troublesome and dangerous for its diffusion potential to other schools in Texas.

The film expertly examined the alignment of U/R guidelines with the school district's governance structure and instructional practice. It highlights an official meeting of the U/R school-community council. Its chairperson, Corne-lio Flores, flanked by the U/R team manager, Roberto Fernández, is featured conducting business and is later interviewed on camera. This segment illustrates the collaborative management approaches prescribed by the U/R planners and trainers who provided Crystal City representatives developmental assistance at workshops and site visits also mentioned in the film. Mr. Flores explains how the U/R program functions in Crystal City. "It's a program we have in schools to improve teaching by training teachers. The school-community council is like an advisor. We put the ideas together and talk to the director or team manager." The film features Mr. Flores's family and children holding the typical Texas backyard barbecue that serves as a vehicle to bring to light the impact of the transformation of the schools on actual students by showing the active partici-pation of youth in high school courses they could not even dream of under the previous school district administration. His children's attainable professional aspirations are described with great parental pride. "Take my Ofelia, for example," says Mr. Flores as the film shows a live news broadcast in which Ofelia is the camera operator, as part of a course. "She will go, God willing, to college. She's been motivated to see what she likes to do, what to study." As the new and transformed school orchestra plays a popular song of the cumbia genre, "El Mudo," for the viewer, Mr. Flores singles out the musical skill of his son. "My Cornelio likes music . . . he wanted to try the saxophone. I never thought that he was going to be that good, because, he's good." The availability of these potential professional paths for his children in the fine arts are symbolic of what the changes mean to the average citizen and student in Crystal City in operational terms. Mr. Flores concludes with the firm belief that "now everybody has an equal right to . . . have a college education."

Decentralization in decision-making had also spread to the classroom level with an innovative approach to faculty and staff development that was born out of necessity. It was a unique articulation of teacher training with field-based experiences in a collegial setting that made trainers and trainees partners in instructional change. Evidently, the lesson of the 1965 fiasco was not lost on the leadership of RUP, some of whom had participated in that first challenge to the established political order in Crystal City. Armed with U/R funds, the school district successfully challenged the certified personnel shortage and a state-supported boycott of the district by nearby institutions of higher education (IHEs). Nearby Texas IHEs refused to offer teacher training courses on site. Through the use of their legal veto power over other Texas IHEs, these institutions also refused to let others assist the Crystal City Independent School District. A solution to this impasse was crafted, in part, by then Dean of Education at San Diego State University, Dr. Tomás Arciniega, who coincidentally had been my Teacher Corps director at the University of Texas at El Paso in 1971. He also played a key role in the success of a mid-management and superintendent administrative certificate program in the district. Drs. Inez Ramírez and Raúl Coy were hired with U/R funds as resident professors by Chicago State University to teach courses on-site. They taught in the afternoons and at night to accommodate the teaching schedules of district faculty, many of whom had moved to Crystal City to volunteer their services, but were not certified to teach in Texas or to hold positions requiring graduate certification. During the day, the on-site professors followed up on their evening instruction with campus-based training; they combined theory with practice and demonstrated effective pedagogical practice in actual instructional situations. Afternoons often were filled with workshops sponsored by U/R and other federal programs to nurture the district-wide faculty and staff development program. This approach was designed with substantial teacher, paraprofessional, administrator, and parent input, and implemented with the authority and the imprimatur of Drs. Coy and Ramírez, who were appointed deputy superintendents. Thus the U/R goal of bringing about school-level change via greater participation by all actors, who were now stakeholders and, in many cases, direct participants in some facet of the educational process, was achieved and well documented in the film.

A singular academic achievement that was unfortunately omitted in the film was the increase in high school graduation rates. More important, graduates of the Crystal City Independent School District began to enroll in significant numbers in colleges, universities, and later, even in medical and graduate school across the United States and Mexico. The use of alumni protagonists of this outstanding accomplishment would have lent significant credence to the success story of the U/R experiment and the efficacy of RUP in Crystal City. A subsequent film on Crystal City produced in 1976 or 1977 by an entity unknown to me, (and who I was unable to locate) does accomplish this task, but lacks the U/R dimension. By 1976, the political landscape in Crystal City was changing. Some educational gains were reaching a zenith and were now available for dissemination by a school system proud of its robust and culturally relevant educational pipeline.

José Angel Gutiérrez expounds on camera how required citizen participation in the political process has a positive effect on the civic character of the population. He singles out "Ciudadanos Unidos" (United Citizens), the political arm of RUP, for recognition in the production of a substantial and capable secondary cadre of leadership, as political offices were rotated frequently. Stanford LTI site-service coordinators attended the Ciudadanos Unidos meetings on Sundays and authored an article in the January, 1975 issue of Urban/Rural that was a companion piece to the documentary. Selective meeting footage and the political campaigning by Ciudadanos Unidos was included in *The Schools of Crystal City*, allowing the viewer to grasp the inevitable partisan nature of politics associated with RUP's takeover and its effect on individual community members. Interspersed with José Angel Gutiérrez's assessment of the political involvement requirements of educators, the views of key opposition leaders who objected to RUP using federal programs for political empowerment receive fair and ample coverage in the film.

Perhaps the most controversial segment of *The Schools of Crystal City* for the Texas and South Texas oligarchy is the finale of the film, with José Angel Gutiérrez's projections on the political and socioeconomic future of Zavala County and the means of arriving at that plateau. He sets the stage by relating that 87 percent of the land is owned by absentee owners—many of whom are key political and economic powerhouses in Texas—making Zavala County a classic case of internal colonialism. Furthermore, he adds, wages in the area "are gross and indecent," poor residents experience a range of unresolved health problems, and they must depart on an annual trek in pursuit of agricultural employment. He forecasts the use of eminent domain, a governmental tool typically employed to confiscate private property for the greater good of a community. He clearly identifies landholdings and gas and oil wells in the county for expropriation, in order to alleviate the economic deprivation of its residents. Those statements are uttered as the film ends with the revolutionary lyrics of "Valentín de la Sierra."

The film was screened at U/R conferences and select educational events. However, the film was not welcomed by some State of Texas officials, who saw the emancipation of Chicanos under a third political party as a threat to the established order. José Angel Gutiérrez's interview in the documentary clearly outlined a path toward the confiscation of land holdings belonging to the oligarchy of Texas, a clear and present danger to their class interests. The potential use of the power of county government by RUP to redistribute the wealth to achieve economic self-determination, on top of other successful strategies that Navarro (1998: 252–269) terms the struggle for economic empowerment, generated fear and concern among conservative Texans, Anglos, and Mexican Americans alike. After all, RUP had managed to spread beyond Zavala County, successfully running candidates for office in other Texas counties with a substantial Chicano population. The party even held a national convention in El Paso, Texas, in 1972. Ironically, according to García (1989: 197), the political containment of RUP by opposing forces in Texas began in various arenas in 1975, the year *The Schools of Crystal City* commenced production.

While *The Schools of Crystal City* delivers a compelling half-hour account of politics and educational reform in a rural community in South Texas, the entire saga does not end with the final scene in the film. Another story, one in which the documentary and I play prominent roles, demonstrates the extent to which old-guard Texas politics and political and educational reform under the aegis of RUP were increasingly at odds. In 1977, a USOE project officer for the U/R program contacted me at Stanford University. He inquired about the nature of the film and who had authorized its public distribution, particularly in Texas, even though regional and Washington, D.C.-based federal officials had screened the film and had not objected to its content.

I outlined the film for him and replied that the Crystal City School District and its U/R project were in receipt of a copy, as per a contractual agreement with the Stanford LTI. He replied in a very serious and official tone that, at that moment, the State of Texas was seriously contemplating charging unnamed persons—namely me, he thought—with outside interference in a local election. Apparently, the incident that triggered the USOE intervention was the public screening of the documentary at the drive-in movie theater in Crystal City just prior to an election, when the entire community got a chance to see it or hear from others about its "inflammatory" content. I could not locate any of my superiors to resolve the issue; it seemed they had disappeared. I was further instructed by the USOE representative to immediately mail to the USOE project officer all existing copies of *The Schools of Crystal City*.

I sent to the USOE a copy of the 16mm film that had approximately one unsynchronized minute of sound/image that was lying around in my office, but I kept the original film and a ¾ " video master. Upon termination of the U/R program and its Leadership Training Institute at Stanford, I brought the film back to Texas in 1978. In later years, copies were made for various academics and residents of Crystal City who requested one. The film had been screened at two National Association of Chicana and Chicano Studies (NACCS) conferences, a Texas Association of Chicanos in Higher Education (TACHE) conference, and several other academic events. Producers of other civil rights era documentaries, such as the *History of American Education* four-part series later depended on valuable footage from *The Schools of Crystal City* to create their own works. My decision to risk keeping the film was made knowing that it was a documentary of historical significance that had to be preserved for posterity. This reasoning proved to be sound. I have seen only one other documentary on Crystal City that also was produced in the 1970s, but I was never able to locate a copy of it.

The decision by the U/R LTI at Stanford University to capture the Urban/Rural experience in Crystal City yielded an insightful documentary. *The Schools of Crystal City* contributes to the understanding of the Chicano civil rights movement in the political and educational arenas by revealing the difficult struggle of a community to emancipate itself. The film captures the indomitable spirit of grassroots people, political organizers, parents, educators, and students who, in the highest spirit of Americanism, chose to stand up and be counted. I cherish my participation in the Crystal City experiment and the U/R program, for I gained substantial experience in educational change politics and a personal sense of satisfaction with my involvement with the Raza Unida Party.

References

Cárdenas, José A. (1995). *Multicultural Education: A Generation of Advocacy.* Needham, MA, Pp. 431-439.

Carter, Thomas P. & Segura, Roberto D. (1979). *Mexican Americans in School: A Decade of Change.* New York: College Entrance Examination Board, Pp. 20-28.

Díaz de León, Luis. (1973). Personal interview in Daly City, CA with Isabel Hernández and Dennis J. Bixler-Márquez. Fall.

ESPNC. (2005). "Five Reasons Why You Can't Blame John Carlos and Tommie Smith: The Black Power Salute." Five Reasons Series. (Video, 28 Min.) ESPN Classic Sports.

The Eisenhower Foundation. (2008). *What We Can Do Together: A Forty Year Update of the National Advisory Commission on Civil Disorders.* Executive Summary, Preliminary Findings. Washington, D.C.: The Eisenhower Foundation.

Fantini, Mario. (1974). "The New Faces of Community Participation in the Seventies." *Urban/Rural, The Newsletter of the Urban/Rural Leadership Training Institute.* May (3), Pp. 3-4.

Galicia, Homero H. (2008). Personal Interview with Dennis Bixler-Márquez, El Paso, Texas, January 23.

García, Ignacio M. (1989). *United We Win: The Rise and Fall of the Raza Unida Party.* Tucson: U of Arizona P, Pp. 197-216.

González, Gilbert G. (1990). *Chicano Education in the Era of Segregation.* Philadelphia: The Balch Institute P, Pp.155-156.

Gutiérrez, José Angel. (1998). *The Making of a Chicano Militant: Lessons from Cristal.* Madison: U of Wisconsin P, Pp. 239-240.

Lindia, John. (1974). "Taking Stock at Midterm." *Urban/Rural, The Newsletter of the Urban/Rural Leadership Training Institute.* May (3), Pp. 2-3.

Mesa, Richard P. (1975). "The Urban/Rural School Development Program, The Urban/Rural Story." *Urban/Rural, The Newsletter of the Urban/Rural Leadership Training Institute.* November, Pp. 1-19.

Mesa, Richard P. (1976). "Implications for Inservice Education of the Urban/Rural School Development Program Experience." In Richard M. Brandt et al, *ISTE Report V, Cultural Pluralism and Social Change. National Center for Education Statistics and the National Teacher Corps*, Pp. 52-70.

Navarro, Armando. (1998). *The Cristal Experiment: A Chicano Struggle for Community Control.* Madison: U of Wisconsin P, Pp. 252-284.

Plan Espiritual de Aztlán (Anonymous) (1969). Appendix A in Thomas P. Carter & Roberto Segura. *Mexican Americans in School: A Decade of Change.* New York: College Entrance Examination Board, 1979, Pp. 393-396.

Resnik, Hank. (1976). *The Schools of Crystal City* (31-minute film). Stanford Center for Research and Development in Teaching, Stanford U.

Resnik, Hank. (1975). "Where Change Is an Everyday Happening." *Urban/Rural, The Newsletter of the Urban/Rural Leadership Training Institute.* January (5), Pp. 13-15.

San Miguel, Guadalupe, Jr. (1987). *"Let All of Them Take Heed": Mexican Americans and the Campaign for Educational Equality in Texas,1910-1981.* Austin: U of Texas P, Pp. 67; 77-80.

Texas Education Agency. (1957). *Report of Pupils in Texas Public Schools Having Spanish Surnames, 1955-56.* Division of Research. Austin, TX.

Tibaldo-Bongiorno, Marylou. (2007). *Revolution '67* (Documentary: 60 Mins.). Bongiorno Productions Inc., the Independent Television Service and P. O.V. /American Documentary Inc.

Tyack, David. (2003*). Seeking Common Ground: Public Schools in a Diverse Society.* Cambridge: Harvard U P, Pp. 149-151.

Urban/Rural, *The Newsletter of the Urban/Rural Leadership Training Institute.* (1973). Urban/Rural, a Bird's-Eye View: Crystal City and San Antonio, Texas. November (1), Pp. 8-9.

U.S. Commission on Civil Rights. (1972). *Mexican American Education in Texas: A Function of Wealth.* August, Pp. 8-10; 29.

UNEARTHING VOICES

¡Mucho Cuidado! Silencing, Selectivity, and Sensibility in the Utilization of Tejano Voices by Texas Historians

James E. Crisp
North Carolina State University

THERE ARE MANY WAYS TO SILENCE UNWANTED VOICES FROM THE PAST bearing messages of inconvenient truth. Michel-Rolph Trouillot, in his classic work *Silencing the Past: Power and the Production of History*, identifies the likely suspects and their methods. First of all there are the heavy-handed actors who deep-six their victims in "real time," burying their voices along with their bodies. Thus, writes Trouillot, did the bayonets of the soldiers of Haitian leader Henry Christophe dispatch his rival Jean Baptiste San Souci from both the field of action and the national memory.[1]

Archivists, who historically have often served the interests of the powerful—the winners, in other words—tend to operate with a bit more subtlety, erasing despised dissenters by the mere failure to assemble the records directly attesting to their deeds.[2] Subsequent storytellers who stumble across the traces of the damned generally find it easy to ignore the ghostly footprints of those who have deviated from the path of the dominant narrative. Written history, in fact, may be wielded as a cultural weapon that cuts a far wider swath than a bayonet. As Fitzhugh Brundage has noted with regard to "memory and history" in Texas, those who use their political power to give shape to a nation's (or a state's) collective historical memory are intentionally creating a product that "forges identity, justifies privilege, and sustains cultural norms."[3]

Much of the Hispanic history of Texas has been subjected to each of these strategies of silencing: in the brutal suppression of dissent, in the wasting away of neglected sources, and in too many historians' casual (or studied) ignorance

111

of the people whose stories run counter to the officially sanctioned narrative of Anglo-American triumph and progress.[4] What Trouillot calls the "practice of silencing," however, can take on even more subtle and deceptive forms.[5] Remarkably, the authentic voices of several prominent Tejanos have been "silenced" by *the very act of quoting words attributed to them*. Take, for instance, the case of José Antonio Navarro.[6]

Navarro is a man whom it is hard to ignore. He was unquestionably the most important Hispanic Texan political figure of the nineteenth century. The first alcalde of San Antonio de Béxar elected after Mexican independence in 1821, he served in the state legislature of Coahuila y Tejas in the 1820s and was elected by that body to the national congress of Mexico in 1835.[7] He declined to accept that post, however, and within a few months was instead a signer of the Texas Declaration of Independence.[8]

In 1845 Navarro became one of the handful of men, and the only native Texan, to have participated in the framing of both the Constitution of the Texas Republic and that of the new State of Texas in the American Union. After serving in both the congress of the republic and the legislature of the new state, he became by the 1850s a leader and elder statesman of the Democratic Party in San Antonio, and in that decade published his *Apuntes Historicos Interesantes*, thereby becoming the first native-born historian of Texas. Navarro County was named in his honor in 1846.[9]

Thus it is hardly surprising to find his name carved into the wall of the recently completed (2001) Bob Bullock Texas State History Museum [TSHM] in Austin. Navarro is one of only four Texans whose words are displayed on the giant "arched limestone panels" that grace the museum's entrance.[10] Upon entering the Grand Lobby of the TSHM, the visitor will see the following quotation, dated 1842, and purportedly a translation from Spanish: "I will never forsake Texas and her cause. I am her son."[11]

The silencing of Navarro's *authentic* voice is not in this case a result of mistranslation from the Spanish to the English. There may be much truth in the Italian pun and proverb *"traduttore, traditore"*—"translator, traitor"—but the betrayal here goes much deeper than the pitfalls of expressing Navarro's thoughts in a language foreign to his own.[12] As we shall see, the date is incorrect, there was no translation—and the words on the wall are not Navarro's at all.

Even in the twenty-first century, the authentic lives and full historical significance of prominent Tejanos such as José Antonio Navarro sometimes seem to be "hidden in plain sight."[13] Consider the case of Navarro's fellow revolutionary and *bejareño* Juan Nepomuceno Seguín, who was branded in 1876 a "notorious traitor" by one of Navarro's earliest and most sympathetic Anglo-Texan biographers.[14]

Today the main drive into the San Jacinto Battleground State Historic Site near the city of Houston has been designated as "Juan N. Seguín Boulevard." In the central Texas town of Seguin, an equestrian statue now tops the tomb of the eponymous hero, whose body was removed in 1976 from his original burial site in Nuevo Laredo to the town that was named in Seguín's honor when he represented its citizens in the Senate of the Texas Republic in 1839.[15]

Neither at the battleground nor in the detailed inscriptions at the base of the statue, however, will the visitor to these sites learn why Seguín became known in the 1840s as the arch-traitor to the Republic of Texas, nor will they learn that he took up arms in that decade not only against the Texas Republic, but also against the United States in that country's war with Mexico. To the credit of the Texas State History Museum, its permanent exhibit on the Texas Republic does call attention to the fact that Seguín and many other Tejanos were forced to flee to Mexico after he was falsely accused of aiding the Mexican army's attack on San Antonio in 1842.[16]

Yet just as on Seguín's tomb, no mention is made at the museum of his armed struggle against Texas and the United States in the 1840s; visitors to the TSHM are much more likely to remember Seguín as the unalloyed Texan hero. According to the current web site of the museum,

> One highlight of the second floor is the "Revolution Theater." Built to resemble the Alamo the day after the battle, this theater features a video presentation on the fight for Texas Independence, told from the perspective of Juan Seguin, a Tejano political and military leader who assisted in the defeat of Santa Anna's troops at the Battle of San Jacinto.[17]

Today, carefully selected Tejanos are often placed front and center in historical celebrations in Texas in a fashion that does not challenge the dominant narrative—and in such a way that critically important aspects of their own lives have been erased from the collective Texan memory.

There was a time, not long ago, when the Tejanos could be completely erased from the history of Texas, in academic settings as well as in popular art and literature.[18] Their lives, as we are reminded by scholars such as Ramón Saldívar and Leticia Garza-Falcón, formed part of a "banished history."[19] Their voices, writes Garza-Falcón, were effectively silenced by a linear meta-narrative of Anglo progress that carried within it both an "ethic of imperialism" and a "rhetoric of dominance."[20]

This was a "dominant narrative" with a very long pedigree. A story of Anglo-Saxon triumph and Mexican degeneracy emerged in the 1830s and 1840s from the throes of the Texas Revolution and the lingering war between Mexico and the Texas Republic (largely written by sympathetic observers from England

and the United States), establishing a template that literally dominated the writing of history in Texas for the next century and a half.[21]

Reviewing the historiography of the Spanish frontier in North America, historian David J. Weber discovered that "Hispanophobia found its most strident and enduring rhetoric in Texas," where "with its particularly vitriolic anti-Mexican variant, [it] also served as a convenient rationale to keep Mexicans 'in their place.'" The "inconvenient fact," noted Weber, "that some Mexicans had joined the Anglo-American rebels was forgotten, and a repudiation of the Spanish past became an essential part of Texans' self-identity." Weber claims that the victorious "Anglo-American rebels controlled not only Texas, but [also] the writing of its history," burdening scholarship in the Lone Star State "well into the twentieth century" and leaving the Hispanic history of Texas "open to distortion and caricature."[22]

Historiographer Stephen Stagner observes that the gentleman scholar and Sam Houston confidante Henderson Yoakum, whose influence in Texas lasted well beyond the end of the nineteenth century, "believed wholeheartedly in the superiority of the Anglo-Saxon race," and "essentially adopted" the "moral and analytical framework" of the "propagandists" of the Texas Revolution.[23] Laura Lyons McLemore concurs, and adds that Yoakum's two-volume History of Texas was joined by works from other shapers of the remembered Texan past who "failed to establish any historical memory that incorporated the diversity of lived experience in Texas."[24]

The turn to "scientific history" in the early twentieth century, led from the University of Texas campus in Austin by the increasingly influential professor of history Eugene C. Barker, did not significantly alter the contrasting portraits of "Mexicans" and "Anglo-Saxons" that had been painted by Texas chauvinists in the preceding generations. Reflecting on the "long shadow" cast by the eminent and erudite Barker, Paul D. Lack concluded in his 1991 survey of the scholarship of the Texas Revolution and Republic that despite his professional skills, Barker "shared the fundamental view that Texas history in the period 1821 to 1836 represented the march of Anglo-American democracy westward in triumph over inferior races."[25]

Barker conspicuously subtitled his magisterial biography of Stephen F. Austin "A Chapter in the Westward Movement of the Anglo-American People," and stated tellingly in the preface to the first (1926) edition that Austin had begun "the transformation of the wilderness that Texas then was into an Anglo-American commonwealth."[26] Barker claimed that rather than having intentions of conquest, Austin instead "strove honestly to make Texas a model state in the Mexican system." But this Austin found to be a "Utopian dream," said Barker, who concluded that "the causes of failure were inherent in Mexican character and experience and are not chargeable to lack of sincerity, of sympathetic forbearance, or of patient, thoughtful labor on Austin's part."[27]

Despite the scholarly rigor of Barker and his colleagues, theirs was a dominant narrative that could sometimes be stunningly oblivious to the realities of Texas history. William C. Binkley was educated in California and spent most of his career teaching at Vanderbilt and Tulane universities, but his deep research and multiple publications on the history of Texas led to his being considered "an ex officio member" of the University of Texas history department.[28] When Binkley delivered the prestigious Walter Lynwood Fleming Lectures on "The Texas Revolution" in the early 1950s—lectures later published in multiple editions by the Texas State Historical Association—not once did he mention the name of a single Tejano.[29] Moreover, when he quite inadvertently alluded to Tejanos collectively, he nevertheless thoroughly silenced them. "The citizens of Goliad," said Binkley,

> boldly proclaimed their position on December 20 [1835] by drawing up an indictment of the conduct of civil and military affairs and concluding with a formal declaration of independence from Mexican rule.[30]

The problem with this statement is that "the citizens of Goliad," a community almost wholly Tejano in population, had by late 1835 mostly abandoned their town due to the impositions made upon them by the Anglo-Texan soldiers who had occupied the *presidio* there. *These* men, and not the citizens of Goliad (as historian Stephen Hardin has noted) were the "unruly rebel[s]" who signed the "Goliad Declaration of Independence" on December 20.[31]

It is worthwhile to note in passing that the conflicting loyalties and difficult choices facing Tejanos at the time of the revolution are suggested by even the briefest biographical sketches of the only two Hispanics among the ninety-one men who signed the Goliad Declaration: [José] Miguel Aldrete and M[ariano] Carbajal. The name of the latter on the document has sometimes been confused with his more famous brother, José María Carvajal, who was (as was Miguel Aldrete) a son-in-law of the prominent Mexican-born *empresario* Martín De León, the founder of the Texas town of Victoria.[32]

The movement for Texas independence split the De León family as well as the men who had married into it. José María Carvajal fought against Santa Anna's forces as a Mexican Federalist in 1835, but unlike his brother-in-law Aldrete, he could not bring himself to support the secession of Texas, and he moved his family to Mexico following the revolution. His brother Mariano died along with most of the ill-fated Texan garrison at Goliad.[33]

Aldrete, one of the largest landholders in Texas, survived both the revolution and the anti-Mexican attacks aimed at the De León family (including those who had supported Texan independence) by aggressive Anglo volunteer soldiers who swarmed into Victoria and the surrounding area after the retreat of the Mexican army in 1836. Aldrete held local judicial offices in Refugio County under the Texas Republic and lived for a time in Corpus Christi before moving to Mexico around the time of the American Civil War.[34]

William C. Binkley's utter neglect of the Tejano role in the revolution (on either side of the conflict) may seem to be an extreme case of the "silencing" power of the dominant Texas narrative, but numerous recent surveys of historical writing in Texas agree with Emilio Zamora, Cynthia Orozco, and Rodolfo Rocha that "the general tendency" of Texas historiography well into the 1960s "was to ignore or misrepresent the historical record" with regard to virtually all Mexican Americans.[35]

Gregg Cantrell, whose own 1999 biography of Stephen F. Austin was the first full-length scholarly examination of the great *empresario* since Eugene C. Barker's intimidating work of 1926, concluded that his predecessor had incorporated in his writings a "whites-only version of the Texas Revolution" that "came to dominate the collective memory of Texans in the twentieth century" and that "left Texans with a highly sanitized" version of history "in which Texas' Hispanic past was largely forgotten."[36]

Cantrell's indictment of traditional Texas history echoed that expressed by Robert Calvert and Walter Buenger in their famous 1991 essay on "The Shelf Life of Truth in Texas." Rather than utilizing historical scholarship to revise the mythic narrative of the past, claimed Buenger and Calvert, the "dominant culture" in Texas "has created and added to the myth in such a way that few openly challenge its premises." The "macho myth of Anglo Texas," they concluded, "still reigns."[37] Not until the 1960s, they found, "did the myth even begin to erode."[38] (Paul D. Lack, one of the contributors to Buenger's and Calvert's seminal anthology, *Texas Through Time*, wrote that real change did not come to the historiography of the period of the Texas Revolution until the publication in the early 1980s of David J. Weber's *The Mexican Frontier: The American Southwest Under Mexico.*)[39]

Arnoldo De León, one of the pioneers in bringing Tejanos out of the shadows of Texas history, and another contributor to *Texas Through Time*, agreed with Calvert and Buenger that the place of Mexicans in the Texan past did begin to shift slightly in the 1960s. "Among the more visible attempts at revision" at that time, writes De León, "were ones designed to rectify the image of the ahistoric Mexican: one genre of publication attempted such a task by . . . resurrecting the old Texas Revolution participants and holding them up as examples of Tejano involvement in the historical process."[40] The very first work cited by De León in this category is a biography of José Antonio Navarro published by

Joseph Martin Dawson in 1969—a work which, as we shall see, conveyed a sanitized and essentially false view of Navarro and also played a pivotal role in causing the bogus "Navarro" quotation to be carved into the wall of the Texas State History Museum.[41]

Tejano historian David Montejano suggested in an essay published in 2000 that Navarro was an example of the kind of "safe leadership" in the Mexican settlements sought by the new Anglo rulers of Texas after the revolution—part of a "conservative landed elite fearful of losing its property and standing in the new order" and thus willing to conform to the dictates of that order.[42] There is no doubt that Anglo-Texans in both the nineteenth and twentieth centuries—both the shapers of a new Texas and the shapers of Texas's remembered past—have tried (but not always successfully) to use José Antonio Navarro for their own purposes.[43]

Standards of historical inclusiveness have broadened considerably since William C. Binkley's day—Tejanos are no longer completely invisible. But the very prominence of the newfound "Texas Heroes" into which Tejanos such as Navarro and Juan Seguín have been transformed in an age of political correctness has often resulted in the misrepresentation of their actual lives (usually through the omission of inconvenient facts) and in the co-option of their voices within the familiar linear narrative of Anglo-dominated progress—rendering these Tejanos "safe" for Anglo-Texan sensibilities.

In the remainder of this essay I will consider four cases, culminating with the alleged Navarro quotation at the Texas State History Museum, that will reveal the pervasive effects of a dominant narrative so ingrained as to distort the interpretation and presentation of primary historical texts—to the extent that the very act of *quoting* Tejanos becomes, with supreme irony, the act of *silencing* them.

Some issues of purely linguistic translation will emerge along the way, but I believe that these four examples, taken from the conflicted lives of three accused "traitors," will reveal that deeper issues of interpretation than mere language are involved. These are cases in which an overarching "meta-narrative" has inexorably affected the way that historians have read the very texts that should have aided their understanding of a complex and multivocal past. Instead, these problematic texts have themselves been forced into the procrustean bedrock of a safe and simplistic "story of Texas."

It should be no surprise that accusations of treason loomed menacingly large in the lives of all three of these Tejano citizens of the Texas Republic: Juan Seguín, Vicente Córdova, and José Antonio Navarro. As historian Andrés Reséndez has shown so brilliantly, shifting boundaries of trade, language, warfare, and nationality meant that the denizens of the Mexican borderlands during the first half of the nineteenth century were beset by conflicting loyalties and often forced into making excruciating choices.[44]

My first example undoubtedly deserves analysis in greater depth than can be provided here, but it is suggestive of how close attention to the actual words of Tejanos can open a window onto a more complex and nuanced reality than is usually found in traditional Texas historiography. The document in question is Juan Seguín's 1842 letter of resignation as mayor of San Antonio.

Seguín was indeed a genuine hero of the Texas Revolution. One of the first political leaders in Texas to call for armed resistance to the Centralist regime of Antonio López de Santa Anna in 1835, this fifth-generation *bejareño* distinguished himself as a rebel cavalry officer, served with Travis at the Alamo before escaping as a courier, and led a Tejano unit under General Sam Houston at the climactic Battle of San Jacinto. After the revolution he served as commandant of the Texan garrison at San Antonio before resigning his commission to accept election to a three-year term in the Senate in 1838. In 1841 he became the first Hispanic mayor of San Antonio under the flag of the Republic of Texas.[45]

Seguín's crisis of loyalty came in the spring of 1842, during his second term as mayor, when Mexico invaded the Texas Republic and briefly captured San Antonio. Officers in the Mexican army spread the false rumor during their occupation of the city that Seguín was in collusion with them. Despite the fact that the mayor was on record as having warned both the city council and the national government of an impending attack, accusations of treason greeted Seguín even as he returned to San Antonio along with the Texan forces that he had joined in pursuing the retreating Mexicans toward the Río Grande.[46]

After being denied his request for a trial or court-martial, which would give public recognition of his claimed innocence, Seguín experienced the further humiliation of seeing his fellow Tejanos, including revolutionary veterans like himself, abused in the streets of San Antonio by the aggressive Anglo-Texan "volunteers" who rushed to San Antonio in the aftermath of the Mexican incursion. Seguín soon withdrew to his *rancho* below the city. There, he suffered the further ignominy of seeing the surrounding homes of his Tejano neighbors burned by hostile Anglo mobs.[47]

On April 18, 1842, Seguín penned this laconic message to the Bexar County Court: *"El estado desordenado en que se encuentra este desgraciado Condado, me obligan a remitir a V[uestro] H[onor] mi presente renuncia del empleo de Presidente de la Corporacion de la Ciudad de San Antonio."*[48] The official, if somewhat disjointed, translation in the original city council minutes renders Seguín's sentence as follows: "The disorderly state in which our unfortunate

County is actually placed in binds me to remit you my resignation of Mayor of the City of San Antonio."[49]

Seguín biographers Jack Jackson and Jesús F. de la Teja have followed the city council's lead in translating "*desgraciado Condado*" as "unfortunate county."[50] Historian Joseph M. Nance uses the word "unhappy" instead of "unfortunate."[51] But neither translation, technically "correct" as each might be, truly conveys the full burden of Seguín's feelings on April 18, 1842.

In Mexican Spanish, the term "*desgraciado*" is "one of the greatest insults that can be directed toward a man."[52] Its use by Seguín in this instance must be read in the larger context of his repeated references to the concept of *honor* as he defended his own position and that of the Tejanos against the assaults and impositions that came their way in the years following the Revolution.[53] The twin concepts of honor and shame—grace and disgrace—are the keys to understanding Seguín's self-exile in Mexico and his decision to take up arms against his former comrades. As Ramón A. Gutiérrez has observed, "public recognition of honor was essential to its value."[54] In the Castilian code of law and custom carried into north Mexico as a part of the cultural baggage of the Spanish colonists and their Tejano descendants, "the infamy of dishonored men was likened to social death."[55]

In their respective prize-winning studies of life on the edges of the Mexican borderlands, both Gutiérrez and James F. Brooks emphasize that not only was the concept of honor "at the very center of the moral system" of the region's Hispanic inhabitants, but *honor* also meant more than anything else "the idea that men's repute rested largely in their ability to preserve, protect, and dominate the well being and social relations of their families and communities."[56] Significantly for the case of Seguín, Brooks adds that in the complex ethnic circumstances of the Borderlands, there existed concurrent with this idea of the responsibility of the man of honor for the well-being of his community the additional "acknowledged (and disquieting) reality that in-group survival depended to some degree on social and economic interactions with out-groups, a continual challenge to men's sense of honor."[57] From the time of his service in the Texas Revolution, Seguín had been one of the prime mediators (as commandant, senator, and mayor) between the bejareños and their Anglo fellow-citizens—who now threatened as never before to become their overlords.

Wounded deeply by his ill treatment in Texas (including the army's refusal to grant him the right of a court-martial in which he could publicly defend his honor), Seguín had intended to retire peaceably to exile in Mexico. But when the Mexican authorities offered him upon his crossing to their side of the Río Grande the stark choice of life in prison or active participation in another Mexican invasion of the Texas Republic, he chose the latter, and in Seguín's words, "by spilling my blood, [to] vindicate myself."[58] After helping Mexican forces capture San Antonio for a second time in 1842, Seguín returned south, shepherding hundreds of hard-pressed and abused Tejano families into their own exile from a country that had betrayed them.[59]

Understood through the prism of honor—and Seguín's determination to avoid its loss—his life choices become not only understandable, but defensible. (To some extent, Seguín did achieve a measure of vindication in Texas during his own lifetime. Upon returning to Texas with his family at the end of the Mexican War in 1848, he found "acceptance by Tejanos and Anglo Texans" alike in San Antonio. In the 1850s he resumed a respected life in politics and elected office in his native city.)[60]

We can see from this first example that close attention to Juan Seguín's actual words—the original Spanish words that most readers of Texas histories have never seen—can suggest a more complex reality and reveal a more authentic account of his life than is allowed by any simplistic division of Tejanos of the revolutionary era into heroes and traitors. Yet today one-dimensional versions of "heroes" such as Juan Seguín are paraded in public celebrations as well as in popular histories in Texas—conveniently erasing the harsh realities visited upon most Tejanos living under the flag of the Texas Republic—while equally oversimplified "traitors" still remain virtually invisible.

If we are to take the Tejanos seriously, and take them whole, the words of a man such as Vicente Córdova also deserve close attention—despite the fact that his alleged treason against the Republic of Texas was never forgiven.[61] If Seguín's words were "under-interpreted" and their full contextual meaning thus unappreciated, then Córdova's have been "over-interpreted"—with a signification imposed upon them that has had the effect of obscuring, just as in Seguín's case, the painful realities of Tejano lives and loyalties following the Texas Revolution.

The declaration of August 10, 1838, issued by Córdova and his fellow-citizens of Nacogdoches has been identified by historian Paul D. Lack as the only Tejano-produced document from the incident known to Texas historians as "Córdova's Rebellion."[62] The men who signed this document (which is reproduced below) were desperate.[63] Even before the Texas Revolution, this eastern outpost of Tejano population near the Louisiana border had been overrun with immigrants from the United States. Competing land claims between old settlers and new arrivals created simmering tensions in Nacogdoches that were exacerbated by the 1835 Texan revolt against the Centralist Mexican government—a revolt that moved toward outright independence in 1836, threatening to put the newcomers in complete control of the legal system and thus perhaps of the lands as well.

At the time of the revolution, Córdova, a former Nacogdoches *alcalde*, was the leader of a predominantly Tejano militia company that was never fully trusted by the new Anglo majority. Córdova's company did not see combat against the Mexican army because an uneasy standoff with Anglo officials and volunteers left the Tejano militia intact only as a "home guard" against potential Indian attacks. Santa Anna's defeat at San Jacinto meant that the loyalty of this unit to the government of the Texas Republic was never put to the acid test of a Mexican advance on Nacogdoches.

After 1836, suspicions of duplicity remained strong on both sides. Old settlers—mostly but not all Tejanos—believed (with good reasons) that their landholdings were vulnerable under the new Anglo-dominated republic. The Texan government—also with good reasons—believed that Córdova and his associates were in treasonable contact not only with dissatisfied Indians (the Cherokees were upset that the Republic had failed to ratify its wartime treaty promising them title to their lands in Texas), but also with emissaries of the Mexican government who hoped to stir up a counter-revolution.[64]

There does seem to be no doubt that covert Mexican military agents were active in the East Texas area, encouraging an uprising among as many of the nearby Indian tribes as would listen to them, and talking secretly to Córdova and other disgruntled Nacogdochians as well. But Paul Lack, who has made the most recent and most thorough study of the Córdova revolt, finds "no evidence of a firm choice by Tejanos to revolt" even as late as July 1838, despite clandestine meetings by Córdova and others from Nacogdoches with those Mexican agents.[65] Lack adds that

> With both sides preparing for war but moving covertly, the question of who initiated battle remains a matter of perspective and mystery. This issue is complicated by the absence of documents left by Tejanos; *except for the proclamation of rebellion*, all contemporary accounts come from Anglo Texas sources."[66]

I would argue that the "proclamation of rebellion" as actually utilized by Texan historians *also* has come from Anglo sources and that since 1838 these traditional English translations of the document have been misleading Texans, including most historians and perhaps even Lack himself. The document, which in one transcription made by a Nacogdoches County official falsely bears the heading "*Pronunciamento*," is in fact a letter addressed to "S[eñ]or Sam Houston" by nineteen residents of Nacogdoches, including Córdova.[67] The Texan president was in their town at the time, taking a summer vacation from his official duties, but rumors of unrest had led him to warn Texas troops and local vigilantes even before his arrival "not to adopt any harsh measures towards the Mexicans in the neighborhood of Nacogdoches."[68]

Events, however, were moving toward a crisis. On August 4, a party from Nacogdoches searching for stolen horses was fired upon by a party of Hispanics that appeared from an inspection of the trail to be part of a larger mounted group. Upon receiving a report on August 7 that "at least 100 Mexicans led by Córdova were encamped on the Angelina River" on the boundary of the lands claimed by the Cherokee, Houston's old friend and Nacogdoches Congressman Thomas Jefferson Rusk activated the local squadron of (Anglo) militia and called for reinforcements.[69]

On August 8 Houston issued a "Proclama," drafted in Spanish, that called upon anyone "assembled with arms in their hands under the false pretext that they are afraid to remain in their homes" to return peacefully to their domiciles. "The honest citizen shall have nothing to fear," said Houston; "the Laws will protect him in his rights as in his properties and in his life."[70] Córdova's letter was Houston's answer.

The president's efforts to prevent a confrontation in the midst of this correspondence were ignored by Rusk and his men, who by this time believed that Córdova had been joined by hundreds of Indians. The Texan militia set out to intercept the alleged rebels in the Cherokee villages west of Nacogdoches.[71] But there was no battle. Córdova and his men retreated, dispersed, and a few of them including Córdova himself disappeared into the uncharted headwaters of the Trinity River. Over the next few months, most of this last group made their way along the edge of the western frontier of Anglo-Texan settlements and across the Río Grande to Matamoros (with some casualties along the way, including a severe wound to Córdova's arm).[72]

Most of the alleged rebels' families and indeed the majority of the Tejanos of Nacogdoches withdrew to rural settlements outside the town. Scores of them (none of whom had signed Córdova's letter) were rounded up and tried for treason early in 1839, but after a raucous trial and forty-eight hours of jury sequestration, only one man was convicted—and his guilt was so dubious that several jurymen and the county sheriff petitioned the new president, Mirabeau B. Lamar, for a pardon. It was promptly granted.[73]

There is much more to this story, most notably the expulsion of the Cherokees of Texas in the summer of 1839 by the militant anti-Indian President Lamar on the grounds that they had been in collusion with Córdova and the Mexican agents, but we need to linger over the fascinating document of August 10 long enough to ask what these desperate men were saying, about Texas and about themselves.[74] Here is their statement, with the original spelling and minus only their signatures:

El Vesindario de Nacogdoches, cansado yá de Sufrir injurias é insurpaciones de sus derechos, no puede menos que tener q. decir: Que hallandose reunido con las armas en la mano para sostener sus derechos individuales, y los dela Nación á que pertenesen, están dispuestos á redamar [sic] la ultima gota de Sangre q. tienen, y confiesan como lo han confesado yá, no conosen á ningunas delas actuales leyes, por las cuales se les ofresen garantias á sus vidas y propriedades; y solo Suplican no se les haga ninguna dejacion á sus familias, prometiendo deVuena fé la vuena comportacion con las deVˢ.—

Agosto 10, de 1838[75]

Traditional Texas historiography brandishes this "proclamation" as undeniable proof of a rebellious conspiracy, but its meaning is far more slippery than any historian has ever acknowledged. Let us begin with the tendentious translation of the verb *"conocer."* In preparing a criminal case against the alleged conspirators, Nacogdoches deputy clerk of court, Adolphus Sterne, began to translate the phrase *"no conosen á ningunas de las actuales leyes"* with the words "they do not know." But then he scratched out the word "know" and instead wrote that these men "do not acknowledge any of the existing laws."

Here is Sterne's complete translation, including all of his stricken words:

The people of Nacogdoches, being tired of Suffering the injuries and usurpations of their rights, they can not do less than say: That they are embodied with arms in their hands to sustain their individual rights, as well as those of the nation to which they belong, they are ready to spill ~~every~~ the last drop of blood, and confess as they have done heretofore that they do not ~~know~~ acknowledge any of the existing Laws, through which they are offered guaranties for their lives and property and only beg that none of their families may be molested, promising ~~that they will~~ in good faith to observe the same towards your families.[76]

Whatever Sterne's motives, his interpretation matched that of Texan Secretary of War Bernard E. Bee, who sent a report of the "rebellion" along with a hasty translation of the Córdova letter to Surgeon General Ashbel Smith from Nacogdoches shortly after the incident. Bee's version of the crucial phrase suggesting treason was that the men with arms in their hands "confess as they have heretofore confessed not to acknowledge nor do they acknowledge the Laws at present (or actually) in existence . . ."[77]

Early Texan historian Henderson K. Yoakum had a bit more leisure to write his more polished translation of Córdova's letter, perhaps borrowing the original Spanish document from Yoakum's close friend Sam Houston, who is reputed to have loaned Yoakum many documents for his use in the two-volume *History of Texas* that he published in 1855.[78] Yoakum's rendering, however, did not substantially differ from that of Bee or Sterne: "[they] declare, as they have heretofore done, that they do not acknowledge the existing laws, . . ."[79]

Twenty years later J. M. Morphis adopted Yoakum's translation *verbatim* in yet another enormous *History of Texas*. After the passage of more than a century, Joseph Milton Nance, in one of his magisterial volumes from the 1960s on Texas border warfare, deftly covered his tracks by *quoting* Yoakum's exact words while *citing* the manuscript Bee translation from the Ashbel Smith Papers at the University of Texas at Austin.[80]

Yet all of these "standard" translations, from Bee to Nance and everything in between, are radically incorrect and undeniably misleading. The verb in the original Spanish is not "*reconocer*"—to acknowledge or to recognize the laws; it is rather "*conocer*"—to be familiar with or acquainted with the laws. The difference in meaning is hardly trivial.

This document is not quite the "*pronunciamento*" as it was labeled by the semiofficial twentieth-century Nacogdoches translator Robert Bruce Blake, nor is it as "bold" and "defiant" as claimed by Joseph M. Nance.[81] It is rather an anguished plea and a cry of "*ya basta*" addressed to Sam Houston, the president of the Republic of Texas, and written in response to Houston's own Spanish-language *Proclama* of August 8, 1838, calling for mutual restraint in Nacogdoches and promising that "the Laws will protect [the honest citizen] in his rights as in his properties and in his life."[82]

In 1995 Jesús F. de la Teja provided an excellent new translation of the document for historian Paul Lack, who has written the best and most thorough account of "Córdova's Rebellion." Here is the key phrase as rendered by De la Teja: "They confess, as they have in the past, that they have no knowledge of the current laws by which guarantees of their lives and property are offered."[83] The difference between De la Teja's translation and that of his many predecessors is stark and unmistakable. Yet even Lack seems to be trapped still in the implications of the old, tendentious translations when he writes in his account that "on August 10, the Nacogdoches Tejanos declared that they had *never accepted the legitimacy* of the Texas Republic."[84] Was this really, as Lack claimed in the same article, a "proclamation of rebellion"?[85]

Despite Lack's claim that the many previous English-language versions of Córdova's letter contained only "minor errors or inelegant translation,"[86] there is a profound difference here and a profound disconnect in Lack's interpretation of Córdova's meaning. This can be highlighted by reference to another crucial phrase in the document: "*sus derechos individuales, y los dela Nacion á que pertenesen*." To what *Nación*—to what nation—are these individuals saying that they belong? For Paul Lack, the answer was obvious: he inserted [Mexico] in brackets as he translated this phrase in an essay published in 1991 in a Texas historical journal.[87] Yet when Lack's erstwhile translator Jesús F. de la Teja was asked in November 2007 to which "nation" this phrase refers, he answered promptly: "It was Texas." These Tejanos (explained De la Teja), like Juan Seguín, tried to be loyal to the Texas Republic following the revolution, but like him they were eventually forced into Mexico's arms from their ill treatment by too many Anglo Texans.[88]

Why did Adolphus Sterne, who should have known better, mistranslate "*conocer*"? My guess is that he and others in Nacogdoches *wanted* a "rebellion"—the result of which could be (and ultimately was) the surrender of the lands of the dozens of Tejanos who were accused of treason (whether or not they had signed the document). Why did Paul Lack, who should have known better, fail to realize the implications of his own translator's words? Perhaps because he believed that loyalties can be to only one "nation" at a time.

It is also possible that Córdova and the Nacogdoches Tejanos had a more limited conception of the "*Nación*" in mind. Provincial isolation and local responsibility for security on the Mexican frontier, writes Ana María Alonso, "fostered the development of a regional imagination of community." The local "organization of warfare itself fostered a parochial consciousness," so that when "peasants' loyalties to their *patria chica*—their "little motherland"—conflicted with obligations to the region or the nation, it was the former that took precedence over the latter."[89]

In my own view, it is the very ambiguity of this fascinating document from Nacogdoches which is its greatest historical significance. It shows—in its original, inscrutable language—the "conflicting loyalties and wrenching dilemmas" that Andrés Reséndez reminds us were the fate of the Hispanic denizens of the Borderlands, including even such icons of Texan patriotism as José Antonio Navarro.[90]

It was, of course, the Mexicans rather than the Texans who accused Navarro of treason, and when they captured him along with the rest of President Mirabeau Buonaparte Lamar's ill-fated Texan Santa Fe expedition in 1841, they tried him, convicted him, and sentenced him to death. Only the promise by his captors in New Mexico that Navarro would not be killed after the Texan capitulation—and the skill of his courageous Mexican military lawyer—saved Navarro from the firing squad.[91]

Navarro nevertheless suffered greatly in the dungeons of Mexico for three-and-a-half years before a daring rescue and escape brought him back to a hero's welcome in Texas in 1845.[92] His long Mexican imprisonment—during which his loyalty to Texas was bent, but never broken—is the central drama of Navarro's life.[93] But many of his Texan biographers—one should perhaps call them hagiographers—have done a disservice to Navarro and to all Hispanic citizens of the Texas Republic by minimizing the painful consequences for them caused by the split from Mexico.

Navarro had signed the Declaration of Independence with great reluctance in 1836, and he admitted to his closest friends in Texas that he never dreamt that he would take part in such a secession movement.[94] The most famous statement attributed to the imprisoned Navarro is this: "I have sworn to be a free Texan. I shall never forswear."[95] While there is no direct evidence that Navarro spoke or wrote these words, they are essentially true—but only as far as they go. The oft-repeated stories of him standing up to his Mexican jailers and refusing offers of fame and fortune if he would only defect—highly flattering to Navarro but undocumented by any contemporary sources—are in all likelihood exaggerated, if not apocryphal.[96]

Navarro's Mexican military lawyer told the judges in his 1842 trial that Navarro had had no choice but to submit to the dominant political forces in Texas in 1836.[97] Navarro himself, pleading for release from prison in 1843, suggested that he was among the delegates to the 1836 Texan convention who, as he put it, "were dragged along by the torrent which carried all before it in this tumultuous assembly."[98] What Navarro actually told his jailers in pleading for his freedom was that he was a man "forever Mexican," who wished to God that the Revolution had not forced him and his fellow Tejanos to make such a wrenching choice between nations.[99]

Navarro has become the symbol of unswerving devotion to Texas, but he was actually quite critical of the surge of Anglo American land grabs in the Texas Republic that were separating many Tejanos from their patrimony.[100] It is also telling that Navarro confided to his friend Reuben Potter that he had accepted—with great misgivings—the importunings of President Lamar to accompany the Santa Fe expedition to New Mexico with the rationalization that if the Texans were successful, Navarro "might prove a useful protector to a Mexican population brought suddenly under the military control of another race."[101]

It is unfortunate that the only book-length biography of José Antonio Navarro published to date provides us, in the context of the Santa Fe expedition, with two of the most egregious examples of "silencing by quotation."[102] The author, prominent Baptist minister Joseph Martin Dawson (who pastored the First Baptist Church in Waco for over thirty years), was a nonagenarian at the time of its publication by Baylor University Press in 1969.[103] In it, he claimed that an anonymously written speech "Address[ed] to the Inhabitants of Santa Fe and of all Towns East of the Río Grande" was not only composed by Navarro, but was "consistent with [his] thought and action throughout his political career."[104]

The speech, never given by Navarro, of course, because of the expedition's capture before reaching its destination, is a bombastic, hypernationalistic example of Anglo Texan expansionist rhetoric. Here are two sample paragraphs:

> You have observed how this Government [of Texas], with the innate vigor of a Hercules, rose from its very birth, invincible, and you see now how well established it is, secure and impervious to the vacuous, boastful, threats hurled from afar by an enemy [Mexico] who was impotent from the beginning in subjugating an infant nation. The day is not far when you will see it become the richest, most powerful nation in America.
>
> It has been evident to you that everywhere a Texan sets foot, he transforms barrenness into fertility. Barbarians disappear, leaving the land to the skill of the farmer. You have witnessed how once [Texans] establish themselves in their duties, small communities take hold, prospering under the aegis of just laws. Commerce and industry flourish, as well as religion, non-corrupted by the abuses of rampant ecclesiastical power.[105]

A close examination of the document reveals that it is written in the hand of an early Texas historian (and Navarro associate) Reuben M. Potter. Correspondence between Potter and President Lamar further reveals that the speech was composed by Potter at the explicit request of Lamar (whose typical rhetoric it strongly resembles). Potter told Lamar that Navarro had reviewed the speech, but "thought it needed only a slight retouching of the style which he gave it by altering a few words."[106] Whatever the final version may have been, the speech recorded in Dawson's biography does not represent Navarro's words—nor, I would argue, do they accurately represent his thinking. Navarro was not an uncritical observer of the Texas Republic, and he knew what could happen "to a Mexican population brought suddenly under the military control of another race."[107]

But Dawson takes the art of silencing by quotation a fatal step further. He adds insult to injury by claiming that when Navarro was being subjected to Santa Anna's alternating bribes and torture in Mexico (none of which have been confirmed by the documentary record), he answered thusly to the dictator:

> I have sworn to be a good Texan, and that I will not forswear. I will die for that which I firmly believe, for I know it is just and right. One life is a small price for a cause so great. As I fought, so shall I be willing to die. I will never forsake Texas and her cause. I am her son.[108]

This, of course, is the longer quotation from which the carved inscription at the Texas State History Museum has been taken.[109] And what was Dawson's source, duly footnoted? It was *Ten Tall Texans*—a little book written for young readers in 1967 by small-town high school math teacher and football coach Daniel James Kubiak.[110]

Dan Kubiak was named Texas Teacher of the Year in 1967, but *Ten Tall Texans* is utterly without scholarly merit or reliability. Needless to say, Dan flew without footnotes. When he needed a quote, he simply made one up, time and time again. And thus Dan Kubiak, and not José Antonio Navarro, wrote the words that are on the museum's walls—a bogus quotation submitted to the museum staff by a Texan academic, but never documented or confirmed by the museum from the historical record.[111]

Dan Kubiak was elected to the Texas legislature in 1968, and spent most of the next thirty years there before being felled by a heart attack in 1998.[112] But it was not a legislator's clout that put Dan's words on the wall. It was good intentions (the desire by both Kubiak in his book and later the museum's creators to include a Hispanic voice in the history of Texas) coupled with a looming construction deadline and a quotation that was just too good to be discarded—and too good to be true.[113]

The lesson to be learned from this "embarrassing history" is that good intentions are not enough; inclusiveness is not enough; a single quotation is not enough; and certainly, this kind of historical ventriloquism is not enough. We need to take the lives of Tejanos seriously and to take them *whole*—along with those of other people who may have been excluded from the dominant narrative of Texas history. We need to hear their authentic voices.

To do so will take hard work by historians digging in neglected places, seeking out those who were once shunned and working in partnership with our museums to bring these voices to the public. We need to take even our familiar heroes far more seriously. This reversal of the process of silencing will inevitably revise the dominant narrative and the collective memory of the history of Texas in a way that will do more adequate justice to both the contributions and the critiques that together constitute the Hispanic heritage of the state.

We should never allow even the most familiar and revered of our society's mythic narratives to be accepted uncritically, nor to be mistaken for legitimate history. Myths offer the false comfort of simplicity, and this simplicity is accomplished by the selective silencing of the past.[114] ¡*Ya basta!*

Notes

[1] Michel-Rolph Trouillot, *Silencing the Past: Power and the Production of History* (Boston: Beacon P, 1995), 43-47.
[2] Trouillot, *Silencing the Past*, 48.
[3] W. Fitzhugh Brundage, "Foreward," in *Lone Star Pasts: Memory and History in Texas*, ed. Gregg Cantrell and Elizabeth Hayes Turner (College Station: Texas A&M U P, 2007), xiv.

[4] For a discussion of the suppression of dissent, the deterioration of sources, and the dominance of an officially sanctioned history in the life story of one particular individual, see Elliott Young, *Catarino Garza's Revolution on the Texas-Mexico Border* (Durham [NC] and London: Duke U P, 2004), 305.

[5] Trouillot, *Silencing the Past*, 48.

[6] "Tejano" is a term used since at least the mid-twentieth century to designate Texans of Mexican descent and ethnicity. In the mid-nineteenth century, the first and usually the only language of virtually all Tejanos was Spanish.

[7] Anastacio Bueno, Jr., "In Storms of Fortune: José Antonio Navarro of Texas, 1821-1846 (M.A. Thesis, U of Texas at San Antonio, 1978), 30, 35, 59.

[8] Navarro claimed illness in declining election to the national congress in 1835. See the letter to Navarro from Diego Grant and José M. J. Carvajal, 29 April 1835, José Antonio Navarro Papers, Center for American History, U of Texas at Austin; see also the *Handbook of Texas Online*, s.v. "Navarro, José Antonio." The only other native Texan signer of the Declaration was Navarro's uncle, José Francisco Ruiz.

[9] *Handbook of Texas Online*, s.v. "Navarro, José Antonio." After first appearing in English translation in San Antonio newspapers in the mid-1850s, Navarro's historical writings were privately published in Spanish in 1869 as *Apuntes Históricos Interesantes*. A facsimile of this edition is included in David R. McDonald and Timothy M. Matovina, trans. and eds., *Defending Mexican Valor in Texas: José Antonio Navarro's Historical Writings, 1853-1857* (Austin: State House P, 1995).

[10] The other three are the artist Tom Lea, the novelist Larry McMurtry, and Sam Houston—who needs no introduction. See the Memorandum of August 1, 2000, from Bonnie Campbell (Curator of the Capitol and TSHM Project Manager) to Mark Alvidrez (Construction Management Project Engineer), "Subject: RFI #578: Quotes for Limestone Panels," [Hereafter cited as "RFI #578 Memorandum."] D[avid] D[enney] Interior Design file, Bob Bullock Texas State History Museum, Austin, TX. Courtesy David Denney, Interim Director, TSHM.

[11] E-mail message, Patricia Lynn Denton (founding TSHM Director) to James E. Crisp, November 9, 2007. The 1842 date for the Navarro quotation on the panel was added after it was selected, as were the dates for the other three panels. See "RFI #578 Memorandum." At some undetermined point in the planning process, the abbreviated word "trans." was added before the date and after Navarro's name, and is today carved into the limestone panel, but as will be shown below, the words are not actually a translation.

[12] Gregory Rabassa, *If This Be Treason: Translation and Its Dyscontents* (New York: New Directions Books, 2005), 3.

[13] The words in quotation marks in this sentence are my own.

[14] Anonymous, *José Antonio Navarro, Written by an Old Texan* (Houston: Telegraph Steam Printing House, 1876; reprint with a preface by Mary Bell Hart, n.p.: Hart Graphics and Office Centers, Inc., 1976), 26.

[15] *Handbook of Texas Online*, s.v. "Seguín, Juan Nepomuceno. Sites inspected by the author.

[16] E-mail message, Patricia Lynn Denton (founding TSHM Director) to James E. Crisp, February 8, 2008. Exhibit also inspected by the author.

[17] See http://www.thestoryoftexas.com/the_museum/about_the_exhibits.html. Accessed November 19, 2007. Video also inspected by the author.

[18] For a discussion of the treatment of Tejanos in Texan historical art, see James E. Crisp, *Sleuthing the Alamo: Davy Crockett's Last Stand and Other Mysteries of the Texas Revolution* (New York: Oxford U P, 2004), 150-178.

[19] Ramón Saldívar, *Chicano Narrative: The Dialectics of Difference* (Madison, U of Wisconsin P, 1990), 19, quoted in Leticia Magda Garza-Falcón, *Gente Decente: A Borderlands Response to the Rhetoric of Dominance* (Austin: U of Texas P, 1998), ix.

[20] Garza-Falcón, *Gente Decente*, 3, 7.

[21] See Stephen Stagner, "Epics, Science, and the Lost Frontier: Texas Historical Writing, 1836-1936, *Western Historical Quarterly* 12.2 (April 1981): 165-181. The leading propagandists of the Revo-

lution and the Republic, writes Stagner, were Mary Austin Holley (Stephen F. Austin's New England cousin), William Kennedy (an Englishman), and Henry S. Foote (a Mississippian). See Holley, *Texas* (Lexington, KY: J. Clarke & Co., 1836); Kennedy, *The Rise, Progress, and Prospects of the Republic of Texas* (London: R. Hastings, 1841); and Foote, *Texas and the Texans: Or, Advance of the Anglo-Americans to the South-West . . .* (Philadelphia: Thomas, Cowperthwait & Co., 1841).

[22]David J. Weber, *The Spanish Frontier in North America* (New Haven and London: Yale U P, 1992), 339-340.

[23]Stagner, "Epics, Science, and the Lost Frontier," 170. See H[enderson] Yoakum, *History of Texas, from its First Settlement in 1685 to its Annexation to the United States in 1846* (2 vols.; New York: Redfield, 1855).

[24]Laura Lyons McLemore, "Early Historians and the Shaping of Texas Memory," in *Lone Star Pasts: Memory and History in Texas*, ed. Gregg Cantrell and Elizabeth Hayes Turner (College Station: Texas A&M U P, 2007), 35.

[25]Paul D. Lack, "In the Long Shadow of Eugene C. Barker: The Revolution and the Republic," in *Texas Through Time: Evolving Interpretations*, ed. Walter L. Buenger and Robert A. Calvert (College Station: Texas A&M U P, 1991), 135.

[26]Eugene C. Barker, *The Life of Stephen F. Austin, Founder of Texas, 1793-1836: A Chapter in the Westward Movement of the Anglo-American People* (Texas History Paperback, Reprint of the 1949 Second Edition; Austin and London: U of Texas P, 1969), vii.

[27]Barker, *Life of Stephen F. Austin*, 448.

[28]*Handbook of Texas Online*, s.v., "Binkley, William Campbell."

[29]William C. Binkley, *The Texas Revolution* (Baton Rouge: Louisiana State U P, 1952; reprint, Austin: Texas State Historical Association, 1979). The Walter Lynwood Fleming Lectures in Southern History are given annually by invited scholars at Louisiana State U.

[30]Binkley, *Texas Revolution*, 102.

[31]Stephen L. Hardin, "Efficient in the Cause," in Gerald E. Poyo, ed., *Tejano Journey, 1770-1850* (Austin: U of Texas P, 1996), 63; see also John H. Jenkins, ed., *The Papers of the Texas Revolution, 1835-1836* (Austin: Presidial P, 1973), 3: 265-270.

[32]*Handbook of Texas Online*, s.v., "De León, Martín."

[33]Joseph E. Chance, *José María de Jesús Carvajal: The Life and Times of a Mexican Revolutionary* (San Antonio: Trinity U P, 2006), 203; Ana Carolina Castillo Crimm, *De León: A Tejano Family History* (Austin: U of Texas P, 2003), 152-53; *Handbook of Texas Online*, s.v., "Aldrete, José Miguel."

[34]*Handbook of Texas Online*, s.v., "Aldrete, José Miguel."

[35]"Introduction," to *Mexican Americans in Texas History*, ed. Emilio Zamora, Cynthia Orozco, and Rodolfo Rocha (Austin: Texas State Historical Association, 2000), 4.

[36]Gregg Cantrell, "The Bones of Stephen F. Austin: History and Memory in Progressive-Era Texas," in *Lone Star Pasts: Memory and History in Texas*, ed. Gregg Cantrell and Elizabeth Hayes Turner (College Station: Texas A&M U P, 2007), 67.

[37]Walter L. Buenger and Robert A. Calvert, "Introduction: The Shelf Life of Truth in Texas," in *Texas Through Time: Evolving Interpretations*, ed. Walter L. Buenger and Robert A. Calvert (College Station: Texas A&M U P, 1991), xii.

[38]Buenger and Calvert, "Shelf Life of Truth in Texas," xxii.

[39]David J. Weber, *The Mexican Frontier: The American Southwest Under Mexico* (Albuquerque: U of New Mexico P, 1982). See Lack, "In the Long Shadow of Eugene C. Barker," 138-144; see also my own very positive evaluation of Weber's contribution in James E. Crisp, "Race, Revolution, and the Texas Republic: Toward a Reinterpretation," in *The Texas Military Experience: From the Texas Revolution through World War II*, ed. Joseph G. Dawson III (College Station: Texas A&M U P, 1995), 32-45, 200-210.

[40]Arnoldo De León, "Texas Mexicans: Twentieth-Century Interpretations," in *Texas Through Time: Evolving Interpretations*, ed. Walter L. Buenger and Robert A. Calvert (College Station: Texas A&M U P, 1991), 30-31.

[41]Joseph Martin Dawson, *Jose Antonio Navarro: Co-Creator of Texas* (Waco: Baylor U P, 1969).

[42]David Montejano, "Old Roads, New Horizons: Texas History and the New World Order," in *Mexican Americans in Texas History*, ed. Emilio Zamora, Cynthia Orozco, and Rodolfo Rocha (Austin: Texas State Historical Association, 2000), 25-26.

[43]Unfortunately, Dawson's deeply flawed work (see note 41) was the only biography of Navarro published in the twentieth century. Two efforts to redress this imbalance are forthcoming. My own chapter-length essay, James E. Crisp, "José Antonio Navarro: The Problem of Powerlessness," *Tejano Leadership in Mexican and Revolutionary Texas*, ed. Jesús F. de la Teja (College Station: Texas A&M U P, 2010), 146-168; furthermore, a long-awaited full-length biography of Navarro by David R. McDonald is planned for publication by the Texas State Historical Association. In the meantime, in addition to the entry on Navarro in the *Handbook of Texas Online*, the best short sketches of Navarro's life are to be found in McDonald and Matovina, trans. and eds., *Defending Mexican Valor in Texas*, 15-32, and Andrés Reséndez, ed., *A Texas Patriot on Trial in Mexico: José Antonio Navarro and the Texan Santa Fe Expedition* (Dallas: DeGolyer Library & William P. Clements Center for Southwest Studies, Southern Methodist U, 2005), xvi-xix.

[44]Andrés Reséndez, *Changing National Identities at the Frontier: Texas and New Mexico, 1800-1850* (Cambridge: Cambridge U P, 2005). My review of this book for the Institute of Historical Research at the U of London may be found at: http://www.history.ac.uk/reviews/paper/crisp.html.

[45]The best available scholarly biography of Seguín is Jesús F. de la Teja, "The Making of a Tejano," in Jesús F. de la Teja, ed., *A Revolution Remembered: The Memoirs and Selected Correspondence of Juan N. Seguín*, 2nd ed. (Austin: Texas State Historical Association, 2002), 1-70.

[46]Ray R. Broussard, *San Antonio During the Texas Republic: A City in Transition* (El Paso: Texas Western P, 1967), 27; Joseph Milton Nance, *Attack and Counterattack: The Texas-Mexican Frontier, 1842* (Austin: U of Texas P, 1964), 11-12, 37; de la Teja, ed., *Revolution Remembered*, 43-45.

[47]Broussard, *San Antonio During the Texas Republic*, 28-29; Nance, *Attack and Counterattack*, 52; John Holmes Jenkins III, ed., *Recollections of Early Texas: The Memoirs of John Holland Jenkins* (Austin: U of Texas P, 1958), 96; Jack Jackson, *Los Tejanos* (Stamford, CT: Fantagraphics Books, Inc., 1982), 82; de la Teja, ed., *Revolution Remembered*, 43; San Antonio City Council Minutes [Republic of Texas], Center for American History, U of Texas at Austin, 59, 80-81 [page numbers are from the WPA transcriptions—see below, notes 48 and 49].

[48]These Spanish words have been taken from the original manuscript San Antonio City Council Minutes for April 18, 1842, held by the Office of the City Clerk of the City of San Antonio, Texas, page 79 (right). Typescripts of these records are also available on microfilm from the Office of the City Clerk. The author is grateful to City Archivist Amanda C. DeFlorio for her assistance in accessing the manuscript records.

Another set of typescripts, prepared during the 1930s by the Texas Works Projects Administration, are available at the Center for American History at the U of Texas at Austin—see below, note 49. The Seguín letter in Spanish may be found on page 103 of the WPA transcriptions.

[49]These English words have been taken from the original manuscript San Antonio City Council Minutes for April 18, 1842, held by the Office of the City Clerk of the City of San Antonio, Texas, page 79 (left). The typescripts prepared by the Texas Works Progress Administration in the 1930s contain both transcripts of the original English and Spanish minutes and a second set of typescripts with both the English text and new translations of the Spanish minutes. The Seguín letter is retranslated therein as follows: "The disordered state in which this unfortunate county finds itself at the present moment, obliges me to remit to Your Honor my immediate resignation of the office of Mayor of the Corporation of the City of San Antonio." San Antonio City Government Records. Journal A: Records of City of San Antonio. TRANSCRIBED, TRANSLATED, AND TYPED By Texas Work Projects Administration[,] Official Project No. 65-1-66-83, Second Set [Translations], Center for American History, U of Texas at Austin, page 107. The English text of Seguín's letter from the minutes may be found typed in virtually identical versions on page 102 of the first set [Transcriptions] and page 106 of the second set [Translations].

[50]De la Teja's more polished translation of Seguín's letter reads as follows: "The turbulent state in which this unfortunate county finds itself at present obliges me to present to Your Honor my resignation as president of the corporation of the City of San Antonio." Juan Seguín to the Bexar County Judge, April 18, 1842, in de la Teja, ed., *Revolution Remembered*, 179. See also Jackson, *Los Tejanos*, 84.

[51]Nance, *Attack and Counterattack*, 53.

[52]Martín Alonso, *Enciclopedia del Idioma* (Madrid: Aguilar, 1958), 2: 1488; see also Francisco Javier Santamaría, *Diccionario de Mejicanismos*, 2nd ed. (Méjico: Editorial Porrua, S. A., 1974), 446; Marcos Augusto Morínigo, *Diccionario de Americanismos* (Barcelona: Muchnik Editores, 1985), 215. All of the following definitions from these dictionaries are for the noun form of "*desgraciado*": Alonso—"*Uno de los mayores insultos que se le puede dirigen a un hombre*"; Santamaría—"*Epiteto injurioso que en Tobasco y otras partes del país vale por cabrón, hijo de puta, . . . etx.*"; Morínigo—"*Insulto grave//El hombre cuya mujer le es infiel//El hijo de mujer pública.*"

[53]See in this regard "Juan Seguín's Address at the Burial of the Alamo Defenders," (February 25, 1837), in de la Teja, ed., *Revolution Remembered*, 156; "Juan Seguín's Address in Senate," (February 1840), in ibid., 174; and Sam Houston's reply to a now-lost letter from Seguín (January 16, 1837), in ibid., 152-53.

[54]Ramón A. Gutiérrez, *When Jesus Came, the Corn Mothers Went Away: Marriage, Sexuality, and Power in New Mexico, 1500-1846* (Stanford: Stanford U P, 1991), 177.

[55]Gutiérrez, *When Jesus Came*, 179.

[56]Gutiérrez, *When Jesus Came*, 176 (first quotation); James F. Brooks, *Captives and Cousins: Slavery, Kinship, and Community in the Southwest Borderlands* (Chapel Hill: U of North Carolina P, 2002), 26 (second quotation).

[57]Brooks, *Captives and Cousins*, 26.

[58]Seguín, "Edited Memoirs," in de la Teja, ed., *Revolution Remembered*, 97.

[59]De la Teja, ed., *Revolution Remembered*, 48.

[60]De la Teja, ed., *Revolution Remembered*, 50-51.

[61]Unlike Seguín, Córdova did not survive the Texas Republic. He was killed in combat at the Battle of Salado Creek, while serving with the Mexican army in the same invasion of Texas in which Juan Seguín participated in the fall of 1842. *Handbook of Texas Online*, s.v., "Córdova, Vicente."

[62]Paul D. Lack, "The Córdova Revolt," in *Tejano Journey, 1770-1850*, ed. Gerald E. Poyo (Austin: U of Texas P, 1996), 99.

[63]Not all of the nineteen signers were Tejanos. They included longtime settler Nathaniel Norris, a free black named Joshua N. Robertson, and two men with Irish surnames (James Quinnety and William Donovan), as well as Córdova and fourteen other Tejanos. See Lack, "Córdova Revolt," 97, 154 (n. 28).

[64]This summary of events in Nacogdoches is taken from Paul D. Lack, "East Texas Mexicans and the Texas Revolution, 1835-1836," *Locus: An Historical Journal of Regional Perspectives on National Topics* 3, no. 2 (Spring 1991), 141-155. Lack's latest and most complete account of the revolt is found in "The Córdova Revolt," cited above, note 62. See also the chapter on "The Córdova-Flores Incident" in Joseph Milton Nance, *After San Jacinto: The Texas-Mexican Frontier, 1836-1841* (Austin: U of Texas P, 1963), 113-141.

Although Lack ("The Córdova Revolt," 152, n.1) states that Nance provides the most complete account of the entire affair, the separate and complementary translations of the Memorandum Book of Mexican secret agent Pedro Julián Miracle published by Malcolm D. McLean make it clear that Nance was mistaken when he claimed (in *After San Jacinto*, p. 117) that Vicente Córdova had accompanied Miracle from Matamoros to East Texas in May of 1838. Córdova first appears in Miracle's camp on July 5, after Miracle's party had crossed the Trinity River; their most substantive meeting was on July 20. See Malcolm D. McLean, comp. and ed., *Papers Concerning Robertson's Colony in Texas* (Arlington, TX: The UTA P, 1990), 16: 544-556.

On July 19, Córdava attempted to make contact by letter with another Mexican agent in East Texas, Manuel Flores. See James T. DeShields, *Border Wars of Texas* (orig. pub. 1912; reprint, Austin: State House P, 1993), 246. The copy of the July 19, 1838, letter from Córdova to Flores cited by DeShields may be found in the Valentine O. King Collection, Texas State Library and Archives Commission, Austin. On August 20, ten days after the "Córdova Rebellion" began, Miracle was intercepted and killed on the Red River, and his diary and papers seized. *Handbook of Texa Online*, s.v., "Miracle, Julián Pedro."

[65]Lack, "The Córdova Revolt," 99.

[66]Lack, "The Córdova Revolt," 99. [My emphasis.]

[67]See note 63, above. The address to Houston is on the obverse of the document cited in note 75, below. The word "Pronunciamento" appears in the Spanish typescript, but not the English translation of the original document, both prepared by Robert Bruce Blake, early twentieth-century Nacogdoches court reporter and County Clerk, in the Robert Bruce Blake Research Collection [hereafter RBB], Special Collections, Ralph W. Steen Library, Stephen F. Austin U, Nacogdoches [hereafter SFA], LII: 263-264.

[68]Lack, "Córdova Revolt," 94.

[69]*Handbook of Texas Online*, s.v., "Córdova Rebellion."

[70]"Proclama," [ms.] August 8, 1838, Nacogdoches County Court Records [hereafter NCCR], Criminal Cases, 1838, (Córdova, Vicente) [Córdova Rebellion], Box 1, Folder 7, SFA; see also the transcript and translation of Houston's "Proclama" in RBB, SFA, LIII: 261-262.

[71]*Handbook of Texas Online*, s.v., "Córdova Rebellion."

[72]Nance, *After San Jacinto*, 123-126.

[73]Lack, "Córdova Revolt," 106-108.

[74]Paul Lack's interpretation of the Córdova revolt as an act of desperation, rather than the inevitable culmination of a treasonous conspiracy, seems correct, but see also, in addition to Nance, *After San Jacinto*, 113-141, the following: John R. Wunder and Rebecca J. Herring, "Frontier Conspiracy: Law, History, Turner, and the Córdova Rebellion," *Red River Valley Historical Review* 7.3 (Summer 1982), 51-67.

[75]Vicente Córdova et al. to S[eñ]or Samuel Houston, August 10, 1838, Córdova Rebellion Papers, NCCR, Civil Cases, Box 26, Folder 15, SFA.

Note: *redamar* likely should be *derramar*—to spill. The Spanish transcription of this document published by Paul Lack in a Mexican historical journal in 1993 contains a number of transcription errors, but none which would alter the basic substance of the message. See Paul D. Lack, "Los tejanos leales a México del este de Texas, 1838-1839," *Historia Mexicana* 42.4 [issue 168] (Abril-Junio, 1993), 902.

[76]Undated translation in Sterne's handwriting, NCCR, Criminal Cases, 1838, Box 1, Folder 7, SFA. Confirmation of the distinctive handwriting is provided by comparison with Adolphus Sterne's signed "Protest Re: Contract with Newspapers to Distribute House Proceedings," August 15, 1850, Memorials and Petitions File, Texas State Library and Archives Commission, Austin.

[77]"Translation Copy," unsigned English version of the August 10, 1838 letter, Ashbel Smith Papers, Center for American History, U of Texas at Austin. The handwriting of Bernard E. Bee may be confirmed by a comparison with Bee's signed letter of August 26, 1838, reporting the Córdova affair to Smith. The letter is in the same file of Smith's correspondence in the Center for American History as the "Translation Copy," but filed separately according to the date of August 10. The translation undoubtedly was sent along with the letter of August 26 to Smith.

[78]*Handbook of Texas Online*, s.v., "Yoakum, Henderson King."

[79]H[enderson] Yoakum, Esq., *History of Texas, from Its First Settlement in 1685 to Its Annexation to the United States in 1846* (orig. pub. 1855; reprint, Austin: The Steck Company, 1935), 2: 246-247.

[80]J. M. Morphis, *History of Texas, from Its Discovery and Settlement . . .*, 2nd ed. (New York: United States Publishing Company, 1875), 400; Nance, *After San Jacinto*, 120.

[81] For the "pronunciamento" designation, see the Spanish typescript of the original document prepared by Robert Bruce Blake, early twentieth-century Nacogdoches court reporter and County

Clerk, RBB, SFA, LII: 263. Joseph M. Nance claimed that the "malcontents" had "boldly and defiantly" replied to Houston's plea for restraint, but Nance interestingly failed to include in his text the translation of the document's final, conciliatory phrase. See Nance, *After San Jacinto*, 120.

[82] "Proclama," [ms.] August 8, 1838, NCCR, Criminal Cases, 1838, (Córdova, Vicente) [Córdova Rebellion], Box 1, Folder 7, SFA; see also the transcript and translation of Houston's "Proclama" in RBB, SFA, LIII: 261-262.

[83] Lack, "Córdova Revolt," 97; 154, n. 28.

[84] Lack, "Córdova Revolt,", 93. [My emphasis.]

[85] Lack, "Córdova Revolt," 99.

[86] Lack, "Córdova Revolt," 154, n. 28.

[87] Lack, "East Texas Mexicans and the Texas Revolution, 1835-1836," 154.

[88] Telephone interview by the author with Jesús F. de la Teja, November 18, 2007.

[89] Ana María Alonso, *Thread of Blood: Colonialism, Revolution, and Gender on Mexico's Northern Frontier* (Tucson: U of Arizona P, 1995), 49.

[90] Reséndez, trans. & ed., *Texas Patriot on Trial*, xiii.

[91] Reséndez, trans. & ed., *Texas Patriot on Trial*, xv, 102-103.

[92] The most reliable account of Navarro's almost miraculous escape is to be found in George Wilkins Kendall, *Narrative of the Texan Santa Fé Expedition*, Library of Texas Number Seven, ed. Gerald D. Saxon and William B. Taylor, (Dallas: DeGolyer Library and William P. Clements Center for Southwest Studies, 2004), 2:237-238.

[93] See Crisp, "Navarro: The Problem of Powerlessness," 147.

[94] R[euben] M[armaduke] Potter, "The Texas Revolution: Distinguished Mexicans Who Took Part in the Revolution of Texas, with Glances At Its Early Events," *Magazine of American History* 2 (October 1878): 585; Jacob De Cordova, *Texas: Her Resources and Her Public Men*, 2nd edition (Philadelphia: J. B. Lippincott & Co., 1858; reprint, Waco: Texian P, 1969), 148, 150.

[95] De Cordova, *Texas*, 152. This classic line, frequently quoted in secondary works, appears nowhere in the known writings of Navarro. The source is a biographical sketch published in 1858 by early Texas historian and businessman Jacob de Cordova, a bilingual acquaintance of Navarro who had come to Texas in 1837. Many subsequent accounts are based on this sketch, written when Navarro was still very much alive and one of the most well-known men in Texas. See the "Introduction" by Dayton Kelley in De Cordova, *Texas* (1969 reprint), iii-vii.

[96] De Cordova, *Texas*, 151-153; Potter, "Texas Revolution," 599-601; Dawson, *Navarro*, 73.

[97] Reséndez, trans. & ed., *Texas Patriot on Trial*, 92-93.

[98] José Antonio Navarro to Don Antonio López de Santa Anna, September 19, 1843, in "Jose Antonio Navarro and Santa Fe Expedition, 1841-1845," [E. C.] Barker transcripts from the Archivo General de México, [Dept. of] Guerra y Marina, typescripts at the Center for American History, U of Texas at Austin, 338: 14-17. [Hereinafter cited as Barker transcripts, AGN.] Quotation from page 16 [my translation].

[99] Navarro to Santa Anna, Sept. 19, 1843, Barker transcripts, AGN, 15 [my translation].

[100] "Remarks of Mr. Navarro on a bill to issue titles to certain lands in the county of Bexar," *Telegraph and Texas Register* (Houston), January 30, 1839, page 3, col. 4.

[101] Potter, "Texas Revolution," 597.

[102] For forthcoming biographies of Navarro, see above, note 43.

[103] Thomas E. Turner, "Introduction," in Dawson, *Navarro*, xiii-xiv; *Handbook of Texas Online*, s.v., "Dawson, Joseph Martin."

[104] Dawson, *Navarro*, 65-66.

[105] An anonymous manuscript of the speech, clearly written in Spanish by the hand of Reuben M. Potter (see note 106, below), may be found in the Papers of José Antonio Navarro III in the Library of the Daughters of the Republic of Texas at the Alamo in San Antonio. The original bears no date, but "June, 1841" has been added to the manuscript in typescript. The "supposed" attribution to José Antonio Navarro is in the heading of a typewritten translation of the document prepared by his grandson José Antonio Navarro III, on June 30, 1936. A copy of the Spanish manu-

script may also be found in the José Antonio Navarro Papers at the Center for American History, U of Texas at Austin. The copy cited by Joseph M. Dawson from the Bexar Archives has not been located.

The translation quoted here, by Dora E. Guerra, was prepared in November, 1977, for the DRT Library, and may be found along with the original manuscript and the copy of the grandson's translation in the José Antonio Navarro III Papers, cited above. A third translation, incomplete and rather inelegant, is provided by Dawson and attributed to Mrs. Earl Boyd of Navarro Junior College in Corsicana, Texas. See Dawson, *Navarro*, 65-66.

[106]See the following letters in Charles Adams Gulick, Jr., et al. eds., *The Papers of Mirabeau Buonaparte Lamar*, 6 vols. (Austin: Texas State Library and Historical Commission, 1921-27; reprint, New York: AMS P, 1973): Potter to Lamar, May 29, 1841 (3: 531 and 5: 474), Potter to Lamar June 5, 1841 (3: 532). My thanks to John Anderson of the Texas State Library and Archives Commission for timely copies of the original Potter letters, which allowed the unmistakable handwriting match with the manuscript attributed to Navarro (see above, note 105).

The manuscript of the speech in Potter's hand in the José Antonio Navarro III Papers at the DRT Library is almost certainly a draft given by Potter to Navarro; the final copy appears never to have made it to Santa Fe, but was likely burned along with the other papers carried by the Texans when the Santa Fe Expedition was captured by the Mexican army in September of 1841 at Laguna Colorada near present Tucumcari, New Mexico.

Navarro biographers David McDonald and Tim Matovina have suggested that Navarro may have translated Potter's speech, but Potter's letters show otherwise; moreover, Navarro did not write or speak English fluently. See McDonald and Matovina, trans. and eds., Defending Mexican Valor in Texas, 19. For Navarro's need for a translator, see Potter, *Texas Revolution*, 602-603. In 1846 Reuben Marmaduke Potter served as Navarro's interpreter during the first session of the Senate of the State of Texas, where Navarro represented Bexar County. See the *Handbook of Texas Online*, s.v., "Potter, Reuben Marmaduke."

[107]See above, note 101.

[108]Dawson, *Navarro*, 73.

[109]See above, note 11.

[110]The quotation in question begins a chapter on José Antonio Navarro in Daniel James Kubiak, *Ten Tall Texans* (San Antonio: The Naylor Company, 1967), 53.

[111]The author has agreed to the request of the Texas State History Museum not to identify the person who submitted the Navarro quotation. The quote was one of many submitted by this person, who was one of about a half-dozen Texas academics who submitted more than a hundred nominations in all. Complete information on the quotations and the process of selection may be found in the D[avid] D[enney] Interior Design file, Bob Bullock Texas State History Museum, Austin, TX.

[112]For all information included here on Kubiak, see the web page "Rockdale State Representative Dan Kubiak Memorial Page (1938-1998)" at <http://forttumbleweed.net/dan.html>.

[113]Telephone conversation with Patricia Lynn Denton (founding TSHM Director), February 1, 2008; see also the "Publisher's Preface," in Daniel James Kubiak, *Ten Tall Texans*, revised and enlarged edition (San Antonio, TX: The Naylor Company, 1970), vii-viii.

[114]A longer version of this paragraph appeared in Crisp, *Sleuthing the Alamo*, 178.

Rev. Gregorio M. Valenzuela and the Mexican-American Presbyterian Community of Texas

Norma A. Mouton*
The University of Houston

THIS IS THE STORY OF A VERY YOUNG MEXICAN BOY WHO TOOK THE opportunity to accompany his "second mother" north to the United States and decided to stay. Not only did Gregorio Valenzuela decide to stay in the north, but he also chose to convert to the Presbyterian Church and devote his life to helping others find the same path to spiritual fulfillment. The interview with Rev. Valenzuela held in his home in San Antonio, Texas, in August of 2007 forms the basis for this story and sheds further light on the person who was willing to stand alone against what at the time was considered a progressive political position. Reverend Gregorio Méndez Valenzuela was born March 12, 1913, in Malpaso, Zacatecas, México to José Valenzuela and Juana Méndez Valenzuela (Ministerial Directory 653). His mother died when he was about two years old, and when the cousin who took care of him proposed to move to Texas, the young boy went with her. He was approximately six years old at the time (Valenzuela "Interview"). Valenzuela attended a rural primary school for farmworkers' children that only offered education through the fifth grade. Valenzuela's first teachers at the rural school he attended in Mackay, Texas, were daughters of Elías Treviño, one of the founders of the Texas-Mexican Presbytery: "De manera que allí fui a la escuela, y a la primaria. Mis profesoras fueron Eudelia Treviño y Hortensia Treviño, hijas de Elías Treviño, uno de los pastores de aquí de San Antonio" (Valenzuela "Interview"). The Treviño sisters provided Valenzuela with a positive example of Protestants early in his childhood. Unfortunately, that school only went as far as the sixth grade. Most Hispanic children in Texas at the time were only given a primary school education under the public system (Ferg-Cadima 9). Any further education for them had to be in private schools, something most Hispanics could not afford.

Between the ages of 10 or 11 and 14 he worked in the fields picking cotton until the farm owner's wife, Mrs. Borden, took him under her wing and sent him to a boarding school in Kingsville (Ministerial Directory 653) for Mexican boys from both Texas and Mexico that provided a work-study program: " . . . yo fui a la escuela allí cuando . . . estaba de Presidente James W. Skinner . . . " (Valenzuela "Interview"). The school was known as the Texas-Mexican Industrial Institute and was founded by the Presbyterian Synod of Texas on May 1, 1912 ("History: In the Beginning"). Today, it is a coeducational school known as the Presbyterian Pan American School. It was through his early education with the Treviño sisters, his close contact with the Borden family, and his later participation in the Tex-Mex Institute that the future Rev. Valenzuela learned about the Presbyterian Church.

After graduating from the Tex-Mex Institute in 1934 (Ministerial Directory 653), he and several other boys were invited to participate in a tour of the northeastern United States for the purpose of publicizing the work of the Institute and soliciting sponsorship for the school from Anglo Presbyterian congregations in that region. They traveled for most of the summer, eventually also visiting New York City. Although they hardly traveled first class and often had to make their funds stretch by eating sparingly, the trip obviously made a lasting impression on the young man. It was the future Rev. Valenzuela's job to give the main address in English explaining the goals and purposes of the Institute (Valenzuela "Interview"). This was an important experience in his life because not only did he use the telling of this experience to regain illegal entry into the United States when he decided to give himself over to the ministry, but it likely disposed him to strive for a better future than he could foresee for himself in Mexico.[1] Upon their return to Kingsville, the future Rev. Valenzuela approached the president of the Institute requesting a recommendation for his participation in the Spanish program at the Austin Presbyterian Theological Seminary. At the time, the program was limited to five students at any one time, and the positions for that fall were already filled. He was told to wait and reapply the following year (Valenzuela "Interview").

Having no particular purpose or activity with which to involve himself after having been refused immediate entrance to the seminary, the future Rev. Valenzuela decided to return to Mexico: "Me voy a ir para México y allá me voy a quedar. Con el inglés que sé. Yo puedo poner una escuela. O puedo hacer aplicación en las escuelas allí que enseñan inglés" (Valenzuela "Interview"). He had never before returned to see his family and had only the address of a sister in Monterrey. After arriving at her door, he found that his father was also living there. His family welcomed him in the humble home, proudly offering him the best they had. He felt bad about taking his sister's bed and forcing her and her husband to sleep on the kitchen floor. After one sleepless night in the home's only bed, he convinced his sister that he would be fine sleeping on the dirt floor in the kitchen and returned the bedroom to her and her husband (Valenzuela "Interview").

While in Monterrey, the future Rev. Valenzuela decided to continue his education and presented himself at the University of Nuevo León. In an interview with the president of that institution, he was told that although his grades at Tex-Mex were excellent, he lacked coursework in both Spanish and Mexican history, which were requirements for his acceptance. He would have to meet those requirements and then reapply (Valenzuela "Interview"). This disillusioned the young man who instead decided to set up a private school. He had twenty-five students and charged them each one peso per week. Unfortunately, Rev. Valenzuela tells us very little about his time as a teacher in Mexico. The money he earned he gave to his sister for his upkeep, but after about a year, he grew nostalgic with memories of his time in Texas and determined to return (Valenzuela "Interview"). He had no U.S. citizenship papers and so his return would have to rely more on luck than anything else. One purpose in returning to the United States was to get the documentation that he would need to facilitate his travel between the two countries and so he left most of his belongings at his sister's house, having every intention of returning (Valenzuela "Interview").

He crossed the border at Reynosa-Hidalgo. At the border he lied and told the U.S. officials that he had been born in Mackey, Texas, but had no documents to prove his claim. They interviewed him, and during that conversation they discovered that he had graduated from Tex-Mex in Kingsville, an institution with which some of the officials were familiar. Having left most of his belongings in Monterrey, he found he only had with him a copy of the speech that he had memorized and presented so many times during the tour of the Northeastern congregations. He showed the border officials his worn copy of the speech and because it was all about the Institute and written in English and since the young man's English was good though accented, the guards decided to let him enter the United States believing the lie of his birthplace (Valenzuela "Interview").

Just after graduating from the Texas-Mexican Industrial Institute and while he waited to accept a scholarship to the seminary in Austin, Texas, Valenzuela was given his first opportunity to preach at Tex-Mex. Valenzuela recounts that conversation when Brother Acevedo, a local minister said, " . . . cuando yo voy a estar unos dos miércoles fuera de la escuela, ¿te quiéres encargar allí de predicar . . . ?" Thus it was that after already having made the decision to enter the seminary, but before beginning his formal training, Valenzuela began his preaching career. Valenzuela eventually rose within the hierarchy of the Presbyterian Church to serve as Secretary of the Texas-Mexican Presbytery. Between 1908 when it was founded and 1955 when it was dissolved, the Texas Mexican Presbytery served all the Spanish-speaking congregations in Texas. Valenzuela's was one of the few voices that opposed the dissolution of that presbytery.

This story is based on the interview with the Rev. Valenzuela, as well as on his sermons and other professional documents. The parallel events in the formation of another central Texas Presbyterian congregation, the Mexican Presbyterian Church of Lockhart, Texas, now known as the Faith/Fe Presbyterian Church of Lockhart, Texas, support and illuminate the difficulties faced by Hispanic Protestants in a climate of discrimination. The Valenzuela material consists of professional papers and a recorded interview. The material from the church in Lockhart, Texas, consists of records and minutes dating from 1925 through 1929 when the church was first formed.

Each set of sermon notes included in the collection varies in length from one to ten pages. Obviously, the longer sermon notes are more thorough and read more like complete sermons than the shorter versions. Most sermon notes include a theme, the biblical reference, and the place, date, and time that the sermon was preached. The interesting thing is that these notes indicate that most sermons were preached more than once and often with many years intervening. Some sermon notes even include notations that show that Rev. Valenzuela preached them to both Methodist and Presbyterian congregations even before his formal break with the Presbyterian Church (Valenzuela "Sermon Notes"). This tells us that the subjects were not limited as to time, place, or denominational doctrine but rather were based on exegesis of the Holy Scriptures. There are approximately 784 sermons in the collection. These include several sermons on the major religious Holy days as well as secular holidays such as Mother's Day along with the usual thematic studies on Christian life and practice (Valenzuela "Sermon Notes").

Rev. Valenzuela organized these sermons with the biblical reference first, followed by the main scriptural text, the theme or subject, and then the theme of the sermon which he refers to as the "introduction." The main body of the sermons is sometimes divided into subtopics and follows the introduction. All of his sermons are typed in Spanish. Most of the sermons are examples of Protestant exegesis governed by conservative hermeneutics or biblical interpretation.[2]

Reviewing this material gives insight into the sociocultural plight of the Mexican-American Protestant who found himself/herself neither totally a participant within the Mexican-American Catholic sociocultural environment nor totally within the Anglo-Saxon cultural milieu. Valenzuela's statements and documents reveal the discrimination confronted by Hispanic Presbyterians who had to work within an established Anglo framework. The discrimination experienced by Hispanic Protestants goes beyond the recognized dichotomy of skin color or cultural heritage and demonstrates the religious discrimination existing within the Mexican-American cultural context. The sociocultural references in these historical records, in both the Rev. Valenzuela's interview and sermons and the Lockhart church records, offer evidence of the discrimination and the difficulties faced by an important segment of the Hispanic community in Texas.

In 1935 Gregorio Valenzuela entered the seminary in Austin (Ministerial Directory 653). While there, he received word that the books and materials he had left in his sister's care had been badly damaged in a flood. Along with his father's death, it was the loss of his belongings that broke the last tie he had to Mexico (Valenzuela "Interview"), and after marrying in Austin,[3] he had no real reason to return to the country of his birth. He had left Mexico as a boy of six years of age and found that the triumphal return he had anticipated had brought him neither the social nor the economic status he had imagined. Although his life up to this point presents some curious anecdotal material, the years of his ministerial training and his subsequent ministry hold more interest for academic analysis. The Rev. Valenzuela was licensed to preach on April 22, 1939, and ordained by the Texas-Mexican Presbytery on April 27, 1941 (Ministerial Directory 653). These dates are not only recorded in the official Ministerial Directory of the Presbyterian Church U.S., 1867–1975, but are confirmed by mention in his Pastoral Record (Valenzuela "Pastoral Record"). That record also contains a list of all the sermons that he preached between 1939 and 1952 along with the membership, recorded marriages and deaths within the various congregations under his care, plus the places where he worked and the salaries he earned. His pastoral record also indicates his year of retirement as 1983. And yet, Rev. Valenzuela told me that he had occasionally been invited to preach as late as 2006. As of 2007, his health no longer permitted him to take the pulpit.

We can see that the choice to join the Presbyterian Church U.S. initially was likely more a situation of circumstance. Had the Protestant denomination that offered to educate and shelter him been another, Valenzuela would just as likely have joined that denomination regardless of doctrinal position. He had, prior to his seminary training, no real appreciation for the difference between Ecclesial, Evangelical, and Fundamentalist Protestant denominations. The Presbyterian denomination was the only one with which he had any personal experience. Rev. Paul Barton, religious studies scholar, in *Hispanic Methodists, Presbyterians, and Baptists in Texas* states that "frequently, . . . [those] who transferred their religious affiliation to the Protestant church . . . were predisposed to accept Protestantism because they had a marginal relationship to the Catholic Church" (46). Not only had Rev. Valenzuela not had any direct contact with the Catholic

Church after moving to the United States, but what experience he had had during his early years in Mexico had been negative.

Hispanic Catholics viewed Protestants as a negative influence, an attitude that led to the exclusion of Hispanic Protestants from the greater Hispanic social community. This exclusion engendered an isolation that placed Hispanic Protestants in a position liminal to both their Anglo co-religionists and the Hispanic Catholics with whom they shared a cultural heritage. Valenzuela quoted a priest from Malpaso, Mexico: "el sacerdote del púlpito decía 'Y quiero decirles a ustedes que no se junten sí hay algún Protestante, que no se junten porque el Protestante es del diablo'" (Valenzuela "Interview"). Thus, as a very small child, Valenzuela was taught that Protestants were evil. Even so, because he had played with the same Protestants that the priest had warned against, he concluded that the priest must have been mistaken. This discrimination against Protestants on the part of the Catholic clergy is supported by R. Douglas Brackenridge and Francisco O. García-Treto in their book entitled *Iglesia Presbiteriana: A History of Presbyterians and Mexican Americans in the Southwest* when they cite an incident recounted in "The Missionary Chronicle" (1842): "On several occasions some Mexican youths attended Blair's Sunday school but were soon pressured by a local priest to stay away" (7). In Valenzuela's case, this discriminatory attitude from the priest coupled with the positive experiences he had among Hispanic Protestants in his early education in Texas predisposed him to reject Catholicism and accept Protestantism.

Arlene Sánchez Walsh in "The Mexican American Religious Experience" states that " . . . conversion to Protestantism for Latinos has often meant estrangement from their families and friends" (27). This social isolation of Protestants advocated by the Catholic Church drove Hispanic Protestants in Texas out of the community that was their natural cultural context. And yet, with a Mexican-American Catholic sociocultural environment that rejected Protestants as evil and an Anglo Protestant attitude that viewed Hispanics as foreign, the U.S. Hispanic Protestant in Texas was left in a marginalized space on two fronts. The same was true for Mexican-American Protestants in California. George J. Sánchez in *Becoming Mexican American: Ethnicity, Culture, and Identity in Chicano Los Angeles, 1900-1945* points out that the estrangement between Protestants and Catholics was imposed by the Catholic clergy: "The contempt of Catholic officials for the work of Protestant denominations with Mexican immigrants was, at times, so virulent that it appeared as if nothing less than a holy war for the allegiance of immigrants was at play in the churches of Los Angeles . . . " (156). This virulence on the part of the Catholic Church also drove a social wedge between the Mexican-American Protestants and their Hispanic Catholic brothers.

Catholics often rejected their Mexican-American Protestant brothers because they had chosen to seek God in a different church. Barton expresses this separation referring to it as a "chasm that separated los Protestantes and Catholics [that] frequently changed the nature of . . . [their] relationships" (49). Anglo Saxons had difficulty accepting the Mexican American because of his ethnicity and the political attitude of segregation that pervaded the society at the time. In 1911, in Laredo, Texas, The Primer Congreso Mexicanista[4] convened to take up matters such as discrimination in education and the officially sanctioned lynching of Mexican Americans (Limón 88–95). This atmosphere of repression and racism precluded complete participation in the Anglo-Saxon culture no matter what the Mexican American's religious preference. Therefore, the Mexican-American Protestant was faced with the need to create his own sociocultural niche. According to Barton, "worship in Mexican-American congregations provided los Protestantes with social and cultural space to develop and express their faith in ways that reflected their cultural values and customs" (85). Both Valenzuela's material and the Lockhart church documents provide insight into some of the difficulties in establishing a separate worship community. Valenzuela's material in particular presents an example of one Presbyterian Mexican-American minister who was unwilling to compromise either his cultural identity or his preferred language of worship in order to accommodate the dominant Anglo-Saxon leadership of his denomination.

The discrimination confronted by Mexican Americans who fled the Mexican Revolution in 1910 was felt not only by the Mexicans who converted to Protestantism, but also by the majority Mexican-American Catholic population. This social tension was an important element in the development of the "México de Afuera" nation building undertaken by immigrants of the Mexican Revolution. The literature developed under the "México de Afuera" banner advocated maintaining family values, praised and protected the concept of motherhood and avoided deterioration of moral values by keeping away from what they considered the negative influences of the Anglo-Saxon culture among which they had to live (Kanellos, "La expresión" 6). But this movement excluded the Mexican-American Protestants by taking a stance against the Protestant denominations that Catholics considered heretical. Paradoxically, the Mexican-American Protestant held dear the same values as the advocates of the "México de Afuera" position, but Mexican-American Protestants were marginalized from this movement by its strong identification with the Virgin of Guadalupe, the patron saint of Mexico. Thus, the Mexican-American Protestant community found itself culturally in an area dictated by its Protestant position somewhere between the Anglo-Saxon worldview and the world vision of its Catholic cultural brothers.

The same moral values espoused by adherents to the "México de Afuera" movement are reflected in a sermon prepared by the Rev. Valenzuela. In a sermon entitled "Grandes preguntas" or "Big Questions" and dated October 17, 1948, there is a section entitled "The Dangers of a Social World." The first danger listed is gambling, and it is described as being the sort that is "sucio y con trampas." This sermon differentiates between playing games of chance and gambling to the point of addiction. This type of addictive gambling is depicted as a vice practiced "en la vida nacional de este país" (Valenzuela "Sermon Notes"). Thus this sermon serves as a warning to Mexican-American Protestants against becoming "Americanized" to the point of allowing their morals and values to deteriorate with the negative influences of the " . . . baja moralidad practicada por los angloamericanos . . . " (Kanellos, "La expresión" 6).

Although the banner of "México de Afuera" gave a national identity to exiles of the Mexican Revolution living in the United States in the early part of the twentieth century, the Mexican-American Protestant community had no such readily available symbols around which to form their ethno-religious identity. Not only had many Mexican-American Protestants already resided in Texas before the Treaty of Guadalupe-Hidalgo, but they also did not identify with the Catholic religion that was at the heart of the "México de Afuera" movement. The Mexican-American Protestants shared a sociocultural heritage with the Catholics, but because of their very conservative moral and religious stance[5] (Weigert, D'Antonio, and Rubel 224–225), they had to turn to their Anglo co-religionists to fill some of those voids. Thus as Juan Francisco Martínez observes in his book entitled *Sea la Luz: The Making of Mexican Protestantism in the Southwest, 1829–1900*, "This new ethno-religious community was forming its identity with an unclear national identity. They were U.S. citizens and Protestants. But even the Protestant missionaries identified them as Mexicans" (131). The early Mexican-American Protestant may indeed have been a U.S. citizen, but he/she could not wholly identify with the United States because the hegemony that was predominantly white Anglo-Saxon Protestant had marginalized him/her. Neither could the Mexican-American Protestant identify with Mexico since he/she was not a citizen of that country. There was no established nation with which the Mexican-American Protestant could readily identify that would satisfy both his/her sociocultural needs and his/her political needs without conflicting with his/her religious position.

Moises Sandoval in *On the Move: A History of the Hispanic Church in the United States* indicates that "the early bishops of Texas showed a decided preference for Europeans over natives" as clergy to serve the Mexican-American Catholic population there (46). The need for European Catholic clergy in Texas was based on the variety and numbers of European settlers to the region in the mid-1800s (Sandoval 45). But even when the majority population in an area was Mexican American as in the case of Brownsville, Texas, the Catholic clergy sent to minister to them was European (Sandoval 45). Although there were larger numbers of Mexican-American Catholics in a particular parish congregation and more congregations in any given city than Protestants, the Protestant churches allowed for the development of local clergy that served their own congregations. Sandoval affirms that the "Failure of the Catholic Church to minister adequately to its Hispanic members is seen as an important cause of conversions. Catholics feel that Protestant churches, typically with small congregations, are more hospitable and build a stronger sense of community. Furthermore, they offer ministers who are from the people themselves, that is, Hispanics" (145). Rev. Valenzuela was one such Hispanic trained by Anglo-Saxon Presbyterians to work among his own people.

Eventually, in 1938, Rev. Valenzuela received his certification from the Austin Presbyterian Theological Seminary (Ministerial Directory 653). That was the highest qualification that a young man with his educational background could aspire to receive through the Austin Seminary at the time.[6] Brackenridge and García-Treto describe the program as a course of studies that "was designed on a two-year plan, with classes held from Tuesday to Saturday. Students were expected to make pastoral calls, to give reports on 'personal work,' to distribute tracts, and to teach and preach on Sundays" (108). They further point out that "the training the men received in the Department did not allow them a career choice wider than that which Texas-Mexican Presbytery could provide" (Brackenridge and García-Treto 109).

Finding himself affiliated with the Presbyterian Church U.S., when the Rev. Valenzuela entered the seminary and felt called to preach the Word of God, he entered a program that from its inception had been controversial. There were so few Anglos within the Presbyterian Church U.S. who considered Hispanic work important, and so few Mexican Americans with deep pockets that funding for no more than the training of five students at a time could be provided.[7] This was most likely why the future Rev. Valenzuela was not accepted the first year he applied. This same contradictory atmosphere continued to pervade the denomination from the inception of the work among Mexican Americans: on the one hand people such as Walter S. Scott, "a leading figure in the development of Mexican American Presbyterian missions" (Brackenridge and García-Treto 20), Henry B. Pratt who aided Scott in his work (Brackenridge and García-Treto 23), and later Dr. James W. Skinner, the first president of the Texas-Mexican Industrial Institute (Brackenridge and García-Treto 101), supported the education of Mexican Americans for the pulpit while at the same time the Texas Synod placed a strong emphasis on financial independence for the churches that funded these students. Ironically, Brackenridge and García-Treto point out that the same financial independence was not required of Anglo congregations: "many Anglo churches in the synod were being assisted by Home Missions appropriations. Moreover, many of these churches had been receiving support for a much longer time than the Texas-Mexican congregations" (119).

And although unlike most other Protestant denominations operating in Texas at the time, the Presbyterians at least had some educational institutions either exclusively dedicated to the training of Mexican Americans or willing to accept Mexican Americans if only on a limited basis. This occurred thanks to the initiative of the Texas-Mexican Presbytery on behalf of its own people. It was only in 1908 that the Texas-Mexican Presbytery was formed as a separate judicatory, but it only had churches in south and south central Texas (Brackenridge and García-Treto 89). Brackenridge and García-Treto state that "even though the newly organized body had the name and formal structure of a presbytery, [it] . . . was not exactly a standard judicatory . . . [it] was simply a channel for distributing its Home Missions funds to the Mexican churches" (90). Brackenridge and García-Treto also affirm that The Texas-Mexican Presbytery's "existence depended to a large extent on its ability to develop an educated ministry and an informed lay constituency, the presbytery, with some measure of success, encouraged the development of educational facilities for Texas Mexicans" (101). The Texas-Mexican Industrial Institute opened in 1912 and The Presbyterian School for Mexican Girls began operations in 1924 while the Austin Theological Seminary opened the Spanish Department in 1921. Still there was much opposition to the integration of Mexican-Americans into the denomination.

The Synod of Texas also despaired at the lack of intellectual preparation and seminary studies on the part of the Mexican-American pastors. But racial discrimination made getting an education next to impossible since public education was not available beyond the fifth grade until the 1930s in central Texas and later in other areas.[8] Only then were Mexican-American children allowed to receive public school secondary education in Texas on a limited basis. Furthermore, de facto segregation continued in Texas schools at least until 1957 (Fighting Discrimination). It would thus seem unrealistic to expect Mexican-American ministers to obtain a seminary education if they could not even get into public secondary schools much less afford to pay for university and seminary. Barton states that "Protestantism . . . assisted rather than prompted . . . [Mexican Americans] to attain their educational goals" (69). Thus it was not a lack of desire to obtain an education, but rather a lack of means to do so that kept Mexican-American pastors from reaching their intellectual potential. As in the case of Rev. Valenzuela, there were those Mexican-American children who were able to get a secondary education through the auspices of the schools established by the

Presbyterian Church U.S., but again the numbers were limited due to limited funding[9] and that still left the problem of university.

We must remember that this was a time in Texas when the Jim Crow laws[10] were closely enforced in the public education system (Ferg-Cadima 12–13), as well as in all areas of social contact between the races. Montejano points out that "In the farm areas of South and West Texas, the Caucasian schools were nearly always divided into 'Anglo schools' and 'Mexican schools,' the towns into 'white towns' and 'little Mexicos,' and even the churches and cemeteries followed this seemingly natural division of people (262). But the attempt to absorb the Texas-Mexican Presbyterian churches into other presbyteries was unsuccessful (Brackenridge and García-Treto 197).

Church records reveal another aspect of the sociopolitical climate of the period. The discovery of the records and minutes of the First Mexican Presbyterian Church of Lockhart really began when my mother was asked to present a speech dedicating a plaque to honor the Mexican school in Lockhart, Texas, her hometown. In order to prepare that speech she searched through official records and came across the minutes of the business meetings of the First Mexican Presbyterian Church of which her father, Ismael Romo, was a founding member. The records she acquired show an active involvement between the Anglo-Saxon and Mexican-American community in the establishment of a Spanish-speaking Presbyterian congregation. It is interesting to note that my grandfather was not previously affiliated with the Presbyterian Church but rather with the Methodist Church. As a Mexican-American Protestant in a small town in Texas in the early part of the twentieth century there were few opportunities to practice your faith in your native language if that language was not English and that faith not Catholic. When a group of Mexican Americans with sufficient capital and political influence was ready to step out and attempt to establish their own place of Protestant worship, the Presbyterian denomination was the one most amenable to helping them. And so it was that they chose to put aside their denominational differences and adopt the Presbyterian faith.

Congregational minutes show that the church in Lockhart took at least two years to establish (Muñoz Dec. 1925).[11] Records dated September 25, 1925, detail the formation of delegates to the autumn meeting of the Presbytery to be held in Austin, Texas. They also list the officers and teachers of the Sunday school program. Furthermore, an official request was made to the Presbytery to supply a student minister from the seminary in Austin to serve the community on a regular basis (Muñoz Sept. 1925).[12] Although the Rev. Valenzuela did not serve this Lockhart congregation, the work with which he was involved while a student at the Austin Seminary was of a similar nature.

In November of 1928, the minutes show that the Lockhart congregation began seeking funds for building their own church structure (Calderón). The most interesting aspect of acquiring the needed loan was that the Mexican-American group of businessmen found it necessary to turn to an Anglo-Saxon member of the community to speak on their behalf in order to solicit the loan. In 1928, racial discrimination and the politics that addressed racial issues espoused the "separate but equal" practices of establishing separate activities for each ethnic community. The Lockhart Mexican-American Protestant community was thus not welcome to worship in the same buildings as their Anglo-Saxon co-religionists and had to build their own place of worship. But even though there were small business owners like my grandfather among the Mexican-American congregants applying for the loan, the bank would not grant a loan without an Anglo Saxon who could co-sign the loan. The same person who helped with the loan,[13] a man named Mr. A.W. Jordan, expressed interest in helping the Mexican-American community since the records show that he donated the land on which they planned to build (Calderón). He gave this land over for their use with the proviso that it would be theirs for as long as it was used to promote evangelical work (Calderón). The sermons written by Rev. Valenzuela were collected as a result of the information gleaned from the minutes of the business meetings of the First Mexican Presbyterian Church in Lockhart. These documents showed that the ministers for the congregation were students supplied by the Austin Presbyterian Theological Seminary.[14] Nearly ten years later, the Rev. Valenzuela studied at the Austin Presbyterian Theological Seminary in Austin, Texas, and, like so many other ministers they went out to churches and communities in various areas of the state just like the church in Lockhart, Texas. The emphasis placed upon the establishment of churches and church bodies that we see in these documents reflects the focus on religion and church involvement[15] that was seen as important by the Mexican-American Protestant community (Barton 106).

Some of the sociopolitical difficulties faced by a Mexican-American Protestant congregation trying to practice their faith in a country founded on freedom of religion were the requirements of Anglo sponsors for loans and road-blocks to seminary educations of equal quality as that available to Anglo Saxons. While such problems were never in the form of laws, the very real hurdles they created acted to deter and prevent progress in religious forums by U.S. Hispanic Protestants. The interview and documents provided by Rev. Valenzuela along with the Lockhart church documents demonstrate some of the problems faced by ministers trying to meet the spiritual, social, and cultural needs of the Mexican-American Protestant community.

Roberto R. Treviño, in his article entitled "Prensa y patria: The Spanish-Language Press and the Biculturation of the Tejano Middle Class, 1920–1940," discusses the "changing self perception of Texas Mexicans" (452). Without addressing religious differences within the Mexican-American community, Treviño analyzes the sociocultural transition from Mexican exile to Mexican American. While Mexican-American Catholics could forge an identification that emphasized their Mexicanness and downplayed any association with the Anglo-Saxon community that their Americanness implied, the Mexican-American Protestant population found itself excluded from the greater Hispanic community by virtue of having chosen Protestantism and excluded from the greater Protestant community because of their ethnicity. Paradoxically, the Mexican-American Protestant was placed on the Mexican-American continuum closer to the American end than the Mexican end because the Mexican-American Catholics were discouraged from socializing with them. Mexican-American Protestants were also socially isolated because of the religious and moral strictures of their denominations.

Another factor in promoting a rapprochement between Mexican American and Anglo Protestants was the acceptance on the part of the greater Mexican-American community of Mexican indigenous cultural markers that included the Aztec pantheon. Treviño refers to the "resurgent Indianism unleashed by the Mexican Revolution " and states that it was "widely reflected in the abundant poetry of the tejano press with "Poems[16] glorifying the Aztec past . . . in which the author appealed to Aztec cosmogony" (456). Such accommodation to a perceived "paganism" was totally unacceptable to the Mexican-American Protestant view. Therefore, an acceptance of President Benito Juárez "whose Indian ancestry made him the epitome of Indianism" (Treviño 456) as a cultural icon was not likely for the Mexican-American Protestant. A similar bias extended to other Mexican national figures that identified with the indigenous movement. This left them with only the Anglo-Saxon culture to turn to for exemplar cultural icons.

Lacking the traditional Mexican cultural icons for their association with the Aztec cosmogony, the Mexican-American Protestants turned to their Anglo-Saxon co-religionists and the North American culture to fill the void. This is reflected in some of the sermons prepared by Valenzuela. On the whole, his sermons contain very few references to either laypeople or clerics in the public eye, but when a reference is used, it is usually taken from the Anglo-Saxon culture. In a sermon that is part of a series on biblical characters dated October 28, 1951, Rev. Valenzuela relates an anecdote about Florence Nightingale and then associates it with the biblical story that is the basis for the sermon (Valenzuela "Sermon Notes"). A sermon dated January 20, 1952, includes an anecdotal reference to Winston Churchill offering his habit of practicing a speech to perfection before presenting it as an example for living a righteous life. Later, in a sermon dated July 10, 1955, Grover Cleveland is mentioned when at his nominating convention in Chicago, Senator Vilas from Wisconsin presents him saying, "We love Cleveland for the enemies he has made." Rev. Valenzuela suggests that Christians should love the church for the same reason (Valenzuela "Sermon Notes"). Please note that in the three anecdotes offered that mention public figures, all four of the figures mentioned are Anglo Saxons. Only one woman is mentioned and she is European Anglo Saxon. Nowhere in Rev. Valenzuela's sermon notes is there a direct reference to any Hispanic figures. This may have occurred either because there were none that had no association with the Aztec cosmogony or because of the training that Rev. Valenzuela received at the Austin Presbyterian Theological Seminary at the hands of Anglo-Saxon professors.

Embracing indigenous symbols on the part of the larger Mexican-American Catholic community served to isolate the Mexican-American Protestants from that community and aided in the development of a sociocultural identity that found itself somewhere between the Mexican Catholic and the Anglo Protestant. This is reflected in the Mexican-American Protestant hymnody that apart from producing its own original music and lyrics preferred to take Anglo hymns and translate them into Spanish rather than to risk translating Catholic hymns that might contain Catholic tenets from Latin into Spanish. Hector Avalos in *Introduction to the U.S. Latina and Latino Religious Experience* states that "the use of Anglo musical forms has figured in conflicts about cultural identity" (252). The same reluctance to be identified in any way with the Catholic Church drove the Mexican-American Protestant to eliminate the celebration of social events such as the "quinceañera" that traditionally includes a mass as part of the ceremonies and dancing in the festivities. Sánchez speaks to the hybridity that this attitude engendered when he points out that "Protestant ministers were . . . hard pressed to alter fully the traditional religious practices of their flock. They often had to make compromises" (156). As noted above, this hybridity was based not on a syncretism with indigenous cultural markers, but rather with Anglo-Saxon Protestant religious symbols and practices.

The liminal space occupied by the Mexican-American Protestant that falls between the Anglo-Saxon Protestant and the Mexican-American Catholic is exemplified in a sermon presented by Valenzuela on June 19, 1949. In this sermon Rev. Valenzuela suggests that both Catholics and Jews, in affirming the religious upbringing of children from birth, are doing what scripture admonishes all believers to do and that Protestants fall short in this area. In this example, Valenzuela admonishes his flock to follow the patterns set forth by both Catholics and Jews in the religious training of their children and conversely to stop following the example of the Anglo-Saxon Protestants that, in his estimation, neglect the religious upbringing of their children or at the very least do not give it sufficient emphasis to assure a pious younger generation. This response on the part of Valenzuela is a reaction similar to that of Mexican-American Catholics regarding the process of "Americanization" imposed upon Mexican-American Catholics (Dolan and Hinojosa 148–149) and Protestants alike by the hierarchies of both denominations (Sánchez 155–157). Ironically, Dolan and Hinojosa cite a priest who equates Americanization with a loss of the Catholic faith (151); this is exactly the same issue that Valenzuela addresses in the sermon cited above.

While the previous example acknowledges a cultural and ethnic tie to the Mexican-American Catholic community, the next example warns against following Catholic practices in matters of religious dogma. A sermon dated April 10, 1955, presents the Protestant position on the crucifixion and resurrection, giving the use of a cross without Christ by the Protestants as a symbol of the resurrected Christ versus the cross with the crucified Christ that he states is used by Catholics (Valenzuela "Sermon Notes"). This is a widely held Protestant attitude toward Catholicism as respects the resurrection.[17] It also reflects the Protestant perspective on idolatry since the Catholic cross with the crucified Christ like "The Virgin of Guadalupe . . . is seen as idolatrous by Protestants" (Avalos 307). The importance of this attitude as presented in this sermon is that it serves as an example of a belief held by one religious community about another. It also drives an ideological wedge between the two communities by presenting two opposing approaches to worship. In the first example, Valenzuela favors a shared sociocultural perspective with Mexican-American Catholics, while, in the second example, he warns against following Catholic religious practices that he views as oppositional to Protestant tenets.

But the most interesting point for me is not the content of the material per se, but the way it was used and the vision that Rev. Valenzuela had regarding his people and his work. The work done by Brackenridge and García-Treto clearly traces the difficulty faced by the leaders of the Texas-Mexican Presbytery and discusses the formation of several ad interim committees beginning in 1942. Rev. Valenzuela served on the third and last of such committees that presented its recommendations in 1951 (Brackenridge and García-Treto 114). The third and final ad interim committee was formed to consider the "feasibility of dissolving the Texas-Mexican Presbytery and placing its churches in the Anglo presbyteries within whose bounds they were located" (Brackenridge and García-Treto 114). The committee recommended a study that was undertaken and took about a year to complete. The results of that study were further considered by the Synod for one more year, thus it was not until 1953 that "the Synod of

Texas voted . . . to instruct its Latin-American Division to devise a plan for the amalgamation of all the churches in the Texas-Mexican Presbytery into the Anglo presbyteries of Texas" (Brackenridge and García-Treto 121). The term "amalgamation" can be read as "assimilation" or "integration," since the goal was to absorb the Mexican-American churches into the existing Anglo presbyteries. In its 1954 session, there were seven elders from the Texas-Mexican Presbytery who requested that the Synod of Texas "proceed at once to integrate their judicatory. [But], G.M. Valenzuela, representing another group of ministers and elders, spoke out strongly against the resolution" (Brackenridge and García-Treto 121). In what was probably considered a progressive move for the times, the Mexican-Americans had to assimilate by dissolving the Texas-Mexican Presbytery and incorporating those churches into the local Anglo presbyteries in which they were located. After much discussion, the Texas-Mexican Presbytery was dissolved by January 1, 1955 (Brackenridge and García-Treto 122).

The Synod of Texas envisioned gradual but positive progress toward financial independence for the churches of the Texas-Mexican Presbytery (Brackenridge and García-Treto 88). While Brackenridge and García-Treto focus their study on presenting a clear and concise picture of the Presbyterian work among Mexican-Americans in the southwest of the United States, they fail to clarify how the political situation faced by the Mexican Americans that engendered the racial discrimination that was their reality made the accomplishment of financial independence a near impossibility for the average U.S. Hispanic church (Brackenridge and García-Treto 91–92).

Records in the Austin Presbyterian Theological Seminary show that Rev. Valenzuela continued to serve the Presbyterian Church through 1963 (Ministerial Directory 653). At that time, while serving as pastor at Jerusalem Presbyterian Church in San Antonio, Texas, Rev. Valenzuela relates an incident where representatives of the Synod of Texas came to his church and in no uncertain terms told him that he should cease preaching in Spanish and only preach in English (Valenzuela "Interview"). Rev. Valenzuela chose to leave the ministry rather than force his congregation to accept that he preach to them in a language that was not their own:

> Y ahora ustedes vienen aquí . . . hagan lo que ustedes quieran hacer porque yo no voy a predicar en inglés. Tenemos clases en inglés, sí, no las estoy desdichando. Tengo un hijo que se va graduar, que está en la Universidad de Texas y una hija que ya se graduó es maestra. Y así es que si ustedes creen que es que porque yo odio el inglés, yo no lo odio. Pero no lo apruebo en mi ministerio. Porque el español es mi idioma, nativa, y creo que puedo alcanzar a más gente en español que en inglés. (Valenzuela "Interview")

And so the records show that from 1964 to 1965, Rev. Valenzuela was "without charge" (Ministerial Directory 653). Rev. Valenzuela worked in a lumberyard for most of that period (Valenzuela "Interview"). Even when he found himself without work as a Presbyterian minister, Rev. Valenzuela accepted the job in the lumberyard only until he could return to the pulpit. Valenzuela recounts the story of accepting the lumberyard job from his friend, Tomás: "'Pues, Tomás, yo te agradezco mucho, pero Dios me llamó para ser ministro, para estar en el ministerio. Y si mientras tanto yo te puedo ayudar . . . Bueno' y le estuve ayudando allí . . . "(Valenzuela "Interview"). Then in 1966 he was approached by the Methodist Church to take over a failing Mexican-American church and the records state that on September 20, 1966, he was "dismissed" to the Methodist Church (Ministerial Directory 653).

The mid-60s were a politically significant moment for Mexican Americans. David Montejano in *Anglos and Mexicans in the Making of Texas, 1836–1986* relates that: "The cracks [in the segregated order] did not rupture . . . until blacks in the South and Mexican Americans in the Southwest mobilized to present a sharp challenge from below in the 1960s. . . . This complex movement accelerated the decline of race restrictions in the cities and initiated a similar process in the rural areas" (264). Paradoxically, perhaps because the term "integration" was applied to the process of assimilating the Texas-Mexican Presbytery into the local Anglo presbyteries, what Rev. Valenzuela wanted was viewed as a segregationist stand when in actual fact what he wanted to accomplish was to preserve his linguistic heritage and better serve monolingual Spanish speakers. Like the position taken by Mexican Americans on the attitude of the national government in the 1960s, Valenzuela's position represented "moral outrage at . . . insensitivity toward Mexican Americans and their needs" (San Miguel 164). Because Rev. Valenzuela took a strong stand on a divisive issue, he was a political pioneer of protest in the Presbyterian Church.

These were just some of the realities lived on a daily basis that made advancement difficult to impossible for the Mexican-American population in Texas at the time that Rev. Valenzuela finished his classes at the seminary in Austin and that transferred directly into the creation, establishment, and evolution of Mexican-American congregations in the Texas-Mexican Presbytery. Consequently, the kind of growth toward independence desired for the Mexican-American congregations by the Synod of Texas was more a dream than a possibility. And yet, Brackenridge and Garcia-Treto tell us that the Texas-Mexican Presbytery, "although hampered . . . by inadequate financial resources, . . . nevertheless conducted its business with a punctilious regard for Presbyterian practice that was not duplicated in any of the Anglo presbyteries" (92). Furthermore, they state that no other presbytery "in Texas had a higher regard for Presbyterian polity than Texas-Mexican Presbytery . . . Paradoxically, . . . no judicatory in Texas had less control over its internal affairs and ultimate destiny" (Brackenridge and García-Treto 92). Hence, according to Brackenridge and García-Treto, the Texas-Mexican Presbytery never really was expected to be independent no matter what the Synod of Texas claimed. If they were not allowed to exercise control over their own destiny, how could they ever gain the pride of ownership required to invest wholeheartedly in any venture?

Only through a better understanding of the groups and sub-groups that make up the Hispanic community can the broad scope of the culture be appreciated. The sharing of ministers and sermons seen in the work of Rev. Valenzuela was a common practice among Evangelical denominations[18] until well into the twentieth century, especially in Spanish-speaking congregations where small isolated communities often had little or no access to ministers on a regular basis.[19] And so, Rev. Valenzuela's life presents us with three major areas for continued study: one is political-historical, another is theological, and the last is literary in the form of the oral narrative. Rev. Valenzuela was a Mexican-American Presbyterian minister so dedicated to working among his own people in their own language that he was unwilling to compromise his work by preaching in English and chose instead to change denominations and complete his ministerial career as a Methodist minister. In his sermons and other documents, as well as in the material from the Lockhart church, are examples of the sociocultural difficulties, the racism, and the educational challenges faced by Mexican-American Protestants in the first half of the twentieth century. When compared to the same sorts of challenges faced by Mexican-American Catholics, it is clear that they were similar, but the methods used by the Mexican-American Protestants to maneuver these situations placed them in a marginalized position between their own culture and the culture of the dominant Anglo-Saxon society in which they lived.

Notes

*The author would like to express her gratitude to the Stitt Library Archives of the Austin Presbyterian Theological Seminary for their help in compiling the information necessary for this article. She would also like to express appreciation to the Recovering the U.S. Hispanic Religious Heritage Project of the University of Houston for their generous grant that made this work possible.

[1] When Rev. Valenzuela returns to Mexico after the tour of the Northeast of the United States and before he returns to dedicate himself to the ministry, he finds that although he considers himself to have made a triumphal return, much like the protagonist of the classic Bildungsroman, unlike the classic Bildungsheld, his education in the U.S. is found insufficient to gain him entrance into the university and he must labor as a teacher with barely enough to cover his expenses while living with his sister (Valenzuela "Interview"). The Rev. Valenzuela makes no direct mention of his subsequent naturalization as a U.S. citizen that gained him the documentation needed to return to Mexico, but that he never used for that purpose.

[2] Further analysis of the homiletic methods and exegesis as applied in these sermons still needs to be undertaken.

[3] The Ministerial Directory shows that Rev. Valenzuela married Velia Falcón in Austin, Texas on March 6, 1939, and that together they had five children.

[4] Information on the Primer Congreso Mexicanista can be found in an article by José E. Limón, "El Primer Congreso Mexicanista de 1911: A Precursor to Contemporary Chicanismo." *Aztlán* 5.1-2 (1974):85-117.

[5] Weigert, D'Antonio, and Rubel undertook a sociological study of Mexican-American Protestants in 1971 that describes the type of moral and religious stance taken by members of various evangelical and fundamentalist churches referred to as members of the 'old church' which would have been the generation prior to those interviewed but contemporary with Rev. Valenzuela: " . . . their realization that Jesus is their personal Savior; that salvation comes through faith and not works; that the role of the saints and the Virgin Mary must be rejected. Furthermore, they now join a church that is more familial, friendlier and simpler. Finally, they come to see that they will lead a better personal life if they do not drink, gamble, etc., although, as mentioned above, these prescriptions are not always insisted upon as they were in the past" (Weigert 224-25). Thus while succeeding generations have become more assimilated to the Anglo-Saxon standards than their ancestors, generations past tended to be more conservative both morally and religiously.

[6] Prior to the establishment of this program at the Austin Presbyterian Theological Seminary, the only possibility for the training of Mexican American pastors was in an "apprenticeship" program begun by Henry B. Pratt in Laredo in 1896. For further details on this program see R. Douglas Brackenridge and Francisco O. García-Treto. *Iglesia Presbiteriana: A History of Presbyterians and Mexican Americans in the Southwest.* 1974. 2nd ed. San Antonio, Texas: Trinity UP, 1987. pp. 23-31.

[7] Brackenridge and García-Treto state that "Recognizing its financial situation, Texas-Mexican Presbytery limited to five per year the number of students enrolled in the Department" (108). Throughout the chapter on the Texas-Mexican Presbytery, these authors draw attention to the inability of congregations in that Presbytery to gain financial independence. Given that these churches could not be self-supporting, it follows that without external financial assistance they would not be able to support more ministerial students at the Austin Seminary.

[8] For a complete discussion on desegregation of schools in Texas see the following: Ferg-Cadima, James A. *Black, White and Brown: Latino School Desegregation Efforts in the Pre- and Post-Brown vs. Board of Education Era.* Mexican American Legal Defense and Educational Fund, 2004. 21 Mar. 2008. N. pag. [Name of Site Missing]. Web. 21 Mar. 2008. <http://www.maldef.org/publications/pdf/LatinoDesegregationPaper2004.pdf.

[9] The Texas-Mexican Industrial Institute began in 1912 with 50 boys. By 1940 there were about 100 boys enrolled. The Mexican Girl's School opened in 1924 and graduated two in 1928. By 1945 there were over 100 graduates. The two schools merged in 1956 and became the Presbyterian Pan American School located at the site of the old Texas-Mexican Industrial Institute. Further details are available at www.ppas.org.

[10] Montejano states that in Texas there was " . . . a separation as complete—and as "de jure"—as any in the Jim Crow South" (262).

[11] Delay in establishing a permanent meeting location for the church can only be speculated. Further study to determine if this delay is attributable to denominational requirements of size and economic independence or to problems in acquiring property for building that could be attributed to discrimination still needs to be undertaken.

[12] The documents do not specify how or where Christian educational materials were acquired.

[13] The Church Minutes of November 11, 1928, give this person's name as Mr. A.W. Jordan, but do not give a first name or any other reference.

[14] A friend said that she knew of a minister still living who had studied at the seminary in Austin and offered to introduce me to him. This was the Reverend Valenzuela. Reverend Valenzuela has gra-

ciously turned over all his professional documents to the University of Houston Recovering the U.S. Hispanic Literary Heritage Project.

[15]In the interview Valenzuela recounted an episode in the establishment of the Príncipe de Paz United Methodist congregation when his daughter, Debbie, insisted on doing her part: "Entonces ella empezó a visitar a puros chamacos. Pues cuando tuvimos la primera reunión, teníamos treinta chamacos . . . Y ella les enseñaba allí . . . Debajo de un árbol." Such volunteer work on the part of women young and old was typical of Mexican American congregations (Brackenridge and García-Treto, 115).

[16]The newspapers that Treviño cites as containing poetry with references to an Aztec past are *El Cronista* (Brownsville), 12 November 1924, p. 2 and 12 October 1927, p. 3 as well as *La Buena Prensa* (El Paso), 15 September 1923, p. 3.

[17]Whether or not this is doctrinally based in either denomination is a point that would be best addressed by theologians.

[18]The same sharing of ministers is noted in the autobiography of Gabino Rendón, *Hand on my Shoulder*, New York (1953), p. 100. Rendón was a Presbyterian minister in New Mexico and Texas until he retired in 1933 (103-4).

[19]Further analysis of documents in the Stitt Library archives needs to be undertaken to clarify this point.

Works Cited

Avalos, Hector, ed. *Introduction to the U.S. Latina and Latino Religious Experience*. Boston: Brill Academic Publishers, Inc., 2004. Print.

Barton, Paul. *Hispanic Methodists, Presbyterians and Baptists in Texas*. Austin, Texas: The U of Texas P, 2006. N. pag. Print. Jack and Doris Smothers Series in Texas History, Life, and Culture 18.

Brackenridge, R. Douglas, and Francisco O. García-Treto. *Iglesia Presbiteriana: A History of Presbyterians and Mexican Americans in the Southwest*. 2nd ed. 1974. San Antonio, Texas: Trinity U P, 1987. N. pag. Print.

Calderón, Eustacio. "Minutes of the First Mexican Presbyterian Church of Lockhart, Texas." 11 Nov. 1928. Minutes. Faith/Fe Presbyterian Church. Lockhart, Texas.

Dolan, Jay P. and Gilberto M. Hinojosa. *Mexican Americans and the Catholic Church, 1900-1965*. Notre Dame, Indiana: U of Notre Dame P, 1994. Print.

Ferg-Cadima, James A. *Black, White and Brown: Latino School Desegregation Efforts in the Pre- and Post- Brown vs. Board of Education Era*. Mexican American Legal Defense and Educational Fund. N. pag.[Name of Site Missing]. Web. 21 Mar. 2008 <http://www.maldef.org/publications/pdf/LatinoDesegregationPaper2004.pdf>.

Fighting Discrimination in Mexican American Education. N. pag. History Matters: The U.S. Survey Course on the Web. *U.S. Latinos & Latinas and World War II Oral History Project*. American Social History Project for Media and Learning (Graduate Center, CUNY) and the Center for History and

New Media (George Mason U). 31 Mar. 2006. Web. 21 Mar. 2008. <http://historymatters.gmu.edu/d/6584/>.

"History." Austin Presbyterian Theological Seminary. N.p. n.d. Web. 30 Mar. 2008. <http://www.austinseminary.edu/index.php?option=com_content&task=view&id=33&Itemid=110>.

"History: In the Beginning." PPAS / History of Presbyterian Pan American. N.p., n.d. Web. 27 Mar. 2008. <http://www.ppas.org/history/hsindex.htm>.

Kanellos, Nicolás. "Cronistas and Satire in Early Twentieth Century Hispanic Newspapers." *MELUS* 23.1 (1998): 3-25. JSTOR. Web. 3 Jan. 2009.

_____. *La expresión cultural de los inmigrantes mexicanos en los Estados Unidos desde el Porfiriato hasta la Depresión*. N.d. Ms. U of Houston, Houston, Texas.

Limón, José E. "El primer congreso mexicanista de 1911: A Precursor to Contemporary Chicanismo." *Aztlan* 5.1-2 (1974): 85-117. Print.

Martínez, Juan Francisco. *Sea La Luz: The Making of Mexican Protestantism in the American Southwest, 1829-1900*. Denton, Texas: U of North Texas P, 2006. N. pag. Print. Al Filo: Mexican American Studies Series 4.

"Membership List of the Sunday School, First Mexican Presbyterian Church of Lockhart, Texas." Oct. 1937. Membership Roster. Faith/Fe Presbyterian Church. Lockhart, Texas.

Montejano, David. *Anglos and Mexicans in the Making of Texas, 1836-1986*. Austin, TX: U of Texas P, 1987. N. pag. Print.

Muñoz, Merardo R. "Minutes of the First Mexican Presbyterian Church of Lockhart, Texas." 25 Sept. 1925. Minutes. Faith/Fe Presbyterian Church. Lockhart, Texas.

_____. "Minutes of the First Mexican Presbyterian Church of Lockhart, Texas." 23 Dec. 1925. Minutes. Faith/Fe Presbyterian Church. Lockhart, Texas.

Sánchez, George J. *Becoming Mexican American: Ethnicity, Culture, and Identity in Chicano Los Angeles, 1900-1945*. New York: Oxford UP, 1993. N. pag. Print.

Sánchez Walsh, Arlene. "The Mexican American Religious Experience." *Introduction to the U.S. Latina and Latino Religious Experience*. Ed. Hector Avalos. Boston: Brill Academic Publishers, Inc., 2004. 11-41. Print.

Sandoval, Moisés. *On the Move: A History of the Hispanic Church in the United States*. Maryknoll, NY: Orbis Books, 1990. Print.

San Miguel, Guadalupe, Jr. *"Let All of Them Take Heed": Mexican Americans and the Campaign for Educational Equality in Texas, 1910-1981*. College Station, TX: Texas A&M UP, 1987. N. pag. Print.

Texas-Mexican Presbytery Records, 1861-1954. Austin, Texas: Austin Serminary Archives, Stitt Library, n.d. Print.

Treviño, Roberto R. "Prensa y patria: The Spanish-Language Press and the Biculturation of the Tejano Middle Class, 1920-1940." *The Western Historical Quarterly* 22.4 (Nov. 1991): 451-72. JSTOR. Web. 22 Mar. 2008.

Valenzuela, Gregorio Méndez. "My Pastoral Record: The Life Ministry of G.M. Valenzuela." Pastoral Record. N.d. Recovering the U.S. Hispanic Literary Heritage Project. M.D. Anderson Lib., The U of Houston, Houston, Texas.

_____. Personal Interview. 8 Aug. 2007.

_____. "Sermon Notes." N.d. Unpublished notes. The G.M. Valenzuela Collection: Recovering the U.S. Hispanic Literary Heritage Project. M.D. Anderson Lib., The U of Houston.

Weigert, Andrew J., William V. D'Antnoio, and Arthur J. Rubel. "Protestantism and Assimilation among Mexican Americans: An Exploratory Study of Ministers' Reports." *Journal for the Scientific Study of Religion* 10.3 (Fall 1971): 219-32. JSTOR. Web. 22 Mar. 2008.

Witherspoon, E. D., Jr., comp. *Ministerial Directory of the Presbyterian Church U.S., 1867-1975.* 1975 ed. Atlanta, Georgia: The General Assembly, 1975. N. pag. Print.

The Female Voice in the History of the Texas Borderlands: Leonor Villegas de Magnón and Jovita Idar

Donna M. Kabalen de Bichara
Tecnológico de Monterrey

C ULTURAL SPACES THAT EXIST IN THE BORDERLAND OR THAT SYMBOLIC space that forms a border or frontier in a cultural sense, are semiotic realities that unfold in unpredictable and indeterminate ways as a result of historical processes. Indeed, as suggested by Clara Lomas, prior to and during the Mexican Revolution of 1910, the U.S.-Mexican border was a sociocultural and political space where, "issue of liberalism, anticlericalism, anarchism, nationalism, class, race, and identity were addressed with revolutionary fervor and articulated through periodical publications, autobiographical narratives, and memoirs by women who became involved not only in Mexico's nationalist strife for a more democratic country but also in calling attention to gender issues" (51). For example, articles written by Teresa and Andrea Villarreal, Isidra T. de Cardenas, and Sara Estela Ramírez in Texas periodicals such as *El Obrero*, *La Mujer Moderna*, *La Voz de la Mujer*, and *La Crónica* addressed nationalist causes, but most importantly, they spoke out against the oppressed social position of women, injustices committed within local communities, and the need for expanded opportunities for education. These same issues were of importance to Leonor Villegas de Magnón and Jovita Idar, two women who have left an indelible mark in the history of Texas, particularly in the Texas-Mexico border area. Because the borderland is a site of cultural exchange, a space where the coexistence of difference is located, I suggest that it is a site of creative ferment. Thus,

158

because each of these female writers can be perceived as pertaining to two worlds, as culturally bilingual, they are able to translate, transform, and create information thereby fomenting cultural dialogue through the written word.

Villegas de Magnón was born in Nuevo Laredo, Mexico, in 1876, and after her mother's death and her father's remarriage she and her brother were sent to San Antonio, Texas where Leonor attended an Ursuline convent school and later on, Holy Cross in Austin, Texas. After her father's death in 1910, and due to revolutionary activity in Mexico, Villegas de Magnón would remain in Laredo where she set up a kindergarten in her home. It is important to mention that due to the scholarly work of Clara Lomas, two of the major works written by Villegas de Magnón have been recovered. In her preface to *The Rebel*, Lomas has noted that the first text, *La rebelde*, was written in Spanish most probably "in the late teens or early twenties" (ix) and the intention of the narrative was to reach an audience within Mexico. In the latter part of the 1940s, Villegas de Magnón wrote another text—*The Rebel*—that was intended for the reading public of the United States. It is in these two autobiographical texts that the reader comes into contact with a narrative voice that presents herself as "the Rebel," "La Rebelde," as founder and "Presidenta de la Cruz Blanca Constitucionalista de Laredo," and "President of the Constitutional White Cross of Laredo." Leonor Villegas de Magnón sees herself as a rebel, as someone whose work contributed to the Mexican Revolution and the cause of Venustiano Carranza. Indeed, in *La rebelde* she tells the reader that "Encantada salí de la presencia del Primer Jefe; en alas de mis ensueños de mujer veía flotar el pabellón mexicano y me sentía heroína, la más valiente [. . .]," "I left the presence of the First Chief enchanted; on the wings of my womanly dreams I saw the Mexican pavilion and I felt like the most valiant heroine" (98).

This "heroína" was not alone in her rebelliousness, an asset she shared with Jovita Idar who was born in Laredo, Texas in 1885. In 1903 Idar received her teacher certification, and her first teaching experience was in Ojuelos, Texas where she is known to have become disillusioned with her inability to affect change in a school system where Mexican children were totally segregated and often excluded from schools. She then began working at *La Crónica*, a family-owned newspaper where she remained at the helm after her father's death in 1914. In 1911 this female activist founded the Liga Femenil Mexicanista that organized a project that would provide free education for Mexican children who did not have the financial means to attend school. After Idar's marriage to Bartolo Juárez she moved to San Antonio, Texas where she began a free kindergarten; however, while living in San Antonio, she also remained active in jour-

---

[1] All translations are mine unless otherwise indicated.

nalism as she became involved as editor of a Methodist newspaper, *El Heraldo Christiano*.

Jovita Idar was also known for speaking out against discrimination, particularly the atrocities committed by the Anglos and Texas Rangers against Mexicans in South Texas. Along these lines she is famous for her journalistic endeavors at *El Progreso*, and she is known to have stood her ground after the Texas Rangers attempted to close the newspaper after she wrote an article condemning Woodrow Wilson's decision to send U.S. troops to the border area. Indeed, in *The Rebel*, the autobiographical narrator presents the following commentary that refers to those like Idar who were contributors to this newspaper: "Through the instigation of *El Progreso*, Laredo became a propaganda center" (83).

The lives of these two women, then, are of special interest in understanding the role of women activists in Texas. Both Leonor Villegas de Magnón and Jovita Idar wrote for *La Crónica* where they expressed their concerns for their compatriots in Texas and Mexico. However, although both women took action during the course of their lives—for example, during the Mexican Revolution Battle of Nuevo Laredo, they crossed the border into Nuevo Laredo to care for wounded soldiers—they were keenly aware of the power of the written word. Indeed, in spite of the limits and prohibitions imposed upon the female subject and her participation in cultural politics in Mexico and the Texas borderlands in the latter part of the nineteenth and first decades of the twentieth century, their writings represent the voice of women who have chosen to speak by putting themselves into the text. Thus, as Cixous argues,

> we must examine women's writing about what it will do. Woman must write her self, must write about women and bring women to writing, from which they have been driven away as violently as from their bodies—for the same reasons, by the same law, with the same fatal goal. Woman must put herself into the text—as into the world and into history (58).

It is precisely an examination of various texts written by Villegas de Magnón and Jovita Idar that are of concern in the present analysis, especially in terms of the type of discourse production evident in each text and the way in which it points to the action of a female author intent on writing about other women, her community and herself.

I suggest that the life experiences of both Leonor Villegas de Magnón and Jovita Idar involved the intersection of two semiotic spheres—those of Mexico and the United States of the early twentieth century. From a semiotic perspective, culture can be understood as "inteligencia colectiva y una memoria colectiva, esto es, un mecanismo supraindividual de conservación y transmisión de ciertos comunicados (textos) y de elaboración de otros nuevos" 'collective intelligence and collective memory, that is, a supra-individual mechanism for the conservation and transmission of certain communications (texts) and the elaboration of new ones" (Lotman, "La memoria a la luz de la culturología" 157). On the basis of this definition, the intersection of the cultural spaces of Texas and Mexico can be defined as a space where memory is shared and where certain texts that deal with that memory are created and conserved.

Laredo and Nuevo Laredo of the early 1900s were cultural spaces where a diffuse ideology of social conventions that make up the "eternal feminine" or "virtues of modesty, gracefulness, purity, delicacy, civility, compliancy, reticence, chastity, affability, politeness" (Gilbert and Gubar 816) continued to circulate. Furthermore, it is important to recall Foucault's comments on societal control of discourse production as a means of understanding the position of women in society: "we do not have the right to say everything [. . .] we cannot speak of just anything in any circumstances whatever, and [. . .] not everyone has the right to speak of anything whatever" ("The Order of Discourse" 52). In spite of these limitations, however, both of these women were exceptions to the traditional Mexican cultural model that situated the woman in a silenced position and within the domestic sphere. That is, because of their educational and class backgrounds—Villegas de Magnón was born into a well-to-do family, Idar was born into a family of journalists, and both were educated as teachers—they were able to more easily choose a different path, that of activism. As suggested by Macías, this active role of women in society is part of the cultural memory of Mexico in terms of the feminist movement. For example, she points out that "with the founding of "La Mujer Mexicana," female teachers, writers, doctors, lawyers, bookkeepers, telegraphists, and other white-collar workers whose ranks had swelled to the thousands from 1880 to 1904 began to speak out on social and economic problems" (13–14). Just as women such as Laureana Wright de Kleinhans, Rita Cetina Gutiérrez, Beatriz González Ortega, and Esther Hidobro de Azualt expressed their desire to become involved in activities to foment Mexico's progress, Villegas de Magnón and Idar would also move in a similar direction in their own sphere of activity in Nuevo Laredo, Laredo, and other areas in Mexico. Ultimately, it is through the discourse evident in their writings that we find evidence of the way in which both women break with certain taboos regarding what women are permitted and not permitted to say.

The Writings of Leonor Villegas de Magnón

Although Villegas de Magnón's *The Rebel* and *La rebelde* are her most extensive texts, I would first like to analyze two of her lesser known essays and articles. I will begin by referring to an untitled handwritten essay that is part of the author's papers that have been collected by Recovering the U.S. Hispanic Literary Heritage Project. This untitled meditation is interesting in that it provides the reader with a glimpse of the female writer's private thoughts. She begins by stating that:

> En mi consciencia suprema tengo Luz, Sabiduría, y Poder necesarios para penetrar ahora esta enseñanzas que estoy recibiendo [. . .] Ese poder así como esos recursos y posibilidades pueden ser puestos en manifestación mediante eso que todo lo que necesito ha sido naturalmente provisto para mi en el plan supremo y afirmando que lo que deseo, ya es mio" 'In my supreme conscience I have the Light, Wisdom, and Power necessary for penetrating these teachings that I am receiving [. . .] This power as well as these resources and possibilities can be manifested through that which is what I need [and] has been naturally provided for me in the supreme plan and affirming that which I desire, is now mine.

The writer further expresses the following thoughts:

> Gracias á [sic] mi consciencia suprema cuya Luz Sabiduría y Poder están en mi y conmigo he comprendido y podido practicar sus enseñanza₃ [. . .] Este poder está en acción en mí constantemente manifestandose [sic] como voluntad firme, carácter determinación, seriedad, firmeza, y resolución. Yo soy una mujer de carácter" 'Thanks to my supreme conscience whose Light Wisdom and Power are within me and with me I have understood and been able to practice its teachings [. . .] This power is constantly in action within me and being manifested as a firm will, character determination, seriousness, strength, and resolution. I am a woman of character.

Of particular importance in analyzing these excerpts is the repeated use of linguistic markers such as "poder," 'power.' That is, Villegas de Magnón contemplates her inner conscience where light, wisdom, and power reside, and which she considers necessary for understanding a particular moment of her life. She perceives this power within her, and she speaks of its "acción," 'action,' within her. The results of this power are expressed in language that presents us with a sense of self that is strong. That is, the use of linguistic markers such as "carácter determinación, seriedad, firmeza, y resolución" emphasize this strong sense of self as "una mujer de carácter," 'a woman of character,' as someone who believes that "Esta vez no debe haber fracaso fracaso [sic] esta vez voy a tener exito [sic] por el poder que está dentro de mi misma." 'This time there ought not to be any failure. This time I will achieve success through the power that is within myself.' This type of discourse production presents the reader with the voice of a female subject whose thoughts stand in stark contrast to the traditional role of women, the "eternal feminine" with its emphasis on compliant, reticent behavior. It is precisely through the written word that Villegas de Magnón breaks through traditional boundaries that are meant to limit female action. She intends to be successful—"yo misma soy exito [sic]" 'I myself am success,' and she expresses this intention through the use of words that are forceful for a woman of this historical period. That is, not only does she state her intention of being successful in her endeavors, she declares herself as success itself. Ultimately she notes that "Por la constante, firma clara y precisa visualizacion [sic] de tu ideal, gradualmente te haces a semejanza de la imagen que has creado" 'Through the constant, firm, clear, and precise visualization of your ideal, gradually you are made into the likeness of the image you have created.' Here we are able to observe the mental life plan of a woman who intends to act and thereby achieve what she has visualized and created for herself as part of her personal life project.

This sense of acting in accordance with what one visualizes in terms of personal ideals is clearly evident in Villegas de Magnón's article, "Evolución Mexicana," written and published in *La Crónica* in September, 1911, soon after Madero's triumphal entry into the capital. The text initially focuses on the "magnífico discurso de Francisco I. Madero pronunciado ultimamente en Cuautla [. . .] Las justas razones que expone serán las dominadores del país y sus maravillosas acciones" 'magnificent speech by Francisco I. Madero pronounced recently in Cuautla [. . .] The just reasons set forth will be those that dominate the country and its marvelous actions.' She further notes his "entendimiento elevado" 'elevated understanding,' as someone who "trata de convencer por medio de la razón y el argumento, poniendo así al pueblo Mexicano á la altura de cualquier nación civilizada" 'tries to convince through reason and argument, thus placing the Mexican people at the height of any civilized nation.' Once again, the reader comes into contact with a discourse that focuses on elevated knowledge and argument based on reason, which is to be the basis of Mexican life where "el machete y el fusil" 'the machete and the rifle' must be left behind.

Another relevant aspect of the article is the writer's critique of the dominant position of the Catholic Church as she states that "La religion mezclada con asuntos interiores del Estado impide el progreso de la humanidad" 'Religion mixed with the inner concerns of the State impedes the progress of humanity.' Here it is relevant to note that, as suggested by Foucault, discourse is never neutral. Indeed, in the article these words are printed in italics so as to emphasize the writer's position with regard to the Church as a cultural elite, as a system of control within Mexican society, one that has limited progress within Mexico, and implicitly, the role that women have been allowed to take within Mexican society.

The female voice of this article then shifts into third person plural: "necesitamos en nuestra patria el militarismo, el ejercito, pero no para combatirnos á [sic] nosotros mismos, no queremos que llene de terror a sus mismos hermanos, pero sí, que nos protege del enemigo extranjero" 'in our country we need militarism, the army, but not in order to fight against ourselves, we do not want [the military] to fill its brothers with terror, but yes, to protect us from the foreign enemy.' The use of the third person plural can be seen as a linguistic form that veils a hidden "I" and that also situates the speaker as part of a cultural collectivity, one that is to be considered as a civilized nation with a national project based on progress, a project that can be defended when necessary with military action. In the last paragraph of the text, Magnón uses only one word in English—"leader"—a linguistic marker intended to revert back to the figure of Madero who cannot be considered "culpable por todos los desórdenes ni las intrigas de los enemigos" 'guilty of all of the disorder and intrigues of the enemy.' She then remarks, "si la causa es buena tiene que triunfar" 'if the cause is good, it must triumph.' Here her discourse stands as a verbal challenge as she addresses her reading public and implicitly states her criticism of those who had opposed Madero's revolt against the Díaz government. One cannot help but think of those such as Henry Lane Wilson who supported dollar diplomacy and who longed for the days when Porfirio Díaz dominated Mexico. Indeed, Wilson´s admiration of Díaz and his negative attitude toward Madero's political project were well known, both in the United States and Mexico. Thus, by speaking out in this article, and, to a certain extent, by addressing Madero's enemies, Villegas de Magnón demonstrates her capacity to make use of the power within her that she speaks of in her meditation.

In July of 1914 in Monterrey, Nuevo Laredo, Villegas de Magnón, as "Presidenta de la Cruz Blanca Nacional" 'President of the National White Cross' presented a speech at a reception offered by the Cruz Blanca. This speech was delivered before Venustiano Carranza, "El Primer Jefe del Ejercito [sic] Constitucionalista" 'The First Chief of the Constitutionalist Army.' She begins her discourse by referring to the Mexican Revolution: "yo comprendí que por procedimientos puramente evolutivas, la revolución iría tejiendo la tela de araña de sus futuros destinos en bien de la república y de los mexicanos [. . .]" 'I understood that through purely evolutionary procedures, the revolution would go on weaving the web of its future destinies for the good of the republic of the Mexican people [. . .].' Once again we find the use of the linguistic marker "evolutivas" or evolutionary which coincides with the previously mentioned article and its emphasis on the writer's vision of Mexico and its road to progress. If we recall her words regarding "exito [sic] por el poder que está dentro de mi misma" 'success by the power that is within myself,' we can certainly understand this speech as Villegas de Magnon's explicit attempt to insert the historic activities of the women of the Cruz Blanca into the history of Mexico's journey toward progress: "Queremos que nuestra obra sea transcendental, que nuestros desintersados esfuerzos obren saludablemente dentro de nuestros procedimientos de evolución" 'We want our work to be transcendental, that our disinterested efforts work healthily as part of our evolutionary procedures.' Thus, she clearly situates her own actions, as organizer of the Cruz Blanca and the actions of those women who worked with her, as transcendental and as relevant contributions to Mexico's evolutionary progress.

In addressing Venustiano Carranza directly, however, Villegas de Magnón uses a veiled discourse: "Yo os pido Sr., que perdone la humildad de mis esfuerzos y los alcances limitadísimos de mi inteligencia ante tan graves problemas" 'I ask Sir that you forgive the humility of my efforts and the limited reaches of my intelligence before such grave problems.' Further, in referring to her activities in organizing the Cruz Blanca during the Revolution, she continues to use a self-effacing discourse as she declares: "Siendo tan débil mi sexo y modesta y humilde obra [. . .]" 'My sex being so weak and [my] modest and humble work [. . .].' In contrast to this seemingly submissive tone of her discourse, which corresponds to the use of the apology in Spanish oral tradition, she ultimately breaks with this linguistic form and presents herself in a forceful manner: "Sin embargo nada me hará vacilar; mi voluntad es firme, mis esperanzas se perpetúan en las llanuras infinitas del porvenir, y mis ideales miran por encima de la cabeza de naturalezas mesquinas [sic]" 'However nothing will make me waiver; my will is firm, my hopes are perpetuated in the infinite plains of the future, and my ideals look above the head of petty natures.' Once again, the reader perceives the voice of a woman, of a speaking subject, who breaks with the constraints of a discourse imposed upon the female as she emphasizes her staying power, her hope, her ideals that found expression in her work during the Revolution as "La Rebelde."

If we compare her speech to Chapter XIV of the autobiographical narrative *La rebelde*, we discover a similar tone. A chapter entitled, "La cena con Ángeles" 'The Dinner with Angels,' refers to a period of time after the Battle of Nuevo Laredo when "Aracelita y La Rebelde [. . .] se acordaron de los días en que velaban por el bienestar de cada soldado [. . .] 'Aracelita and The Rebel [. . .] remembered the days when they looked after the well-being of each soldier [. . .]' (91). This chapter is clearly in keeping with Villegas de Magnón's project of inserting her actions and those of the women who worked with her into the history of the Mexican Revolution. Indeed, within this chapter alone we find ninety repetitions of the phrase "La Rebelde," which is always capitalized within the text, and the "Cruz Blanca" is mentioned forty-six times. All of these references take place in the space of less than thirty-one pages, and they can be interpreted as the intention of a singular female subject who insists on her own contributions and those of the White Cross during the Mexican Revolution. Furthermore, in this same chapter we find that "La Rebelde" is told by a certain Sr. Múzquiz that she should wait to receive orders from the Primer Jefe. Her response is clear: "¿Órdenes?" repitió La Rebelde, "es que nunca he recibido órdenes de nadie" y notando la expresión de sorpresa en la apacible cara del señor Múzquiz dijo como disculpándose "es que yo sé lo que tengo que hacer" 'Orders?' repeated The Rebel, 'I have never received orders from anyone,' and noting the surprised expression on the gentle face of Mr. Múzquiz, she said as though excusing herself 'it's that I know what I must do' (94). In this passage the reader encounters the voice of a woman unaccustomed to taking orders, yet she is keenly aware that the male listener is taken aback by her response. She is also aware of the prohibition placed on female speech; that is, she realizes she has overstepped the boundaries set for her as she attempts to adjust her discourse for Mr. Múzquiz: 'I know what I must do.' Here the reader once again recalls the meditations of this author, her sense of being "una mujer de carácter," a woman who responds to her conscience and exercises her determination through specific actions. Ultimately, then, we find a female voice that has set out to inscribe her actions and sense of determination into her text.

The Writings of Jovita Idar

The same resolute voice that is evident in the writing of Villegas de Magnón can also be perceived in articles written by Jovita Idar. In Idar's article, "El Primer Año de Vida," published in *La Crónica* on January 8, 1910, two types of information can be observed: a firm statement regarding the continued journalistic activity of *La Crónica* as well as information regarding civic and cultural life in Laredo. For example, the author notes that : "'LA CRÓNICA' entra en su segundo año de vida [. . .] firme en sus propósitos de seguir una carrera honrosa, sin bajesas y sin humillaciones, defendiendo con entusiasmo y con franqueza los intereses del elemento méxico-tejano" "'LA CRÓNICA' enters its second year of life [. . .] firm in its intention to continue its honorable course of action, without vile deeds and without humiliation, defending with enthusiasm and frankness the interests of the Mexican-Texan element.' Here Idar's discourse involves linguistic markers that point to a sense of strength and determination— "firme en sus propósitos," as well as a refusal to be humiliated by those who have leveled attacks at a personal level and against advertisers and subscribers of the newspaper. This declaration of resolve implicitly refers to those who write for *La Crónica*. For example, she declares that there are those who have taken action "contra nosotros" 'against us' and whose intention is to "hacer desaparecer a LA CRÓNICA y de matarrnos de hambre" 'ensure that LA CRÓNICA disappear and starve us to death.' In response to these intentions she further states that "entonces jugamos el todo por el todo y contestamos las amenazas con energía y firmeza que no esperaban nuestros detractores" 'therefore we risked everything and we answered the threats with energy and firmness that was not expected by our detractors.' Like the writing of Villegas de Magnón, Idar's discourse can be interpreted as contestatory. For example, the title of the newspaper is consistently presented in upper-case letters and we find a discourse that is firm as it emphasizes those detractors who intended to silence the newspaper. Idar further points out that certain liberals from Texas and Mexico "pusieron a nuestra disposición su pluma y su inteligencia para combater la gangrene que en todas partes corrode el organismo social" 'placed at our disposal their pen and their intelligence so as to combat the gangrene that everywhere corrodes the social organism." It is through the written word, then, that Idar responds forcefully to those who would attempt to silence "LA CRÓNICA" as a representative voice of Texas-Mexicans.

Throughout this article, phrases such as "sin fijarnos en la amenaza" 'paying no attention to the threat,' "sin flaquear" 'without weakening,' "contestando golpe por golpe" 'responding blow for blow,' stand out in her text. Of interest is the fact that it is through the written word that the author actively combats "golpe por golpe," the corrosive effects of social "gangrene." She then specifically mentions that "Redactada "LA CRÓNICA" casi todo el año por los jóvenes Clemente y Eduardo Idar y por la Srita. Jovita Idar, encargándose el Director únicamente de la sección editorial, diariamente aumentaba más y más su circulación [. . .]" "LA CRÓNICA" written almost the entire year by the young men Clemente and Eduardo Idar and by Miss Jovita Idar, with the Director only taking charge of the editorial section, its circulation increased more and more each day [. . .].' She further declares that those who "quieren dirigir el hogar y fanatizar a la mujer, se nos echaron encima" 'want to rule the home and fanaticize women, attacked us.' Although the portion of the text that follows is damaged and illegible, it is possible to read phrases such as "los dardos de la gente de sotana [. . .] entorpecieron nuestra marcha" 'the arrows of the people of the soutane [. . .] hindered our march.'

It is through the discourse production evident in the article that the reader comes into contact with the voice of a woman who, by stating her name in print, situates herself as an important societal contributor, together with her brothers. Interestingly however, and in keeping with the cultural practice of this era, she places her name after those of her brothers. Yet she presents herself as an active member of a family unwilling to back down from threats. To those who would see women who write as fanatics, she presents a female voice that contests the confines of social configurations that include the hierarchy of the Catholic Church that attempts to continue to define relationships between men and women that are "power-asymmetrical" (Fowler 63). However, like the voice of Villegas de Magnón that emphasizes the power within the female, Idar too demonstrates this inner power as a woman capable of using forceful language to contest the taboo concerning women's active role in society.

As a means of defending her position and that of her cultural community, the second portion of the article defines actions involving civic initiatives such as the construction of dams. She also points to construction of a kindergarten, a "Club de hombres de negocios" 'the businessmen's Club,' "La liga cívica" 'the civic league.' and the construction of a rail line between Laredo and Rio Grande City that is supported by other newspapers throughout Texas. So as to emphasize the presence of "méxico-tejanos" she then specifically mentions other Spanish-named newspapers: "*El Cosmopolita*" (Alice); *El Heraldo* (Laredo); "*El Aldeano*" (Uribeño); and "*El Porvenir*" (Brownsville). With regard to "la liga cívica," it is interesting to note that she points to the support of the "inteligentes e instruidas Sra. Leonor V. de Magnón y Srita. Profesora Zenaida Salinas "'the intelligent and learned Mrs. Leonor V. de Magnón and Professor Miss Zenaida Salinas.' Noteworthy is her description of these women as intelligent and learned as well as active in civic affairs. This description clearly contests those who try to "fanatizar a la mujer," especially those women who like herself, Villegas de Magnón, and Salinas, refuse to confine themselves to the domestic sphere only.

In addition to listing those works that will benefit this region, Idar then goes on to point to "artículos científicos, literarios, y filosóficos" 'scientific, literary, and philosophical articles that have been published in "LA CRÓNICA." Thus, her voice situates the newspaper as an instrument of protest, of social and civic improvement, and as a cultural space that includes writing in the area of science, literature, and philosophy. This newspaper, together with others of the region and specific members of the community such as the Bruni, Ortiz, and García of Laredo as well as Luis Volpe C. Guerrero, people from Zapata, Sr. Manuel Guerra of Rio Grande City, give voice to the méxico-tejanos.

In the article "A La Memoria de Mi Inolvidable Amiga Sara Estela Ramírez," 'In Memory of My Unforgettable Friend Sara Estela Ramírez,' her text article with all uppercase letters: "SARA ESTELA NO HA MUERTO!" 'SARA ESTELA HAS NOT DIED!' Ramírez, like Idar, took her training as a teacher. As a female activist, she was also a supporter and vocal leader of the Partido Liberal Mexicano that proposed a number of governmental as well as educational reforms in Mexico. Ramírez, who published many of her essays and poetry in *La Crónica*, is described by Idar with phrases such as: "vida ejemplar" 'exemplary life,' "elevada y noble carácter" 'elevated and noble character,' "luminoso reflejo de su culta inteligencia y de su tierno corazón" 'luminous reflection of her cultivated intelligence and her tender heart.' It is significant to note that just as in the article "El Primer Año de Vida," where Idar uses adjectives such as "inteligentes e instruidas" in referring to Villegas de Magnón and Zenaida Salinas, she also emphasizes Ramírez´s intelligence. Through these discursive references and the naming of specific women, the author points to a semiotic space and a particular cultural community of women whose worth resides in their intelligence as well as in their tenderness and their ability to care for others. Furthermore, she implicitly situates herself along with them when she calls Sara Estela "Mi Inolvidable Amiga" 'My Unforgettable Friend." Idar then writes, "No lloremos por ella, su dulce nombre y el recuerdo de su vida quedan entre nosotros, como ejemplo de los más elevados sentimientos, de su patriotismo inmaculado." 'Let us not cry for her, her sweet name and the memory of her life remain with us, as an example of the most elevated sentiments, of her immaculate patriotism.' What would seem to be a simple article recalling "estrechísimos lazos de cariño" 'very close bonds of affection,' in fact confirms that the effect of Ramírez´s patriotic life stands as an example that "queda entre nosotros" and will continue to circulate in the cultural memory of Texas Mexicans, especially as a model for other women to follow.

"POR LA RAZA: LA NIÑEZ MEXICANA EN TEXAS" 'FOR THE RACE: MEXICAN CHILDREN IN TEXAS' is another article written by Idar, under her pseudonym of A.V. Negra ("Black Bird"), published in August of 1911. In it she notes that "Nuestra Patria está demasiado ocupada en sus asuntos interiores para poder atender á [sic] sus hijos que, por los azares de la fortuna ó por cualquier otra causa [. . .] se han visto obligados á salvar a los linderos de la Patria para internarse en terreno extranjero" 'Our Country is too busy with its internal concerns to be able to attend to its children who, by fortune's chance or for whatever reason [. . .] have been obligated to cross the borders of our Country to be interned in a foreign land.' Once again we see a focus on the plight of Idar's compatriots, especially the children of Mexico who have been forced to leave their homeland and live among foreigners. She further notes the imperative of having to educate these children "si queremos que no estanque el desenvolvimiento mental de nuestros compatriotas" 'if we do not want the mental development of our compatriots to stagnate.'

The author is clearly aware that "el extranjero" 'the foreigner' views Mexicans with "desprecio" 'disdain' because of their lack of education. She emphasizes this lack by speaking of "la ignorancia crasa de una inmensa mayoría de nuestros compatriotas" 'the crass ignorance of the immense majority of our compatriots.' The article emphasizes the need for education, specifically in terms of conserving the mother tongue as a way of preserving a sense of identity of those who have been forced to migrate to the United States. For example, she declares that: "Con profunda pena hemos visto á [sic] maestros mexicanos enseñando inglés á [sic] niños de su raza, sin tomar para nada en cuenta el idioma materno" 'With deep shame we have seen Mexican teachers teaching English to children of our race, without taking into consideration the mother tongue.' These passages demonstrate the author's concern regarding the ignorance of Mexican children, yet she also criticizes another type of ignorance: that of Mexican teachers who would seem to blatantly disregard the importance of teaching Spanish rather than English as a means of preventing "adulteraciones y cambios que hieren materialmente el oído de cualquier mexicano, por poco versado que esté en la idioma de Cervantes" 'adulterations and changes that materially offend the ear of any Mexican, even though he might be minimally versed in the language of Cervantes.' Careful observation of this passage points to the author's explicit concern regarding the importance of conserving the mother tongue of Mexicans, yet implicitly she would seem to be commenting on the necessity of conserving a sense of racial identity that is closely tied to linguistic usage.

Idar's project as expressed through this article is similar to Villegas de Magnón's emphasis on evolutionary progress in Mexico. For this progress to affect all Mexicans, Idar specifically proposes that, because neither the Mexican or U.S. governments will do anything for the children of Mexico who are in dire need of education, "nosotros, los padres de niños mexicanos, debemos unirnos para sufragar los gastos que una escuela requiere" 'we, the parents of Mexican children, should unite so as to pay the costs that a school requires.' On the basis of the argumentation evident in the article, these children are caught in what Homi Bhabha has termed "in-between spaces" (2). As Idar further argues, since the welfare of "niños mexicanos" will not be provided for by nation-states, it must be the collective community that takes responsibility for the educational process. The author ends her article by insisting once again that "la niñez mexicana en Texas necesita instruirse" 'Mexican children in Texas must be educated.' She sees education as a means of assuring that these children cease to be considered as an annoyance by the "extranjeros que nos rodean" 'foreigners who surround us.' Thus, the author expresses the importance of education as a means of maintaining language usage and therefore a clear sense of Mexican identity within Texas. It is through articles such as this one that the reader comes to understand why Idar was known as a woman concerned and committed to her own cultural community within Texas.

Conclusion

As Pierre Bourdieu has noted, language is what "makes the world" or determines the way in which that world is understood. He further argues that "the theory of practice as practices insists [. . .] that the objects of knowledge are constructed, not passively recorded, and [. . .] the principle of this construction is the system of structured, structuring dispositions, the habitus, which is constituted in practice and is always oriented towards practical functions" (*Logic of Practice* 53). The purpose of language for both Villegas de Magnón and Idar can be understood in terms of knowledge about a particular cultural world evident in the intersecting semiotic spheres of Texas and Mexico. Furthermore, as Emma Pérez has argued, "women as agents have always constructed their own spaces interstitially" (33). By speaking out in their writing, then, the voices of Villegas de Magnón and Idar become an interstitial intervention or what Pérez defines as "third space feminism," which takes place "within and between dominant male discourses" (32). The third-space writings of these women are in fact creating an alternative history and can be seen, then, as depositories of knowledge regarding a specific historical period. That is, through their writing they have contributed to the construction of an alternate system or habitus within Texas. One of the aspects of the world being presented in the texts of each of these women writers has to do with what Bourdieu has termed "regionalist discourse" that is intended to "impose as legitimate a new definition of the frontiers and to get people to know and recognize the region that is thus delimited in opposition to the dominant definition" (*Language & Symbolic Power* 223).

Ultimately, I would suggest that the discourse of both Villegas de Magnón and Idar functions as a kind of "symbolic power" that stands in opposition to the confines of dominant cultural systems. Both of these women have left their mark in Texas history as they represent themselves as women of strength, capable of speaking out through the written word as they contest certain rules, values, and dispositions of a cultural field that traditionally marginalized the female voice. Indeed, both Villegas de Magnón and Idar were keenly aware of their assigned roles within the habitus, and although they had developed a sense of what was expected of them, they openly challenged the regulating processes that functioned within their culture as they undertook life projects that moved beyond the confines of cultural practices that limited the female role in society. They chose to create texts that function as independent intellectual forms and as mediators that attempt to enter into dialogue with and affect a change in the reader's perspective.

Works Cited

Bhabha, Homi K. *The Location of Culture*. London: Routledge, 1994.

Bourdieu, Pierre. *Language and Symbolic Power*. Ed. John B. Thompson. Trans. Gino Raymond and Matthew Adamson. Cambridge, Massachusetts: Harvard U P, 1991.

_____. *The Logic of Practice*. Trans. Richard Nice. Stanford: Stanford U P, 1990.

Cixous, Hélène. "The Laugh of the Medusa." *Feminisms: An Anthology of Literary Theory and Criticism*. Eds. Robyn R. Warhol and Diane Price Herndl. New Jersey, Rutgers U P, 1991.

Foucault, Michel. "The Order of Discourse." *Untying the Text: A Post-Structuralist Reader*. Ed. Robert Young. Boston: Routledge & Kegan Paul, 1981.

Fowler, Roger. "Power." *Handbook of Discourse Analysis Volume 4: Discourse Analysis in Society*. Ed. Teun van Dijk. London: Academic P, 1985.

Gilbert, Sandra and Susan Gubar. "The Madwoman in the Attic." *Literary Theory: An Anthology*. Malden, MA: Blackwell Publishing, 2004.

Idar, Jovita. "El Primer Año de Vida." *La Crónica*. Laredo, January 8, 1910.

_____., "A La Memoria de Mi Inolvidable Amiga Sara Estela Ramírez." *La Crónica*. Laredo, August 27, 1910.

Lomas, Clara. Preface. *The Rebel*. Ed. Clara Lomas. Houston: Arte Público P, 1994.

_____. "Transborder Discourse: The Articulation of Gender in the Borderlands in the Early Twentieth Century." *Frontiers: A Journal of Women Studies* 24. (2003): 51-74.

Lotman, Yuri. "La memoria a la luz de la culturología." *La semiosfera I: Semiótica de la cultura y del texto*. Trans. Desiderio Navarro. Madrid: Ediciones Cátedra, S.A., 1996.

Pérez, Emma. *The Decolonial Imaginary: Writing Chicanas into History*. Bloomington, Indiana U P, 1999.

Villegas de Magnón, Leonor. Untitled Essay. Recovering the U.S. Hispanic Literary Heritage Project Archives of Leonor Villegas de Magnón.

_____. "Evolución Mexicana." *La Crónica*, Laredo, September 7, 1911.

_____. "Discurso de la señora Villegas de Magnón, Presidente de la Cruz Blanca Nacional presentado ante el Primer Jefe del Ejercito Constitucionalista, Don Venustiano Carranza , en la recepción ofrecida por la Cruz Blanca Nacional." Monterrey, N.L., July 7, 1914.

_____. *The Rebel*. Ed. Clara Lomas. Houston: Arte Público P, 1994.

_____. *La rebelde*. Ed. Clara Lomas. Houston: Arte Público P, 2004.

Contributors

Monica Perales, Assistant Professor of History at the University of Houston, received her B.A. in Journalism (1994) and M.A. in History (1996) from the University of Texas at El Paso, and her Ph.D. in History from Stanford University in 2004. She is the author of *Smeltertown: Making and Remembering a Southwest Border Community* (University of North Carolina Press, 2010).

Raúl A. Ramos, Associate Professor of History at the University of Houston, is the author of *Beyond the Alamo: Forging Mexican Ethnicity in San Antonio, 1821-1861* (University of North Carolina Press, 2008). He received his A.B. in History and Latin American Studies from Princeton University in 1989 and his Ph.D. in History from Yale University in 1999.

Dennis J. Bixler-Márquez obtained his M.A. and Ph.D. from Stanford University and B.A. and M.E. from the University of Texas at El Paso, where he is the director of the Chicano Studies Program. He is the lead editor of *Chicano Studies: Survey and Analysis,* 3rd ed.

James E. Crisp is Associate Professor of History at North Carolina State University. His most notable work, *Sleuthing the Alamo* (Oxford, 2004), was published in 2009 as *Confrontando El Álamo: La Última Lucha de Davy Crockett y Otros Mitos de la Revolución de Texas* by the Fondo Editorial de Nuevo León. His biographical essay on José Antonio Navarro is in *Tejano Leadership in Mexican and Revolutionary Texas* (Texas A&M, 2009), edited by Jesús F. de la Teja.

Francis X. Galán received his Ph.D. in history from Southern Methodist University in 2006, and was formerly Visiting Professor of History and Mexican American Studies at Our Lady of the Lake University in San Antonio, 2008-2010. Currently a Lecturer at the University of Texas at San Antonio and Our Lady of the Lake, he is revising his dissertation about Los Adaes, the forgotten capital of Spanish Texas, into a manuscript for publication.

Mark Allan Goldberg is a Ph.D. candidate in the Department of History at the University of Wisconsin-Madison. He is interested in exploring the connections between health, race, colonialism, and nation-building in the borderlands. When he's not working, Mark likes to spend time with his family, read, and listen to and make music.

Donna M. Kabalen de Bichara is an Associate Professor and Chair of the Humanities Department at the Tecnológico de Monterrey. As a member of the Research Center, "Memoria, Literatura y Discurso," her research focuses on minority culture in North America, Mexican-American literature and women's literature. She has written numerous articles, and is completing a manuscript on a comparative analysis of the border autobiographies of four Mexican-American women.

Norma A. Mouton's dissertation, *The Autobiography of Conversion in U.S. Hispanic Literature* (University of Houston, 2009), focuses on writings by U.S. Hispanic Protestant authors, from the late nineteenth century to the present. She is currently a lecturer at Sam Houston State University in Huntsville, Texas.

Virginia Raymond is the Director of the Texas After Violence Project in Austin, Texas. Raymond earned her law degree from the University of Texas at Austin in 1985, and completed her Ph.D. in English, Ethnic and Third World Literature at UT Austin in 2007. She has published articles in the *Texas Handbook Online* and *La Voz*, the publication for the Esperanza Peace and Justice Center in San Antonio.

Emilio Zamora is a Professor in the Department of History at the University of Texas at Austin. He has authored three books, co-edited three anthologies, assisted in the production of a Texas history text, and written numerous articles. His latest publications are *Claiming Rights and Righting Wrongs in Texas, Mexican Job Politics during World War II* and *Beyond the Latino World War II Hero: The Social and Political Legacy of a Generation* [co-edited with Dr. Maggie Rivas-Rodríguez].